THE FARTHEST PLACE ON EARTH

North Korea - Truths and Myths
From the Most Isolated Country in the World

AVRAHAM TASHACH

Production by eBookPro Publishing
www.ebook-pro.com

THE FARTHEST PLACE ON EARTH

Avraham Tashach

Translation from Hebrew: Kaeren Fish

Contact: zambodrora@gmail.com
ISBN 9798333893314

CONTENTS

PREFACE *(More than a Prelude)* 5

CHAPTER 1: *Reviving a Dream* 20

CHAPTER 2: *From Potential to Reality* 28

CHAPTER 3: *Black Hole Shock* 40

CHAPTER 4: *Getting Used to an Alternative Reality* 66

CHAPTER 5: *Comfortable in the Alternative Reality* 93

CHAPTER 6: *Back to Earth* 113

CHAPTER 7: *Getting Started* 145

CHAPTER 8: *First Tour – September 2016 (The Nuclear Explosion)* .. 158

CHAPTER 9: *A Fortunate Accident* 188

CHAPTER 10: *Second Tour, Fall 2016*
(A Second Fortunate Accident) 232

CHAPTER 11: *October 2016 – Third Group* 271

CHAPTER 12: *"Nuclear War" (?)* 287

CHAPTER 13: *September 17 – "We're Going to War!"* 312

CHAPTER 14: *May 2018 – A New Dawn* 332

CHAPTER 15: *Seventieth Anniversary Celebrations –*
Celebrating "Victory" 346

CHAPTER 16: *Thoughts in Conclusion, or:*
Who Isn't "Disconnected from Reality?" 379

KOREA – HISTORY 384

ACKNOWLEDGEMENTS 399

INDEX 400

PREFACE

(More than a Prelude)

In 1988, after twenty-three years of service in the Israeli Air Force, I started a new chapter of my adult life – this time as an overseas tour leader.

Over the course of twenty-eight years, I led about 350 tours on six continents, gaining exciting experiences and new insights along the way. I fulfilled countless dreams: I saw the Great Wall of China, the Taj Mahal, Machu Picchu, and the Galapagos Islands; I looked out over the ruins of civilizations; participated in the Carnivals in Rio and Venice; visited nightclubs in Paris and shows in Las Vegas; watched glaciers cracking, volcanos, towering waterfalls; admired the cherry blossoms in Japan and the glorious fall foliage in the US Northeast – all this and more became part of my routine.

Dreams that I wasn't even aware of, came true. Cities around the world, mountain ranges, great rivers, volcanic islands and coral islands, rain forests on every continent, deserts, the most famous nature reserves in the world – visiting all of these was how I made a living. The most important museums in the world were my "workplace." I was exposed to adherents of all the major religions and the strange rituals of religious sects in Vietnam, Tibet, Mexico, Guatemala, Africa, and even in the heart of Europe. The year 2016 was my 29th year as a tourist and tour guide, and, as in Taoist philosophy, two opposites coexisted within me, not in conflict, but rather complementing one another. On one hand, I believed that I had seen and experienced everything and that the chances of still being surprised by anything were extremely small. On the other hand, I never felt that it was enough; I never got bored, and dreams that were fulfilled made way for new dreams, as well as older ones that had yet to be realized.

One old dream that still buzzed around in my head was to go back in time and to experience Communist totalitarian rule. The fall of the Soviet Bloc left one remaining "reserve" – North Korea.

*

And then came the biggest shake-up of my life. I found myself in North Korea, face to face with the most distant, secluded and mysterious culture on earth. Finally, this long-forgotten dream came true. The exposure to North Korea was an unexpectedly powerful experience. Nothing had prepared me for this other-worldly reality; it instantly sparked my alertness, washed over me and seized control of my mind with surprising intensity. My thoughts remain captive to that unique sphere of existence, even now, six years later. After that first encounter I returned to North Korea another seven times, as a tour guide for groups from Israel. The visit was short, but eventful. At the time, the pendulum of current events was swinging between nuclear war and the (slim) hope for a sane relationship between the world powers, with the flames of conflict contained at a level that was under control and tolerable for all sides. The start of the period of my trips coincided with the North Korean experiments with nuclear bombs and missiles. These led to increasingly bellicose rhetoric on the part of the leaders, which seemed to be leading to inevitable war – nuclear war. But then, as in ancient Greek theater, a *deus ex machina* introduced a twist in the plot: there were meetings of the leaders of North and South Korea, culminating, of course, in the summit meetings between the ruler of

North Korea, "little rocket man" Marshal Kim Jong Un, and the "dotard," US President Donald Trump. I was fortunate enough to visit North Korea during that period of transition between the "brink of war" and the "doorstep of peace." As such, my familiarity with service providers and tour guides deepened and turned into friendship that was built on the foundations of honesty and mutual respect. Our conversations likewise developed into heart-to-heart, personal chats. Especially surprising were the discussions about current events. **This book expresses and reflects the world-view of members of the North Korean middle class** with whom I developed a direct relationship, and the truth as they see it.

The tourists that I led also described the visit to North Korea as a powerful and special experience, and agreed that the unique story of North Korea is fascinating to almost anyone who is exposed to it. Wherever I go (in Israel or around the world), when the people around me discover that I have been to North Korea – and especially when they hear that I have been there several times – the shining eyes full of wonder, the curiosity, push all other topics aside, and the story of North Korea becomes the center of discussion – far more so than any other of the other countries that I have visited. I find myself "put on the spot" to tell, to describe, to answer questions. Each time I have been invited to speak in public (with time constraints, of course) the end of my speech is just the beginning. I am bombarded with questions, thoughts, arguments. The widespread curiosity and the many questions that I have been asked about North Korea, along with my own life-changing experience, are what prompted me to write the story of North Korea as it revealed itself to me.

My story is unique insofar as I was fortunate enough to be, over and over again, in the right place at the right time, in the right circumstances. It's important to me to convey the North Korean story, which is very different from the story that is familiar to the general public. Since the North Korean story was developed in the West *ex parte*, it is based on very little knowledge, a great deal of hypothesis, and a fair amount of false and biased information. Like every other Westerner arriving in North Korea for the first time, I brought with me a collection of myths which, as such, required no proof. The deeper I was drawn into the special story of the Koreans, many of the exclamation points in my mind began to curl themselves into question marks. My aim in this book is to try to question some of the prevailing myths so that readers might allow some firmly-held convictions to soften and make way for questioning, as happened to me and to the groups that travelled with me.

*

This book is a personal story, describing my experiences and the questions and insights that gradually evolved during my repeated visits, and which were reinforced through the presence of dozens of Israeli tourists who accompanied me. Naturally enough, discussions developed that were enriching to all participants, myself included.

In addition, the book includes useful information, historical facts, and descriptions of sites for the benefit of those interested in traveling to this mysterious destination. My story isn't about the regime, and makes no pretense of removing the veil of secrecy surrounding the North Korean leadership – for the simple reason that visitors to North Korea are not exposed to the workings of the regime and its secrets. Instead, the book tells the story of members of the middle class whom I repeatedly met and worked with. It also tries to create some cracks in the hard but thin shell which, for the world, surrounds the story of the Korean nation (both halves) – a nation that was a victim of the Second World War, and which paid an even higher price in the Cold War.

*

My dream was to be a combat soldier. When the time came for my enlistment in 1965, the IDF policy was that graduates of vocational high schools were automatically assigned to technical roles in the army. To evade this fate I volunteered for the Nahal (a Hebrew acronym for Fighting Pioneering Youth) program, combining military service and farming. Towards the end of my basic training in the Nahal program, just when it seemed that the strategy had been successful, I received an order to transfer to the Air Force.

There I was given a technical job in the maintenance structure. Dissatisfied and unhappy, I requested over and over to return to the IDF combat structure. The Six-Day War, occurring while I served on the maintenance team for a squadron of fighter planes, changed my approach to military service. Watching all the planes take off filled me with emotion and pride. I understood that while the pilot is the spearhead, without maintenance technicians none of this could happen. The hangar where I was stationed was at the end of the far end of the runway, where the planes approached to land. Without knowing why, I found myself counting the planes as they returned. I counted two, another four, and eventually twenty. Twenty-four planes had taken off; four were missing. They would no doubt be returning any minute, I told myself, and continued to wait patiently. The minutes passed, and gradually it dawned on me that they would not be coming back. This was war. For the first time in my life, as a nineteen-year old youth, I realized that loss and bereavement are part of reality, not just lyrics in the War of Independence songs that I had grown up on. As a member of a youth movement I had grown up – like most of my generation – with the ethos of the "silver platter" described in the famous poem by

Nathan Alterman.[1] Alterman had presented an anonymous girl and boy; now, at this moment of glory, the "silver platter" was real and bore the names and faces of people I knew and admired.

My view of military service was completely changed. My change in attitude found practical expression a year later. With my date of discharge from mandatory service already approaching, I joined an Air Force delegation to the US to study and to train in maintaining Phantom planes. Participation in this course entailed staying on for permanent service in the Air Force – an option that had not crossed my mind up until that point.

*

For nine months in 1969 we were with the US Air Force, mostly in California. At the time, the reality of life in the US was light years removed from Israel, and, for the first time in my life, I experienced culture shock. The economic gap between the two countries was dramatic, certainly for me. Having grown up in a working-class family, at twenty I didn't yet have a driver's license, owing to the cost. In Israel, only wealthy people owned a vehicle of any type; even American cigarettes were a status symbol. And here I was now, with a driver's license, like most members of the delegation, driving a private "American" car. In Israel, the Dodge Dart was the luxury limousine that transported the General Chief of Staff, while on American TV it was advertised as "your great little car." In Israel, TV broadcasts were scheduled three times a week, in black and white, while American TV offered an end-

---

1   Its symbolic image of a young girl and boy wearing battle gear and covered in dust, foretold the colossal human cost – 6,000 lives - of the establishment of the State of Israel. At the end of the short poem, the pair identify themselves as the "silver platter" upon which the Jewish State would be handed to its inhabitants.

less choice of channels broadcasting continuously, all in color. In short, the youngster that I was had discovered a new world.

At the same time, 1969 was a special year in American history, with the Woodstock Festival marking the apogee of the Flower Children. It was a year in which this superpower became bogged down in Vietnam, and the anti-war protests reached a peak. The student protests, the demonstrations, and the draft-dodging coalesced into a wave that threatened to engulf the US. The streets of Los Angeles – and even more so San Francisco – were full of young people who had run away from home and were preaching "make love, not war." They regarded anyone associated with the military with pity, at best; more often with outright hostility.

As great as the gaps may have been in terms of lifestyle, the differences between ourselves and our American peers was much greater when it came to our respective perceptions of military service. During the period after the Six Day War, adulation of the Israeli Air Force was at an all-time high not only in Israel but also, in the US and around the world, among American Jews and – even more so – among the US Air Force personnel with whom we were in day-to-day contact. We were young and enthusiastic, filled with a sense that we had been part of the victory in this utterly moral war – a war that was viewed as a fight for the country's very survival. Many people viewed us as heroes. We regarded ourselves as having performed our duty well, with the results reflecting this. The American Air Force soldiers we worked with on airplane maintenance had returned from service in Vietnam, or were preparing for a tour of duty there. The victory of the IDF and the Israel Air Force, in comparison with the Sisyphean war in Vietnam, aroused their frustration, along with esteem bordering on admiration for us. They would jokingly propose "an offer we couldn't refuse" – three generals in return for one: General Motors, General Electric and General Dynamics – in return for General (Moshe) Dayan.

11

Our American peers viewed their own country and their military service in a completely different light. I could not understand how American youngsters could even imagine not giving of themselves for their country. The explanation that the Vietnam War was an unnecessary and unjustified war sounded to me like a pitiful excuse, since it's not the soldier who decides, but rather the country's leaders. Like everyone else, I became accustomed to the abyss separating my world-view from that of the Flower Children. I learned to live with the contempt that I would encounter in the street, where my military haircut was a sharp contrast to the long hair of Americans my age.

Most of the time, of course, we were busy with our course, but on weekends we hiked and got to see the wonders of the Western US. Fantastic San Francisco, which was the bastion of the youth protest, was our destination more than once. On one of our trips we visited the home of an elderly (to our youthful eyes) woman named Sarah. Out of the blue, Sarah asked us, "What do you think of the Flower Children's long hair?" Without giving myself or my companions a moment to think, I blurted out my adamant and unequivocal response: "Awful, ugly, quite unacceptable. It's for brats and punks on drugs." Sarah took a deep breath and then drew out a dollar bill, pointed to the portrait of George Washington and to his hair, and, in the silence that followed, turned to me and asked what I thought of the man. I was struck dumb. Sarah, in her wisdom, did not pursue the discussion. The lesson I learned then has remained with me for more than fifty years, to this day. Thinking back, I think it was Sarah who managed to make the first crack in my simple, one-dimensional world-view. The exclamation mark began to wobble.

Ultimately it turned out that those young men and women, the Flower Children, had understood through their senses that which the leaders were unable or unwilling to understand. The "domino effect" theory was the basis for the West's justification of the Vietnam War. The theory maintained that the fall of South Vietnam into the hands of the Communist North would lead to neighboring countries – Laos, Cambodia, Thailand and Burma – falling into Communist hands, too, followed by all the Third World countries, in Asia, Africa, and Latin America. The Vietnam War ended with the Paris Peace Accords signed on January 27th, 1973. From a military point of view, the US army had been victorious. Two years later, on April 30th, 1975, South Vietnam fell to the Communist North, with no real resistance.

The Vietnam War was never declared a war by the US, and as a "non-war" it claimed more than two million Vietnamese lives (the great majority – 1.8 million – Northern Vietnamese), and some 58,000 American troops. The domino effect did not happen. The non-aligned countries did not become part of the Communist Bloc. On the other hand (in a separate chain of events), the Communist Bloc evaporated.

Two American presidents – Bill Clinton and George Bush Jr., both draft-dodgers, each entered the Oval Office after defeating the respective war heroes George Bush Sr. and Al Gore.

Perhaps the Flower Children were right after all?

The Six-Day War and the trip to the US paved the road that I followed up until the age of forty. The idea of permanent service in the Air Force maintenance corps became a logical possibility. More than a conscious choice, it was just the way things turned out.

*

On the eve of the Jewish New Year, September 26th, 1973, I was visiting my parents' home. As usual, I had brought a *Maariv* newspaper with me. My parents' Hebrew was reasonable, but they still preferred reading the Yiddish newspaper – *Letzte Neis* ("Latest News"). The headlines, as the New Year approached, proclaimed that our security situation had never been better, and that no war was foreseen on the horizon for the next decade. Minister of Defense Moshe Dayan declared that it was better to have Sharm el-Sheikh under our control without peace, than to have peace without Sharm el-Sheikh, since it ensured free passage for ships to Eilat. For a while the Soviet Union allowed Jews to emigrate to Israel; the national mood was at an all-time high, and we viewed ourselves as an invincible superpower. Every soldier serving in the Air Force was regarded as a strategic expert; certainly I was, after my service with the US Air Force and after being part of the arrival of the Phantoms in Israel. My father and I talked; we liked to argue: he, the Yiddish-speaking exilic Jew, and I – not a Sabra, but nevertheless (in my own eyes, at least) a representative of the New Jew, the Israeli devoid of the "blemishes of the Diaspora." In the midst of our discussion, and in response to the headlines, my father said, "*Avremele – dos yahr svet zayn a-krig*" ("This year, there will be a war").

"No," I told him, "We are strong; we have Phantoms. The Egyptians won't dare declare war; they know that if the Six-Day War lasted three hours,[2] the next war will last thirty minutes."

"Maybe," my father replied, "but war is going to break out."

I continued to dismiss his words. "Do you know how many casualties they'll have?!"

"Sadat will be willing to risk even a million casualties; he'll declare war," my father insisted.

"Where do you get this from, Dad?" I asked.

"Sadat said it," he replied.

"So what if he said?" I argued, but my father was adamant: "Sadat has to take back the Sinai; he will do anything to break the deadlock on Sinai."

---

2 Most of the air force of Egypt, Syria and Jordan was demolished within three hours.

"Why does he have to take back the Sinai?"

"He promised, and for him it's a matter of honor."

"And what about our honor?" I challenged him.

My father, a European Jew who didn't speak a word of Arabic, looked at me and answered with a question:

"Would you kill your daughter for honor? He would!"

I wasn't convinced. What nonsense he was talking, I thought to myself. After all, Dayan had said...

Ten days later, the Yom Kippur War broke out. I spent the entire war at the Bir Gifgafa and Bir e-Thamada airfields in the Sinai, some of the time under bombardment by the Egyptian Air Force. The news reports were laconic, offering little information, and I – situated right in the eye of the storm – was still convinced that this was not war, but rather a series of incidents, the likes of which we had seen many times before. Our leaders surely could not have been mistaken.

It was only when the war was over and I returned home, met people, and heard about friends and acquaintances whom I would not see again, that a more realistic picture started forming in my mind of what had gone on. My discussion with my father replayed itself over and over in my head; my father had been right!

About six months later, in May, 1974, the atmosphere in Israel was grim. Protest movements were fueled by the damning preliminary report of the Agranat Commission (appointed to investigate the IDF failings that had led to the Yom Kippur War), which had been submitted in April; the public as a whole was in shock at the sudden drop from the heights of glory of the Six Day War to the terrible cost of the Yom Kippur War. My father was extremely ill, but nevertheless when I visited we discussed current events, as usual. The hot topic at the time was the Disengagement of Forces Agreement with Egypt. And then, out of nowhere, my father said, "Soon there will be peace with Egypt."

Showing my father some indulgence, I politely replied, "Yes; if not in my lifetime, perhaps in my children's lifetime." My father grew angry. Talking was difficult for him; with great effort he lifted his hand and shook his finger at me, demanding, "Don't you talk to me like that. Say what you think, regardless of my condition." Since he was so adamant, I changed my tone and said, "Dad, where did you invent that from?" And he repeated his mantra: "Sadat has to get the Sinai back." He rested for a moment; talking had cost him much effort. Then he went on, "He has no money for another war. In order to get the Sinai Peninsula back, he will have no choice but to make peace!" I didn't answer. It was clear to me that, with the end of his life approaching, this was his heart's desire.

My father passed away at the end of May 1974.

*

On November 19th, 1977, two years and five months after my last conversation with my father, Egyptian President Anwar Sadat landed in Israel. (Chief of Staff Motta Gur had difficulty internalizing the significance of the moment: "He's bluffing.") Another two years and a bit passed, and on March 26th, 1979, a peace treaty was signed between Israel and Egypt on the White House lawn in Washington. The entire Sinai Peninsula (including Sharm el-Sheikh) was returned to Egypt. Among those spearheading the process that led to the agreement was Moshe Dayan, the man who had declared, "Better Sharm el-Sheikh without peace, than peace without Sharm el-Sheikh." During the Yom Kippur War, Saudia Arabia had announced that the Baab el-Mandeb strait was closed to Israeli ships. Although not a single cannon had been moved to back this up, it turned out that the declaration was enough, and access to the port of Eilat had ended. Once again Dad had been right!

A textile worker who lacked the means to complete elementary school (although an extraordinary intellectual by virtue of his reading, conversations and arguments with educated members of his circle of friends), who had never served in the army (eye problems), and who had not grown up on Western culture, armed only with his "secret intelligence" – the *Letzte Neis* – analyzed the situation and anticipated processes better than the political and military experts and most other people. My father was neither a genius nor a prophet. His secret was simple: he looked at the facts and the data with no preconceived opinion and without falling into the trap of conventional thinking, and arrived at simple conclusions. We might say that my father was the young boy in the story of "The King's New Clothes." As for me, thanks to my conversations with him, the exclamation marks in my mind moved aside, making room for questions.

*

Age forty – the minimum age for military retirement – was knocking at my door. Concurrently with my service I completed an MBA degree in Organizational Behavior at Tel Aviv University, since it was clear to me that the next chapter of my life would be centered around the human element. I thought about retirement and what it means, and arrived at the definition that retirement is a psychological situation in which a person is occupied mainly with his hobbies. Armed with this insight, the path to deciding that what I wanted to do was mainly to travel, was short. In my childhood and youth, books about voyages and explorers had fascinated me. I sailed with Magellan around the world, I joined Columbus on his "voyage to India," I helped Vasco da Gama to round the Cape of Good Hope; together with James Cook I mapped the coasts of Australia and New Zealand, and I was even present at the unforgettable meeting where Henry Morton Stanley greeted David Livingstone with the immortal line, "Livingston, I presume." My past as a counselor in the Scouts movement and at the IAF technological college, the ease that I feel in the presence of people, and the fact that sometime in my childhood I seem to have been blessed with the gift of the Blarney Stone[3] – along with my love for open spaces and being on the move, led me to decide that I would spend my time and make my living from touring. Or, more precisely, leading tours. At the age of thirty-nine I signed up for a course for guiding groups traveling overseas, and at the age of forty I retired from service in the Air Force.

About a month later, I was already leading my first group to Romania and Hungary on behalf of Rimon Tours. As mentioned previously, 28 years later, in 2016, I could look back on over 350 tours to six continents and over a hundred countries. In my third year as a guide I led a group on a trip that included Italy and Yugoslavia (our company's last tour to Yugoslavia, before the war and the breakup of the country). During that tour we spent a day sailing in the Dubrovnik archipelago, during which I had a discussion with one of the tour participants. He was about thirty years older than me, and our conversation turned to the topic of my job. The traveler expressed great empathy for the unconventional lifestyle imposed on me by my occupation, and asked, in a general way, about my financial remuneration for such frequent absences from home. I told him, "I'll be honest with you: the pay is nice, but that alone wouldn't justify the sacrifice. This work isn't going to make me rich." I still haven't forgotten his response, and his thoughtful expression as he gazed at me, wagging his finger in my direction. He said, "Listen to me well,

---

3   According to Irish legend, this stone, brought by the Crusaders from the Holy Land and set into the battlements of Blarney Castle in Ireland, endows anyone who kisses it with the "gift of the gab."

Mr. Tashach. Life is a flash; in that flash, one has to accumulate as many experiences as one can." After a brief pause, he added, "You're going to be rich; very rich!"

CHAPTER 1

Reviving a Dream

I t was a fine, wintery Friday morning in February, 2016. My wife and I were walking along the Nahlat Binyamin pedestrian mall in Tel Aviv when my phone rang. On the line was Chaim Peres, director of Tarbutu, a division of Rimon Tours. He started, "Tashach, I have a crazy idea: North Ko...." I interrupted before he could finish the sentence: "North Korea??!! I'm prepared to pay to visit there!" "North Korea," Chaim replied calmly, and continued, "I've been thinking that Tarbutu, as a relatively new company, with a human cultural orientation, needs to find a niche that hasn't been touched by anyone else." I wasn't really listening to what he was saying. My thoughts were racing backwards in time, to my first two tours as a guide.

*

It was the summer of 1988. I had recently retired after twenty-two years of service as an officer in the maintenance corps of the Israeli Air Force. As a retiree, I had decided to devote myself to my hobby – traveling the world. I took a course training guides for group tours overseas. Although I was a former officer and had accomplished a few things in my life, including attaining a B.A. and an M.B.A., I was eager to embark on my chosen second career. When the assignment was finally announced, I was disappointed, and also hesitant: was this really what I wanted? The tour in question was to Romania and Hungary, a far cry from the destinations I had been dreaming about. The director of the tour guide department decides what the company's needs are, and when the company has a problem, you have to take on the assignment, because that's what's needed. He told me, "You'll have a local guide with you; study the material, let the local guide help you. This is actually a test for you: if you succeed, there'll be more to come; if not, it's a sign that you aren't cut out for this work." Suddenly you feel that you've gone back more than two decades, to basic training. In fact, not even basic training; more like the pre-enlistment tests for army units. Your dreams? Your hopes? Their time will come. After some consultation and deliberation, I decided to take the leap.

July, 1988. After a short but tiring night flight, I found myself at Bucharest Otopeni Airport. There I was – after growing up in Israel, some studying and some instruction from the US Air Force, and some touring around the US, Britain, and Western Europe. I considered myself a man of the world and thought I understood more or less how things worked. All of a sudden, with no warning, I was in freefall! With no parachute or safety net, just falling into a deep pit; the pit of a reality completely different from anything I had known or anticipated. And within this reality, for which I was unprepared, I was expected to function, lead, and display confidence and calm.

This was my first encounter with life under totalitarian rule. It was the period of Ceaucescu's regime. The country was decrepit. The choice of food available to the tourists raised several eyebrows. People would swarm us, hoping to get their hands on a piece of chewing gum. Jeans were worth their weight in gold. Instant coffee and nylon stockings were a distant dream, to say nothing of a pack of long Kent cigarettes, which was worth a month's salary in Romania.

I had grown up in the free, open, liberal atmosphere in Israel, where authority was all but non-existent and where "Who does he think he is, anyway?" could refer to a university professor, the IDF Chief of Staff, or a Nobel Prize winner; it frequently referred to a government minister who wasn't to one's political taste. For someone from that sort of background it is exceedingly difficult to deal with a reality in which one's interlocutor avoids making eye contact, and in which fear, evasion, appeasement and slyness are vital ingredients in the recipe for survival.

It was utter culture shock. A few examples out of the totality of events and experiences that I was exposed to may illustrate what I mean. My guide in Romania, by the name of Ilya, was a young, intelligent and pleasant chap... with no experience. Like me, he was leading a group for the first time. Despite this, we did a reasonable job of running the tour, and got along well. I might even say that we became friendly, despite the age difference. On the third day of the tour, at the top of a mountain in Poiana Brasov, Ilya turned to me and asked if I wanted to see a really beautiful view. I looked around – the view was breathtaking; what could be better? Ilya insisted, "Come, I'll show you." We moved away from the group, climbing up onto a huge rock from which we could see anyone who might approach, and Ilya invited me to sit down. There was a brief moment of silence; I looked at the view, and politely murmured, "Truly beautiful." And then Ilya looked at me and asked, "What do you think of Romania? The politics, the economic situation, and so on." This took me by surprise. I was a little fearful of replying, and so I began which some general statements that didn't really mean anything. Ilya didn't give up, and slowly our polite exchange turned into an in-depth discussion of the situation in Romania, the economic and psychological state of its citizens, and of course the tyranny and its implications. For the first time in my life I was talking directly with a victim of tyranny. This was the twentieth century, in the heart of Europe.

The tour group I was leading included an elderly, single man, with no close family. When we arrived in Bucharest, he approached me and asked me to come with him to his room, since a distant relative was going to visit him. I didn't understand what my role was in this meeting, but I acquiesced to what I viewed as his slightly odd request. We were sitting in his room when the relative arrived. The two of them embraced with great emotion. The visitor extricated himself from the embrace and addressed both of us, in Romanian, of course, asking loudly, "Well, how is Romania? Isn't it wonderful?" My tour participant almost shouted his response in the affirmative, and the relative, who understood that I didn't speak Romanian, turned to me, pointed towards the light, and with movements of his mouth indicated that I should agree: "Da, da." Like an actor in a play, I quickly took on my role, and as expected of me, sprouted superlatives in English as to the wonders of Romania. It was a rather disturbing experience, quite unlike anything I had encountered at first hand; I had only heard about it in stories, movies, or theater. Again – the end of the twentieth century, in the heart of Europe.

On the last night of the tour we slept over at the second-most luxurious hotel in Bucharest. At dinner I decided to distribute all the remaining packs of cheap Israeli chewing gum that I had on me and that had I had been using as tips. I was in good spirits. The tour was nearing its end, and I was enveloped in a sense of relief at having made it through my first assignment, and the joy of success. Every waiter that passed by received a precious treasure: a pack of chewing gum. At some stage, after all the waiters had already received their rewards, the waiter who had been the first to receive a pack of gum came over, got down on his knees and, bringing his hands together in a gesture of pleading, requested another pack, explaining that he had two children. The end of the twentieth century, in the heart of Europe.

*

Two weeks after the end of the first tour, I was back in Romania with another group. (The first one must have been successful, or there wouldn't have been a second.) This time, the local guide was older, and more experienced; a fantastic guide named Carmen. On the second day we were in Neptun, a summer resort on the Black Sea. We organized ourselves in the hotel and then went down with the group to swim in the sea. The members of the group wandered off, some going to swim, others to sit on the beach. The vacation feeling in Neptun was completely different from the heavy, gloomy atmosphere of Bucharest. Suddenly Carmen turned to me and asked, "Do you know how to swim?" I nodded. After all, I had grown up in the coastal town of Bat Yam; the sea had been a central part of my childhood. Carmen didn't even wait for my response; she said, "Let's swim." She headed out towards the open sea, swimming away from the beach, and I stayed close by her. The further we swam, the more I wondered what was going on. Then she stopped, looked around, noted that no-one was nearby, and – like Ilya, the previous guide – engaged me in conversation about life in Romania. Carmen was older than Ilya, and she spoke out more clearly, more brazenly, and far more critically than he had. Again, I felt confused and perplexity. Here we were at the end of the twentieth century, in the heart of Europe.

This tour, too, ended in Bucharest. On the next-to-last night, at dinner, there was a very unpleasant anti-Semitic incident. A drunken waiter got angry at a Romanian-born group among my tourists, yelled insults at them, and shut off the lights in the dining room. The acting manager rushed over and, taking in the scene, apologized, sent the waiter out, and showed Carmen that he had reported the incident in the hotel log book. The next day the senior manager came in to work and saw the report. He called Carmen and informed her that he had questioned the waiter and had concluded unequivocally that the whole incident was a fabrication meant to smear the hotel.

Carmen, greatly distressed, came to me and said, "Come, we're going to write a complaint in the hotel's complaint book." I didn't know what that meant. I told her, "Do whatever is needed; you know better than I do how the problem should be dealt with."

About an hour later, Carmen came back and said, "The hotel manager wants to talk with us."

"I'm with you," I said, and we headed to his office. When we entered, the manager seated us at a table laden with a feast. An abundance of food, Romanian wine, Sibiu salami, Tuica liqueur.... I sat down, slightly confused, trying to make sense of what was happening. The manager and Carmen engaged in lively discussion in Romanian, which, of course, I couldn't understand. I watched from the sidelines, trying to understand this drama without translation. Carmen turned to me and said, "The manager wants us to withdraw the complaint. Don't agree to it." Again I told her, "Carmen, I'm with you." Suddenly the manager, who understood a bit of English, got up from his seat, walked over to me, got down on his knees, his hands spread on the floor, and bent to kiss my feet. I thought I had seen enough in Romania, but until this moment, I realized that while I might have seen a lot, I had understood very little. Hurriedly I stood up, and fled from the room. End of the twentieth century, in the heart of Europe!

*

On the first tour, after Romania, we went on to Hungary. Arriving there, I asked the local guide a few questions about our conduct during the tour of Hungary, based on my "interesting" experiences in Romania. Her brief and blanket response was, "Forget Romania; here everything is different." Indeed, the real-

25

ity of Hungary was different in every way. After what I had seen, Communist Budapest looked much closer to Paris than to totalitarian Bucharest.

On the first evening, I was immersed in a sense that my journey from Bucharest to Budapest, more than a geographic move from east to west, was a cultural journey in the same direction, and even more than that – a journey forward in time.

About two years later, the Communist Bloc collapsed, and Romania, among the other countries of Eastern Europe, began moving westward on the continuum of time and culture.

*

Although I had witnessed totalitarianism and the drama of the collapse of the Communist Bloc, I felt that it had been something of a missed opportunity since, in real time, I hadn't truly internalized what dictatorship means for everyday life. Those had been my first two tours as a guide, and my mental and emotional energies had been focused mainly on the tour and the participants.

In my own head, by training and in my work as a guide, the human element is the center of my world, and, consequently, the main topic that I seek to convey. The way I see the world, if one has no knowledge of the past, one cannot understand the present. The realm of history encompasses countless different aspects. What interests me is the day-to-day life of people in different places, during different periods, living in different cultural worlds.

The sense of the missed opportunity gave rise to a desire to experience what life was really like under absolutist rule.

My career took me to Bulgaria, Yugoslavia, China, Vietnam, and Cuba, all under Communist rule (in some cases, this was soon to end). "No, this isn't it," I told myself. The feeling of a lost opportunity didn't dissipate; on the contrary, it grew more intense, along with an irrational desire to go back in time, in order

26

to make up for the missed chance. This desire became somewhat problematic with the disintegration of the Communist Bloc.

On December 17th, 2011, the ruler of North Korea, Kim Jong-Il passed away. Two days later, his son, Kim Jong-Un, was declared his successor, perpetuating the dynasty. This piece of news breathed new life into the dormant dream in my head, igniting the idea of giving totalitarian rule another try. The way I saw it, a trip to North Korea would certainly fit the bill of a journey backwards in time to make up for my tours to Romania in 1988.

Having made the decision, the next step was a Google search: "Tourism to North Korea." To my astonishment, a large number of websites were offering tours. I chose one of them. The introduction on the site provided some background about the tour, followed by the itinerary, and then a registration form. I narrowed my focus to this site, and continued. I chose a route and date for my tour, all the time knowing that the moment I identified myself as an Israeli, the registration would lock me out. I continued, filling in my address and then passport information; so far no problem. The next step was filling in credit card details. I filled it in; everything proceeded normally. Now all I had to do was to press "Enter," and I was set to go. My hand, hovering over the keyboard, began to shake. Logical thinking took over my brain: What are you doing? Where are you going? Are you crazy?!

Logic emerged victorious. The hand hovering over the keyboard quickly moved slightly over and clicked on "Delete." The idea was set aside, pushed to the very back of my mind. After all, not every dream can be realized.

*

And now, on this sunny, wintery Friday morning in February 2016, my wife and I were strolling down the Nachalat Binyamin pedestrian mall, when my phone rang...

CHAPTER 2

From Potential to Reality

The bombshell phone call breathed new life into the idea that had all but faded into oblivion. The thought that this crazy dream had been reborn and suddenly appeared to be achievable, overpowered me completely. Throughout Saturday, that was all I could think about. My thoughts oscillated between the tour in question and my first encounter with totalitarian rule in Romania. Sights from the past came to mind, and I began projecting them into the future. The combination of imagination, anticipation and anxiety painted a confusing picture in my head.

On Sunday morning I headed impatiently to the office. "Chaim," I addressed the director of the Tarbutu division without preliminaries, "What's happening with the tour to Korea?" I feared that over Saturday – the Jewish Sabbath – the idea had dissolved. Chaim, in his usual quiet and to-the-point tone, told me, "In principle, it's all set; we've made contact with a tourism service provider representing a tourism company in North Korea. All we need to do is to choose a date, and we're ready to move ahead." Before I had a chance to rejoice at this news, Chaim continued, cooling my enthusiasm: "I've consulted with Yaki (Yaakov Ben Menahem, CEO of Rimon Tours), and we decided that before moving ahead and spending money, we'll first check whether there's a potential market, and whether it's actually viable to run a tour to North Korea. We're going to publish an ad; we'll see whether there's a response, and its scope, and then we'll decide accordingly."

I left his office confused and frustrated. On one hand, his plan was realistic and seemed to make sense. On the other hand, I feared that lack of interest might kill the idea of the trip before it had a chance to be born. I was consumed by thoughts. My mood swung between cautious optimism and gloomy pessimism as to the chances of the trip happening. To stay calm, I decided to ignore my emotions and to think logically, so I could see things more clearly. I was about to lead a tour to Peru and Ecuador in March, and at the end of April I was going to be leading a tour to South Africa. That left a short, clearly-defined window of time in April in which I could participate in a learning tour. By the time the ad was published and the responses assessed, that window of opportunity would have closed. Moreover, the only obstacle in the way of moving ahead was the financial consideration. And that was a problem that could be solved.

The next day I was back in Chaim's office. "Chaim," I said, "About the North Korea trip – let's turn it around. In this case, we have to put the wagon before the horses."

"Meaning?" he asked.

I told him, "Quite simply, I'm going! Without any connection to the ad. You can publish the ad; if there's no response, I'll pay for my trip. If people are interested, my trip will be paid for as planned, by the company."

On the spot, with no hesitation, Chaim answered, "Done."

That's how the idea on the part of Chaim and the company to pioneer tours to North Korea dovetailed perfectly with my crazy dream and with the fantastic professional challenge that it represented for me. Now we needed to turn the ideas into reality.

*

Once the final decision had been made, we took action, starting with filling in forms. All the office staff accompanied my registration process, filling in the simple participation request forms that were sent to me by the service provider, scanning my passport and a high-quality photograph, and waiting for the response, which arrived the next day. There was a small problem: on my Israeli passport, for some reason, my date of birth appeared as 00.00.1948, and the service provider wasn't sure how the Koreans would deal with that. Determined not to allow a technicality to spoil the party, I proposed that I would fly to Korea with my European passport. Once again, the passport was scanned, along with a passport photo. The same day I received approval for the trip, and a few days later my visa approval arrived by email. The visa forms would be waiting for me in Beijing. Together with the approval we received four printed pages of recommendations as to preparations for the trip and, especially, behavior during the tour. The following is my summary of the material after making eight trips:

Instructions for Tourists in North Korea

1. The tour includes all meals – full board.
2. List of anticipated expenses during the tour, including the recommended tips for guides and driver.
3. During the trip only foreign currently may be used (euro, dollars, yuan).
4. Dress – casual, but shirts showing messages of a political nature should be avoided. At least one set of "respectable" clothing should be packed, including shoes.
5. No holy books allowed (a deliberate barrier against potential missionary activity), nor Lonely Planet travel guide books.
6. Upon arrival at the airport, you will be asked to present for inspection any book or newspaper of any type in your possession.
7. Communications in North Korea:

    a. Communications for locals: All the Koreans we came into contact with had smartphones, mostly of Chinese manufacture. But communication is limited to within the borders of North Korea, in terms of calls, internet, and apps. In other words – a complete disconnect from the outside world.

    b. Communications for tourists: No access to outside phone lines or internet. Complete disconnect, with the exception of the land line from the hotel room. Outgoing calls using the telephone in the hotel room are easy, and not especially expensive. It is technically possible to receive incoming calls, but this can be problematic, mainly because of language limitations of the recipients of the call – the reception clerks.

Rules of Etiquette During a Tour to North Korea:

1. In North Korea, leaders are regarded with great respect. Visitors are requested to comply with the norms of behavior in the country in general, and with regard to the leaders in particular.

2. Upon arrival in North Korea, all baggage is scanned. In addition, one has to prepare for manual inspection any electronic/communications equipment (cameras, phones, laptop computers, etc.), along with whatever books or newspapers one has brought.

3. Following passport control, passports are deposited with the authorities; they are returned to the passengers at the airport before they leave the country.

4. Photography: unlimited, except when it comes to military installations or military personnel, close-ups of people, or partial photographs of statues or pictures of the leaders.

5. Throughout the tour, participants must remain with the group. Do not leave the hotel at night. Any request to leave the group setting, during the day or at night in the hotel, must be addressed to one of the guides, who will do whatever he/she can to help.

6. The tour organizers conclude on a positive note: "We have extensive experience with our Korean guides; they make every effort to fulfill any reasonable request by tourists. Please give them a chance; cooperate with the local guides and local custom; and relax – a most enjoyable experience awaits you."

Hallelujah, I was registered for a tour to North Korea as part of a multi-national group. The trip was scheduled for April 13th. We checked with the Ministry of Foreign Affairs in Israel whether there was any formal obstacle to entering North Korea. Surprisingly enough, the country did not appear on the list of hostile states; there wasn't even a travel warning.

On the outside, the trip was moving ahead; on the inside, I was riding a rollercoaster of excitement, anticipation and curiosity, alternating with discomfort in the face of the unknown, anxiety, and fright.

Visa for North Korea

*

Yaki decided to join me on the trip. The technical arrangements were now behind us, and we had everything we needed: flight tickets, a hotel in Beijing, a meeting place and contact person from whom to collect the visas; flight tickets to Pyongyang, a tour itinerary, and pages of instructions. Now I had a different sort of preparation to do: it was time to learn and try to understand the place I was going to, and who I would be meeting there. I bought a book – the only travel guide book available – *Lonely Planet* (which, of course, I could not bring with me into North Korea), and consulted encyclopedias, Wikipedia, and online op-eds, printing out whatever I could find. I looked for relevant clips on YouTube and found a good number, bookmarked them, and decided to make time to watch and learn. I searched for any available sources of information. Once I had collected enough raw material and sat down to start studying it all, I suddenly decided, on the spur of the moment, that I didn't want to learn anything; I wanted to arrive in a state of ignorance. I would see, feel, and internalize, and when I got back to Israel I would compare my experiences with the information I had collected. (The more times I went back to North Korea and the more I think about it with hindsight, the happier I am with the decision I made.) Still, I couldn't go with no preparation whatsoever. I focused on reading up on the history of Korea, especially in the twentieth century, and a very general portrayal of the country's leaders and the period of their rule (see the box below). Inter alia I realized that I would be in North Korea on April 15th, birthday of the Father of the nation, Kim Il-Sung. (I wasn't aware yet of the importance of the occasion.)

The following is a summary of my preparatory reading:

Leaders of North Korea

President Kim Il-Sung: April 15th, 1912 – July 8th, 1994
Period of rule: 1948-1994 (Eternal President)
Portrayal: Freedom fighter, liberator from Japanese occupation, Founding Father, author of the constitution, fought for Korean unification.

*

Chairman Kim Jong-Il: 1941 – 2011
Leadership: 1994-2011 (Eternal Chairman)
Portrayal: Served the homeland all his life, perpetuating the revolution with all his might, leading with confidence during difficult times (famine, collapse of the Communist Bloc)

*

Marshal Kim Jong-Un: 1982-
Leadership: 2011 –
Portrayal: Continuing the revolution, leading a technological revolution that is rapidly driving the country towards a promising future

History (20th century)

1905: Japanese conquest
1910: Annexation to Japan
1945: Liberation (following the Japanese surrender to the US)
1945: Division of Korea along the 38th parallel
(US influence in the South; Soviet influence in the North)
1948 (August): South Korea declares independence
1948 (September): North Korea declares independence
1950-1953: Korean War

Other than some basic information, I didn't study in preparation for the trip. But my mind was working non-stop. I tried to imagine the reality that I would encounter during the visit. Images of the future tour arose in my mind in a rainbow of hues – gloomy grey, rosy pink, and everything in between. The images and their colors became entangled, resulting in fitful sleep and sudden awakenings. Waking up drenched in a cold sweat, I would calm myself with clear, rational thoughts.

As noted, there was no problem as far as the Foreign Ministry was concerned; not even a travel warning. Still... North Korea was constantly in the news, and the news wasn't encouraging. The following are some of the relevant headlines from the beginning of 2016 until our scheduled date of departure, in mid-April:

On January 2nd, 2016, a fourth nuclear test was carried out – the first in three years (the previous one had been in April 2013). On February 10th the headlines announced that the Chief-of-Staff of the North Korean army, Ri Yong-Gil, had been executed. There was no mention of how, but reports mentioned that in May, 2015, Defense Minister Hyon Yong-Chol had been executed in public by a firing squad using an anti-aircraft gun. On February 29th, a clip appeared showing American student Otto Warmbier pleading for his life, confessing to a "hostile act against the Korean people." The crime had taken place on January 2nd; on March 16th, he was sentenced to fifteen years of imprisonment and hard labor.

The news painted a frightening and very bleak picture. The North Korean rulers, and life in the country, were surrounded by mystery. But the little that did emerge pointed to a regime that was totalitarian, cruel, and – more than anything else – unpredictable to the point of lunacy, with not the slightest regard for its citizens, much less anyone else. In view of this public image, it was not surprising that people reacted the way they did upon hearing that I was going to North Korea. Conversations went more or less as follows:

"Where are you going?"

"North Korea."

"You mean South Korea, right?"

"No, North Korea."

"What?! Where that crazy guy is, the one with the funny haircut?"

"Yes, there."

"Aren't you afraid? You know what happened to that American?"

"I know. Yes, I'm afraid. But I'm going."

"You know they're going to show you only what they want you to see..."

"Yes. Again, I know, but I'm going."

"But you understand that whatever you see is just a show for tourists."

"I understand. But I want to go. I want to see the show; it must be the greatest production in the world..."

"Did you buy a return ticket, or just one-way?"

"One-way, of course. No point in wasting money."

"You must be going with a foreign passport."

"Correct. But only because of a technical problem. The guy I'm traveling with is going with his Israeli passport."

"What? They allow Israelis into North Korea?"

"Yes, they allow it, and it may surprise you to hear that there's no ban on travel there on the part of the Israeli government, either."

"Wow. Scary. Take care..."

It's hard to ignore the reactions of acquaintances, friends, and family who care about you. Their responses, the prevailing public opinion, the unknown, and, in addition, the pages of instructions and rules of behavior that I had received, all intensified my fears and undermined my confidence in the decision I had made.

At some stage I decided to try again to deal rationally with my fears. I decided that the Korean security authorities must certainly have access to world internet, and they must have tools for dealing with the Hebrew language. Moreover, throughout my stay in the country I would be monitored – in other words, filmed and recorded, and my possessions would be exposed to scrutiny and searches. All this led directly to an all-encompassing decision: I would act and behave precisely in accordance with the guidelines and instructions. (On each of my return visits to North Korea, those same assumptions, which I never managed to either prove or disprove, remained the basis for all my conduct in the country. At this stage, prior to departure, they helped me to deal with my fears.)

I had no illusions that a trip to North Korea would show me what really went on there. This wasn't, nor was it meant to be, a research trip. I just wanted to see and sense the place, as though watching a play. When you go to the theater, you watch a drama onstage. If the backdrop shows a house, you know that it isn't really a house, but as a spectator you still regard the space as though it were a real house. You aren't interested in what happens backstage. All I wanted was to a spectator in a reality show, but much later I was able to say that I had also been exposed to some of what was happening behind the scenes. Not in great depth; I managed to see just a little of what went on beyond the screen separating the audience from the stage. And so the main image that remains is the image of the stage. I certainly make no pretense at understanding more than that.

In addition to all my anxiety about the "objective" reality, there was also a fear that related to my own personal circumstances. I was going to enter the country with a European passport; it was entirely possible that they would riffle through my bag and find my Israeli passport, since I needed it in order to leave China. They would then start looking for information about me on the internet, and since I had already come to the realization that Hebrew isn't hieroglyphics, the authorities would discover that I had been an officer in the Israeli Air Force. Israel is an ally of the Great Satan – the US. They would have a super-spy on their hands. Wonderful.

I was having trouble sleeping. I feared that if I shared my thoughts with my family – certainly with my wife – I would transfer my anxiety to them and make them fearful, too; all this time I was outwardly calm and confident. So the only option left was to consult with myself.

The "consultation" led to simple, practical decisions: to conduct myself on the trip as I do when driving on the road; to ignore the fear and its source in factors that were not under my control, and to take great care to behave in accordance with the rules, instructions, and road signs. I would be especially cautious, and in the case of the slightest doubt, I would consult with the local guides.

As for my Israeli passport, I decided to take action. At the moment when I had to deposit my European passport, I would hand over my Israeli passport as well, and would explain to the clerk that I was an Israeli; I would also declare that I was a retired officer of the Israeli Air Force.

It is difficult to describe the relief and calm that replaced my fears once I had made these decisions. I was eager and ready for the journey.

CHAPTER 3
Black Hole Shock

April 11th, 2016. Yaki and I set off. We waved goodbye to friends, family and work colleagues, but this was no ordinary goodbye. It was more like the sendoffs for ships during the voyages of discovery: wooden ships with sails, at the mercy of the wind to progress, using the most rudimentary navigational methods, and with a supply of food limited in both its quantity and its diversity. Everyone wished us a safe return, and of course plied us with "practical" advice: "Take care of yourselves," "Don't get up to nonsense," "Don't try any tricks," "You know that...."

*

Yaki and I were in Beijing. It was two days before we were due to join the multi-national group for the tour to North Korea, and we still knew nothing about its composition. Our tour was organized by URI – a company that the Operations Department at Rimon had selected as the most serious option, based on the speed of response to our inquiries and its professionalism. Of course, the choice had involved taking a chance and some measure of intuition, too, and it turned out to be successful, leading to effective, ongoing cooperation (we worked together on nine groups between 2016 – 2018).

To give us an opportunity to evaluate a competitor who seemed serious and professional, on the morning of the second day Yaki had a business meeting with the director of another tourism company that organized tours to North Korea. The main reason for Yaki joining me on the trip was intellectual curiosity. The business initiative had been that of Chaim Peres, CEO of Tarbutu, but since Yaki was already here, and ultimately the aim of the trip was to bring groups to North Korea, we set up the meeting.

Tours to North Korea are not marketed directly by the Koreans. A number of Western and Chinese companies have been approved by the Koreans as agents for organizing and marketing them. Obviously, they compete with one another for clients. The meeting was a business meeting, and since the business aspect isn't my department, I found myself in the position of a participating observer, following with interest the discussion between Yaki and the tourist agent, who was trying to present the advantages to be gained by teaming up with his company for our future tours. My observation of them led to my first surprise (it would not be my last) with regard to the North Koreans. From what this agent (who was English) was saying, I gathered that he represented a North Korean company that was a competitor to the company we had planned our trip with. To the best of my understanding, under the Communist system – and certainly in a country that zealously upholds socialist ideals – the entire economy is in the hands of the government. In Romania I had encountered just one tourism company – a state tourism monopoly. I had found a similar situation in my initial encounters with the "socialist" world in Yugoslavia, Bulgaria, China, Vietnam and Cuba. So where was competition in North Korea coming from? I didn't delve into the question in depth, but somewhere in the recesses of my consciousness a light went on. I had to be open to identify situations in which all kinds of exclamation marks regarding "clear facts" about North Korea should perhaps become question marks...

*

At 11:00 on the morning of April 14th, 2016, we were at Beijing Airport, Terminal 3, next to Loi Café. There were supposed to meet Yuan, the URI representative; she would give us our flight tickets and visas for North Korea. We arrived early, which gave us time for coffee and an opportunity to start identifying our fellow travelers. This initial encounter at the airport allowed us to make brief acquaintance. The group numbered nine participants. Aside from Yaki and myself there was a youngster of about thirty, named Ambrose, from Singapore, and Todd and Charles from Hawaii, both around forty. Later on, they told us that, as socialists, they had chosen this tour in order to observe at close hand the economic system that they believed in. There were another three Americans of about the same age: Brian, Michael, and the only woman in the group – Gina. They had booked the tour out of curiosity. All three were employees of United Airlines, and knew each other. Last was a friendly guy named Mike Hoer from Utah, USA. Mike had long-standing, in-depth familiarity with totalitarian culture in the East – Communist China. Over the course of the tour he and I forged a friendship that deepened over many conversations, giving rise to insights that would be of great importance and help for my future tours. I went on to seek his advice on the sorts of questions and situations that arise in North Korea, and we remain friends to this day.

One woman and eight men of three nationalities would quickly bond into a nice, supportive group that was fun to tour with, on the basis of the common denominator we all shared: curiosity and a strong desire to decode the North Korean enigma – or, at least, to remove one of the countless layers of camouflage concealing the greatest political riddle of the early twentieth century.

Yuan, the URI (meaning "We," in Korean) representative, arrived as planned, distributed the visas and tickets, and directed us to the Air Koryo counters. There was a brief, to-the-point check before the flight, then border control, and we found ourselves waiting for the short flight to Pyongyang via Air Koryo – the North Korean national airline, rated for four years running by the British Skytrax website as the world's worst airline.

With this less-than-encouraging information in mind, we boarded the plane, a Russian Tupolev Tu-204 airliner. Smiling air stewardesses guided us to our roomy, leather seats with informational and propaganda pamphlets in the seat pockets. We perused the pictures showing North Korea, many of them, of course, starring the ruler, Marshal Kim Jung-Un. The plane filled up completely. The great majority of the passengers were tourists like ourselves. Takeoff was exactly on time. The flight duration was around an hour and a half. Immediately after takeoff, the air stewardesses distributed drinks. After the round of drinks we received a light meal – the Korean version of a hamburger. Following the meal, another round of drinks. I looked around. It seemed that the natural tension had softened somewhat among the passengers, and I found myself wondering: On what basis had this airline been awarded the title, "Worst airline in the world?" (Incidentally, it turned out that while I just wondered, others had protested, and Skytrax changed the rating to "not rated," owing to the small number of respondents. Moreover, Tripadvisor awarded the North Korean airline a decent, medium-level rating, with three and a half stars out of five).

During the flight all passengers received three forms to fill in: an entry form, a health questionnaire, and a customs declaration that demanded, inter alia, a list of foreign currency, electronic communications and photography devices, as well as books, in our possession. Among the pages of instructions we had received from the tour agent there had been copies of these forms and instructions for filling them in. The instructions could be summarized in two brief commands of universal validity: Declare the truth! If you have any doubt, don't fill in anything, and explain when you're asked. Like all the other passengers, we too were soon absorbed in filling in the forms. When I reached the section with the foreign currency declaration, I took out the money I had in a pouch hidden under my clothing, and counted it to be sure that my declaration would be accurate. As I was doing so, I stole a glance around and noticed that those around me, sooner or later, were doing the same. Apparently, they had all received the same instructions, and they had all decided that they should not annoy the North Korean authorities. Like everyone else, I turned the time on my watch half an hour ahead. The time in North Korea is half an hour ahead of China, and half an hour behind South Korea and Japan.

*

Around an hour and a half after takeoff, according to schedule, we arrive at the Pyongyang Sunan International Airport, North Korea. I am eager to see the country for the first time, but at the same time I find myself hesitating. I am full of anticipation without knowing what to expect; mostly, I am preoccupied with the entry procedure that awaits me, hoping that I won't face any obstacles or unexpected problems: dual passport; an inaccurate declaration; a search turning up something suspicious; or the like. The natural tension in view of the process ahead overshadows my excitement at arriving at my destination and at the realization of a long-held dream.

A skybridge leads me to a terminal with shiny grey granite flooring. I am struck by the cleanliness. My initial surprise is replaced by tension surrounding the formalities. At the entrance is a health inspection counter. Two uniformed personnel take the three forms I hold out to them, and select the health questionnaire. They barely glance at us or at the form, hand the other pages back to us, and with a courteous hand gesture point us in the direction of the border control counters that are about ten meters away. There are ten border control counters, with six to ten passengers in front of each of them. One by one we approach the counter, and my turn arrives. In rudimentary English the policeman asks for my passport, my visa form, and my entry form. After a brief and businesslike review, he stamps the visa. The passport receives no stamp! The policeman hands the documents back to me, adding, "Welcome to the Democratic People's Republic of Korea." That's it! I'm in North Korea! So far, it's immeasurably faster and simpler than the procedure I had imagined, but this is surely not the end of the story. The main challenge is still ahead of me, and all of us. Further along in the hall is the baggage carousel. Only one flight arrives at a time in Pyongyang. All the passengers line up along the lone carousel that is active. As our suitcases arrive we head for the baggage check stations. All our luggage will be subjected to inspection and scanning. I hold a packet in which I have prepared everything that will undergo careful scrutiny. In my case, this includes only a cellphone and a video camera that the company has provided me with. Others are carrying cameras, portable computers, tablets, books, and more. While we wait, a uniformed policeman approaches the first person in line, asks for his passport and packet of items, and passes it on, behind the checking counter. The wait in line lasts about fifteen minutes, but the tension surrounding the inspection makes it seem longer. When my turn comes, I approach the official. He looks towards me, points to the equipment that I am carrying and to my passport, and asks me to affirm that it all belongs to me. Upon my affirmation he politely allows me to enter the Arrivals hall. The entire process has taken less than an hour since the moment we landed. If only it was like that in all airports around the world. My mind quickly flips through recollections of nightmare arrivals in Romania, Yugoslavia, Bulgaria and China, two decades ago, and even Cuba in recent years. I think to myself: it isn't at all as I thought.

The Arrivals hall isn't big. The terminal isn't big either; it's more or less like Terminal 1 at Ben Gurion airport, in Israel – at least in terms of size, but not in terms of the gleaming, spotless cleanliness. Around me in the hall are kiosks selling water and mementos. The word "nice" – perhaps even "very nice" – sums up my airport experience thus far.

The arrival procedure is, by definition, individual, and thus as I emerge I look around for the others. Near the entrance I immediately spot some members of the group crowded around someone who, it turns out, is one of our guides for the trip. Before I even have a chance to enjoy the sense of relief it suddenly occurs to me that, in my enthusiasm, I have forgotten to take back the video camera. (Cameras are foreign to me; as it see it, the best way to do photography is to observe with one's eyes and then save images to the brain. Later on I manage to forget the camera again.) But in my excitement I'm not even irritated at myself. I approach our guide – a young man of about thirty, not tall, rather chubby and round, his placid face beaming goodwill. I introduce myself by name, and ask for his name. "Mister Li," he answers. I tell him about the video camera that I've forgotten at customs control, on the other side of the curtain. Mister Li isn't overly concerned. He turns to a woman who looks around forty, standing at a slight distance from us. She is of medium build, with a face that conveys stern rigidity. They exchange a few words. The woman turns to me in a tone much calmer and more pleasant than her appearance suggests. "I am Miss Li," she introduces herself, adding, "I will be your guide for this tour." I glance at Mr. Li, and back at her, as though asking whether they are related. With a knowing smile she says, "No, I'm not related to Mr. Li. The name 'Li' is very common in Korea." Immediately she looks serious again, resumes a businesslike air and asks me to describe the camera and the manufacturer. I give her a brief description and she gestures for me to follow her. Quite matter-of-factly, and to my surprise with no restriction, we go back to the customs area. Miss Li asks me at which counter I did the check, and I point to it. We approach what appears to be the manager's counter, and before we even reach him, the manager standing there hands me the camera, casually and with no formalities. The story of the camera comes to an end. Now, in accordance with the written instructions we received prior to the trip, and spurred by the fears that I fed my mind, telling myself that the fact that I was an Israeli who had "sneaked" into North Korea with a European passport would be discovered, and would put me – and maybe Yaki too – at risk, I turn to Miss Li and ask, "Where do we deposit our passports?"

"With me," she answers, and holds out her hand to receive the passport. I pull out both of my passports, the European and the Israeli, presenting the Israeli one first and launching into the speech I have practiced at length:

"Here are my two passports, the European one and the Israeli one. I entered Korea with my European passport, because my birth date in the Israel passport is 00.00. 1948, and I thought it might cause a problem."[4]

---

4   As I spoke, I recalled "The Poem of the Soviet Passport" (1929) by Vladimir Mayakovsky (1893-1930). Despite having been born into the Russian nobility, Mayakovsky identified with the ideas of the Communist Revolution and was one of the most prominent revolutionary poets. After the Revolution, he traveled extensively by train throughout Europe. Passport checks would be carried out during the journey. In the poem, he describes how the attitude of the officials towards the passengers would differ depending on their passports: British, American, Polish, or Scandinavian. When the officials see his red passport, decorated with the hammer and sickle emblem, their faces express disgust

I take a deep breath and go on:

"Let it be understood, I'm an Israeli, my home is in Israel, all my family is in Israel."

Another brief pause, and I continue my "confession": "I'm a retired Israeli Air Force officer, after twenty-two years of service."

Miss Li takes both passports with an air of apathy that is almost insulting. My speech seems to have made no impression whatsoever; she doesn't offer any response. Her body language and demeanor seem to say, "Israeli, Turkish, Polish; what's the difference?" I feel as though a great weight has been lifted from my shoulders, and, with the addition of the camera that is now back in my possession, my mood improves tremendously.

I go back to the Arrivals hall. Some members of the group are chatting with Mr. Li; others are walking around the terminal hall. At the stalls selling souvenirs and drinks, all business is conducted in foreign currency: euro, dollars, or Chinese yuan. I note that all the Koreans I have met thus far display a badge on their clothing showing one or more of their leaders. I point to the badge on Mr. Li's lapel, and say, "I would like a badge like that too. Where can I buy one?" Indicating the souvenir shops, I ask, "Which of them would have it?" Mr. Li answers with an embarrassed smile, "You can't buy a badge like this. It's only for citizens of our country; we receive it."

This was actually the first casual conversation I had with a citizen of North Korea. Later on I would come to understand that

---

and contempt. Mayakovsky describes how he pulls out his passport and launches into a speech whose essence may be summed up as follows (in free translation): "I, Vladimir Mayakovsky, hand this precious document over to you for your inspection. Read it and envy me; I am a citizen of the Soviet Union!" The poem was published only in 1930, after his death (by suicide), and remained a fixture of the Soviet educational system up until the collapse of the USSR. There is no graduate of the Soviet educational system who did not learn the poem by heart.

I had made two mistakes: firstly, I had pointed with my finger at images of the leaders. Secondly, I had sought to buy as an entertaining souvenir the pin that Koreans wear with "religious" honor and pride on their lapel. But as a visitor who had only just arrived, it was clear to my hosts that I wasn't familiar with the local customs. Moreover, it seems that I wasn't the first to make these mistakes; later on, when I came back again and again, I saw many other people do the same. They make mistakes, and are forgiven.

The minutes went by. The terminal started to empty out, and eventually we found ourselves the last ones there. I wondered about this and asked Mr. Li where Miss Li was, and why we weren't setting off. His answer was that there was a small problem with one of the members of the group, which Miss Li was dealing with. "It will take just a few minutes," he told me. A few minutes passed, as we waited in the empty terminal, and eventually Miss Li and the tourist arrived. She was matter-of-fact and ready to go; the tourist explained with a smile that his portable computer held a film that was forbidden to bring into Korea, and he had been asked to delete it. We were slightly worried; he maintained his calming smile and described the customs officials' conduct as polite and efficient. We boarded our bus and noticed that the terminal was being locked. Our tour of North Korea was beginning. First experience: The only international airport in the country, in the capital city. A lone plane lands, the passengers are processed, and then the airport is closed; they "roll up" the terminal for the day! Truly, a unique experience. Not mind-blowing, but it introduces a reality that will reveal itself in the days to follow, an alternative reality that exists only in North Korea.

*

We are on the bus. Nine travelers – six Americans, two Israelis, and one Singaporean. Miss Li holds the microphone; she introduces the driver, Mister Li (as the second guide), and herself (as the head guide). The bus makes its way out of the parking area to the highway leading to Pyongyang, the capital. The road twists to the right, and again I look with astonishment at the airport as it is locked behind us.

Miss Li starts her tour. While she is explaining, my eyes are glued to the road. I try to internalize the view, to find something unusual. Actually, it's not clear to me what I'm looking for, or what I expect to see. In front of me is a two-way street in reasonable condition, green fields, farmers working the land, others walking on the sides of the road. Nothing really fascinating. At the same time, Miss Li is giving a brief presentation of Korea – North and South, together and separately: territory, population, climate, geographic structure, and a brief historical review, taking care to call her country DPRK – the abbreviation for the Democratic People's Republic of Korea.[5] Miss Li continues her historical survey, carefully navigating her way around potential landmines. The facts and data that she is providing are objective and arouse no antagonism. We listen carefully to what she is saying, while trying to take in our first sights of the DPRK. At one point we interrupt with a question – "May we take photographs?" and are answered with a smile, in the affirmative.

Our question leads her to what seems to us – and, I believe, even more to Miss Li – as the most important part of her open-

---

5   Throughout all my visits to North Korea, the locals have called their country "Korea." They talk about "South Korea" or "the other part of Korea" only when visiting the border area, and during the tour at the War Museum – which commemorates the Korean War!

ing lecture: the rules of etiquette to be followed on the tour. She begins as follows:

"We know that our rules of etiquette are different from those in the countries that you come from. We also believe that rules of etiquette differ between any countries. We ask you to respect our customs, just as we will respect you and your customs when we come to your countries."

In a very friendly and non-threatening tone, Miss Li sets forth the instructions, not before noting, "We, citizens of the DPRK, have great honor for our Leaders, and it's important to us that you respect the honor with which we regard them."

She goes on: "If you have in your possession a picture of one of our Leaders, which you might find in your room, or which you took from the plane, or which you bought at a souvenir shop, we ask: Do not sit on it, don't cut it or crumple it, and certainly don't throw it into the trash.

At certain sites, when we come to statues of our Leaders, you will be asked to bow. If this custom disturbs any of you, we respect you and ask that you stand aside until the others have finished the brief ceremony in keeping with our custom. Only after the bow are you invited to take pictures of the statues. But please – when you photograph, take care to photograph the figures in full, so that no part of the Leader's body is cropped. Also, we do not use a finger to point at someone else, and certainly not at pictures of the Leaders, or statues or emblems of them. If you wish to point to them, please do this," and she demonstrated: "Extend the whole had towards what it is that you wish to point to, in a loose, open movement, with the fingers of the hand not flexed; a sort of gesture of respect."

I tried it. Try it yourself – and see how simple and respectful it is. Now I understood my mistake in pointing at the badge showing the leaders on Mr. Li's lapel.

The rules of respect and conduct are simple and clear. Miss Li continues with her instructions:

"Photography. You are invited to photograph as you wish, subject to the following limitations: You may not photograph military personnel or military installations. You may photograph people up close, but only after receiving their permission; as to photographing the Leaders – we have already discussed that. For your safety (?!) we ask that you do not go about alone. During the day, we will be together anyway. After we reach the hotel, you are requested to remain inside. If you wish to go out, ask Mr. Li or myself, and we will be glad to accompany you. In general, we are here to assist you in everything. If there is anything that is unclear, ask us. If there is anything that you want, or request, we will do whatever we can to help you."

The rules of conduct, which sounded more like a request for cooperation, in terms of both their content and their manner of presentation, helped to break the tension we were feeling and left us all – travelers and staff alike – with a feeling of calm and tranquility. Later on in this tour, and to an even greater extent in the tours that followed, I realized that these rules of conduct are simple, logical, and easy to carry out, and they should be treated like traffic rules in a country where people drive on the left side of the road: one simply becomes accustomed to the local custom, and respects it.

Our guide's speech lasted about half an hour, as we covered twenty-five kilometers from Sunan Airport, and we found ourselves at the gateway to Pyongyang.

*

Pyongyang, capital of North Korea, the seat of government as well as the cultural and economic center of the country. Pyongyang! Around three million inhabitants, about fifteen percent of the country's population. Its area is about two thousand square kilometers (in comparison, Greater London is around 1,600 square kilometers), with the Taedong River running through the city from east to south-west. I am full of curiosity. In fact, I am altogether caught up in anticipation of the sights of the city, and to tell the truth, I don't know what to expect. So I decide to set aside any sort of expectation, and simply to give myself over to the sights. The first encounter with the city isn't impressive. The residential buildings recall the construction projects in Eastern Europe after the Second World War, or the immigrant neighborhoods built in Israel in the 1950s. Despite the unimpressive architecture, the streets are notable for their cleanliness; the sidewalks are wide enough to accommodate a great many pedestrians, and some locals are waiting in a very orderly line for the bus.

We enter the city from the north, and in front of my eyes I see evidence of the "facts" that everyone knows about the poverty and disrepair even though this is a capital city. On the other hand, nothing has prepared me for the sights that reveal themselves after about five minutes' driving inside the city. All of a sudden, the scenery changes completely, as though a new slide show has replaced the previous one. While there is none of the traffic congestion that we associate with a city of three million inhabitants, the streets are far from empty of cars. The city is built on generous, spacious lines: parks, monuments, and many public buildings alongside nice residential buildings. It's a very impressive city! We continue our panoramic drive, but something is disturbing me; there is something strange about the appearance of the city. Seemingly everything is "right," but there is something that doesn't add up.

We approach the Immortality Tower obelisk that marks the beginning of Ryomyong Street; further along is Kim Il-Sung University (the events on this street in April 2017 will be described at length later on). Immediately after it, on the opposite site, is another monument: Friendship Tower, dedicated to the Chinese nation and its army, which helped North Korea during the Korean War. This is the only acknowledgement of Chinese participation in the war. The role of China and of the USSR in the war is played down in the North Korean account. On the left is the Kaeson Youth Park, which includes a modern amusement park with enticing rides. Looking ahead, I see the Arch of Triumph at the center of a huge square. Adjacent to the square is Kim Il-Sung Stadium. Our eyes are drawn to a huge mural depicting Kim Il-Sung's victory speech on August 15th, 1945, upon Korea's liberation from Japanese occupation.

I try to ignore my urge to decipher the strangeness of the city and to concentrate instead on the sights, but the riddle continues to nag at me. Slowly, from behind utter surprise of entering Pyongyang, the capital, my mind starts to make sense of it: as in the games of my childhood, when I would look for the slight differences between two almost identical pictures, I try to discern how this city is different from other cities around the world. It is the mural that all of a sudden illuminates, in a flash, the strangeness of the city. Unlike anywhere else I have been, there is no signage showing company names on office buildings; no advertisements, no commercial slogans, no sign of any banks. Restaurants and stores do not show off their wares for passersby to see; they do not invite people to eat, buy, enjoy. Instead, there are countless painted murals and propaganda boards in the streets, praising and glorifying the homeland and, of course – mainly – the leaders. Pyongyang: an alternative reality, only in North Korea.

We do not make a stop; later on in the tour we will visit the square and its environs. We hurry on to the Mansudae Grand Monument. Owing to the delay at the airport, there is time for only one stop before dark, and the guides choose this site. The bus continues on its journey, passing by the Chollima Statue – a winged horse on a pedestal. "The mythological Korean horse gallops hundreds of kilometers in a day," Miss Li explains. "The mythological horse is allegorical; it symbolizes North Korea and its gallop towards the country's bright future." We are at the foot of Mansudae (Mansu Hill). The bus turns right, while all eyes look to the left, to an enormous, tall, wide structure built in the style of a Chinese pagoda. This is the Great People's Study House. The Study House looks out onto Kim Il-Sung Square. Another right turn, and all eyes are still looking to the left: on the hill is another giant structure: the National Assembly building, seat of the North Korean parliament. The bus makes yet another right turn and once again, on the left, another giant building appears: the Museum of the Revolution. We are now facing Mansudae – Mansu Hill. The bus makes a steady, gentle climb to the parking lot. On our right is the Mansudae Water Fountain Park.

We reach the Mansudae Monument. To the left, looming tall, are the heads of the two statues of the leaders. It's the middle of April; the sun is starting to set, and we need to conclude our visit before dark. The lower the sun dips, the colder it gets. We are not properly equipped for the chill of the evening, but our curiosity urges us to hurry up and disembark. Li Mi-Soon (Miss Li's full name) asks us to listen to her instructions. She emphasizes again, in the tone reserved for sacred sites, the respect that Koreans have for their leaders:

"The statues of the Leaders at Mansudae are the main site in Korea where we express our thanks to our Leaders. We customarily express our appreciation with flowers, and with a bow."

Miss Li points to a few stalls and continues, "Whoever would like to, is invited to purchase a bouquet of flowers and to lay it at the feet of the statues of the Leaders. A bouquet costs five euro." Since Yaki and I have agreed in advance that we are here to participate in the show, we see this as an opportunity for a "brief appearance onstage," and before Miss Li can complete the sentence, Yaki and I exchange glances and I jump up and say that we are interested. Following our example, all the other members of the group likewise express their wish to lay flowers. Mr. Li collects the money, and while he goes off to buy the bouquets, Miss Li continues with her instructions:

"During the ascent and the ceremony, it is appropriate not to chatter, and certainly not to talk loudly. Hands should not be placed in pockets. First we will lay the bouquets, then we will stand in a line and bow together. Only after that can we take photographs. During the photographs we will take care not to photograph only parts of the Leader. For those using video cameras, please take care to film the Leaders consecutively, and take care that when shifting the focus of the camera from the Leaders to the surroundings and background, the filming should be halted so that the frame doesn't cut the image of the Leader."

After we confirm that we have understood the instructions, we get off the bus. As noted, daylight is receding and it is already quite cool, but all our attention is focused on the statues of the leaders, about a hundred meters to our left, atop the hill. Mr. Li returns with the flowers and hands each of us a bouquet. I am busy trying to photograph the statues. Mr. Li turns to me in a soft tone and says, "Avraham" – he has already learned the names of all nine members of the group – "We do not photograph our Leaders in profile." He goes on to explain, "After we lay the flowers and bow, we can take photographs." For a moment I am distraught; I dare not make mistakes like this! But Mr. Li's tone and body language are tranquil and calming.

Holding the flowers, proceeding quietly and respectfully, we start to ascend the gentle slope leading to the monument. The path leading to the top of the hill is paved and wide, with grass and flowers on both sides, and speakers hidden within the foliage play quiet music. We walk for about two minutes, and then the site is revealed to us in all its glory. My gaze is drawn to two statues, 22 meters tall.[6] In the background is a gigantic mural of Mount Paektu, on the wall of the Museum of the Revolution. We climb about ten steps leading to a raised platform. The statues stand on a base that is taller than a person, and the base itself rests on a sort of "stage" that is about a meter higher than the platform that the visitors stand on. Li Mi-Soon wastes no time: she arranges all of us – nine travelers and two guides – in a row, about ten meters from the stage, and then asks us all to draw closer and lay the bouquets. We follow her instructions, setting down the bouquets at the feet of the statues of the leaders, and then turn around and, with our backs to the statues[7], come back into the line. After we are all in order, we again face the leaders. Li Mi-Soon asks that we follow her example. She makes a deep bow, and we imitate her. The bow lasts about three seconds. Then we gather around her; she starts by telling us about the site, then reminds us the rules for photography, before freeing us to photograph, observe, and take in the site. I am seized by a profound embarrassment. How is it that I – an enlightened liberal – am moved by this pagan ritual that is so foreign to me, part of a totalitarian religion, at such a megalomanic site? I push these thoughts to the back of my mind and concentrate on what I am seeing. Darkness is beginning to fall. The city lights come on, but rather dimly. Against this background, the monuments stand out prominently: to the

---

6   For the second time this evening – and again, with a cynical smile – a poem comes to me. The sight of the statues reminds me of my matriculation examination in Hebrew literature, featuring the poem by Saul Tchernichovsky, inspired by a statue of Apollo: "I come to thee and here before thy pedestal I kneel..."

7   Thus refuting many publications that declare it forbidden to turn one's back on the statues of the Leaders.

left, about five hundred meters from us, is the Chollima Monument. Opposite us is the Workers' Party Monument, and a glance to the right shows the Juche Tower.[8]

After a few minutes we start making our way back to the bus. Owing to the cold, I unthinkingly put my hands into my pockets, and feel a light tap on my shoulder. Mr. Li politely reminds me that we are not supposed to put hands into pockets. Having been "caught in the act," I apologize, my voice betraying my alarm. Mr. Li is reassuring: "It's okay; I understand. It takes time to get used to our etiquette."

Mansudae – Monument and Myth

Mansu Hill ("Mansu" means "Long Life;" "dae" means "hill" – thus, "Hill of Long Life") is only about thirty meters high, but its location in the heart of Pyongyang lends it undeniable advantages. The monument was built in 1972, at the initiative of the heir apparent (at the time), Kim Jong-Il, in honor of the sixtieth birthday of his father, the "Great Leader," President Kim Il-Sung. In 2011, with the death of General Kim Jong-Il, a statue of him was placed alongside that of his father. The hill commands an impressive panoramic view of the capital. At its center are the two enormous bronze statues. The leaders face the city, looking out over the nation of laborers, as well as the three central, most significant monuments: about five hundred meters to the left of us is the Chollima Monument; opposite us, exactly 2,016 meters away (an allusion to Kim Jong-Il's birthday: 2 = February, 016 = 16th, 1941), is the Monument to the Founding of the Korean Workers Party, and to the right, on the other side of the river, at a distance of about three kilometers, is Juche Tower.

---

8   Each of these monuments will be discussed in greater detail below.

In the background is the Museum of the Revolution, and on the wall of the museum is a huge mosaic showing Mount Paekto. To the left is the statue of the (Eternal!) Great Leader, President Kim Il-Sung. As in all pictures and statues of him, he is wearing formal, stately garb. His face projects a loving, fatherly smile, as appropriate to the Great Leader. To his right is his successor, his son, the (Eternal!) Chairman, dressed in workers' garb, with the serious expression of a man who is engaged in running the country. The figure of the present leader, Marshal Kim Jong-Un, is absent.

On either side of the statues there is a red granite monument depicting a group of more than two hundred figures. These sculptures depict the fundamental myths of North Korea: one shows the struggle against the Japanese; the other – the heroic revolution.

The site is more than a monument; it is a manifesto.[9] The organization, in this case, is the state, and the manifesto includes the essence of the fundamental principles and ideas of North Korea. These are:

The Revolution: The ideology of revolution defines North Korea and differentiates it from South Korea. As noted, on each of the sides of the statues of the leaders there is a battery of red granite figures. One of these monuments is dedicated to the Revolution; the other, to the war of liberation from Japanese occupation. In

---

9   According to Wikipedia, a manifesto is a "published declaration of the intentions, motives, or views of the issuer, be it an individual, group, political party or government." Monuments in general, and in North Korea in particular, may be works of art, but the art is a by-product. The work's main purpose is to convey an overt message and – perhaps no less importantly – a covert one. In this sense they are similar to Western churches, especially Byzantine or Medieval Catholic churches (particularly those in Romanesque or Gothic style).

addition, the Museum of the Revolution is the wall upon which the background mosaic – Mount Paektu – appears.

Mount Paektu: This mountain, included in the national emblem of North Korea, is the tallest mountain in the country, reaching 2,774 meters. It is a volcanic mountain in the north-western part of the country, on the Chinese-North Korean border. The crater lake in the caldera is the source of three rivers, two of which trace the country's land borders. The Yalu River forms the border with China; the Tumen River forms the border with Russia.

Mt. Paektu is the formative myth of both parts of Korea. According to Korean mythology, it was here, in the year 2333 B.C.E. that Dangun, founder of Korea's first Imperial Dynasty, Gojoseon, was born.

In addition, Mt. Paektu also plays a central role in contemporary myth: North Korea is Korea! Mount Paektu and its environs were the base for the resistance against Japanese occupying forces, led by Kim Il-Sung and his wife, Kim Jong-Suk, who is regarded as a brave fighter and national heroine. It was here, in 1941, during the battle to liberate Korea from Japanese occupation, that Kim Jong-Il was born.[10]

Figures of leaders: President Kim Il-Sung is always shown in stately clothing. He is the Great Leader. His paternal visage projects indulgence and determination: determination against the enemy, indulgence and love towards his children – the people. He is portrayed in this convivial manner wherever his image appears, anywhere in the country.

---

10 According to a Western source (backed up by official documentation), Kim Jung Il was born in Russia, in the village of Vyatskoye. Kim Jong-Suk, his mother, died when he was a child in 1949, in childbirth, together with the baby.

Chairman Kim Jung-Il is always in working clothes: busy, occupied, altogether given over to the people, and leading them on the path of the revolution.

The image of the present leader, Marshal Kim Jong-Un, is absent. There is no statue or picture of him to be seen in the streets or town squares. The message is, "I don't have time for commemorations; I am busy leading the country forward into the future." His figure hovers over everyday existence. Pictures of him are shown on television, in the press, and in performances, and he is heard on the radio and on TV.

Dynasty: This is the first and only dynasty in the Communist world. The seventy-five year rule of the Kim family is rather remarkable. There are certainly those who attribute the achievement to cruel tyranny. Even assuming that that is indeed the nature of the regime, it is not unique in the Communist world, and therefore there must be some other element to explain this phenomenon. The Mansudae Monument presents at least one conspicuous clue: a close connection with the past. The contemporary myth is bound up with the formative myth of Mount Paektu. Whereas elsewhere in the Communist world there is a struggle against formative myths, here they are enlisted in support of the ruling family.

Monuments: Visitors to the site, like the statues of the leaders, look out over the city and over three prominent monuments, each with its statement. The Juche Tower is dedicated to the most important and central idea in the North Korean ideology: self-reliance. The Workers' Party Monument, of course, symbolizes the revolution. The Chollima Monument indicates the direction: a gallop towards a better future.

What about the US? As noted, at the sides of the statues of the leaders are two reminders of heroic battles: the Revolution, and the struggle against the Japanese. Why is there no hint of the great enemy, the US? Perhaps because the US is politically connected to the establishment of North Korea, and if any mention is made of the US in the military context of WWII, its decisive role in Japan's defeat might lead raise inconvenient questions. Nevertheless, the US stars in countless murals, museums and monuments as the great enemy of North Korea and the source of all its difficulties.

*

Our first encounter with Pyongyang is drawing to an end. Back on the bus, on the way to the hotel, Li Mi-Soon tells us, "I'm proud that all the members of the group chose to honor our Leaders with flowers. I hope that you enjoyed the visit, and once again I thank you for the honor that you showed to our Leaders." After a drive of about ten minutes, we see in front of us the central train station of Pyongyang, a starting or end point for the train journey between Pyongyang-Dandong and Beijing. Immediately after the train station we arrive at our hotel – Koryo Hotel, the best tourist hotel in the city. Officially it rates five stars. The hotel comprises two 45-story towers. At the top of one of the towers is a revolving restaurant. The hotel also features a swimming pool and gym (which we will have no time to use) as well as a great number of restaurants and stores. As the bus pulls to a stop at the entrance to the hotel, three porters pounce on it, and before we even have time to disembark, all our baggage is already waiting in the lobby. The lobby is grand; at the entrance, on the right, is the reception desk and a café; on the left is a sort of cafeteria which we will visit to drink beer. Opposite is a restaurant, which looks promising, and on each side are elevators for the two towers. Our guide returns from the reception desk, distributes the keys to the rooms, and issues instructions regarding the rest of the evening and the timetable for tomorrow. She reminds us that we are not to leave the hotel without a guide. "We will meet in another hour for dinner," she tells us. In response to my question as to the possibility of communications with Israel and the costs involved, she asks me to accompany her to the reception desk. The cost is reasonable, and one can call directly, with a dedicated international dialing prefix, from the hotel. It sounds simple, and too good to be true. We'll see later, I think to myself, and go up to my room.

My room is a standard hotel room, rather generous in size; a sort of mini-suite. There is an entrance room with a sitting area next to the window, a bedroom, and of course a bathroom. I take a few minutes to examine the room in greater detail, and with an unprofessional air start looking around for monitoring equipment: a camera, or a microphone. I find nothing, of course, and I remember my basic assumption: I know that I am constantly under surveillance, and I have already decided to ignore it completely. (I maintain this policy in all my future visits to North Korea.) I continue to look around at the room and its furnishings; the bathrooms, the wardrobes. Kettle – yes! Coffee/tea/sugar/milk – no. I find the electrical socket only after a thorough search: it is near the floor, nowhere near the table or any other surface. In other words, one can boil water in the kettle only when the kettle is on the floor. Oh well. In the bathroom I find thin towels (like the kitchen towels back home), soap, and shampoo. There is a hair dryer. The bedroom has two single beds. In short: reasonable and functional, but not luxurious. I'm not surprised. Over the course of my trips to Russia and other Communist countries, I have already come to understand their approach to what makes a "good hotel" for Western tourists: relative splendor in the public areas, with rooms that are more modest, but reasonably comfortable. We meet for dinner at one of the hotel restaurants. It's a buffet-style meal. Owing to some delays, we are the last to arrive. The choice of dishes isn't great, but since none of us has come to North Korea for the specific purpose of culinary experiences, we take it in our stride. After the meal, our guide gathers us to tell us about plans for tomorrow. After the technical details like breakfast, timetables, etc., she gets to the point, telling excitedly, "Tomorrow we will visit a sacred site! Please dress in your most dignified clothes. We will be required to conduct ourselves according to strict rules. Before we leave, we will instruct you as to the rules of etiquette, and, if you have no objection, we will review your appearance." No, no objections, we think to ourselves – as though any other possibility exists. It is now approximately 21:00. After a day crammed with attractions that have pushed our adrenaline levels sky high, we don't feel ready to sleep. We are in the lobby of the hotel with our two guides, when Mike, our new friend, and Yaki, have an idea. They turn to Li Mi-Soon and tell her, "We're going to the train station." Li Mi-Soon tenses and barks, "No! You can't; it's dangerous!" Mike and Yaki reply, "That shouldn't be a problem, the station is here," and they point in the direction of the station, "Just two hundred and fifty meters away." Li Mi-Soon dismisses the idea, telling them, "Tomorrow, if you like, we can go." They yield – one can't push too far. We remain in the lobby, chatting over beer. By the end of the first day, the group of six Americans, two Israelis and a Singaporean have melded into a unit. Analyzing the day's events, we are all in agreement: it's been amazing. I got up to my room; now it's time to talk with my wife and to update Chaim. I lift the phone receiver, dial the hotel prefix for an international line, continue with the Israel dialing code, and then my wife's number. A few seconds' wait, and we are talking. Drora can't believe it: I had foreseen a complete disconnect, communication difficulties, and... here we are talking;

mainly a call for me to reassure her. The myth of the complete disconnect dissolves on the first day of my visit to North Korea. Next, I call Chaim. My report is factual and emotionless; it's all simple and easy. But emotions aside, I am lost in thought. It's strange; I think to myself: I'm not particularly excited, but I am very confused. Nothing matches the script I imagined before my arrival. It is the ordinary telephone calls, especially, that rattle me. The thoughts race in my head; they are not organized, but rather a hodgepodge of flashing images with no words, appearing randomly with no logic. On one hand, everything is different: different from what I have seen thus far on my trips around the world, but at the same time also different from what I had imagined. On the other hand, everything is normal: the landing, the entry procedure, the bus, the guides (and one can talk with them, and even exchange smiles), the hotel, dinner, sitting in the lobby with friends, talking on the phone – my life's routine. I am in bed alone with my chaotic thoughts, and, surprisingly enough, I am soon overtaken by a deep sleep that brings much-needed rest.

CHAPTER 4

Getting Used to an Alternative Reality

It's our second day in Pyongyang; my first morning in North Korea. I'm an early bird by nature, and this morning I wake up especially early. The thoughts from last night, which I managed to put aside in order to fall asleep, reappear and demand my attention. I do not succumb, but evade them by getting the day started. As instructed by our Korean guides, I take my most "dignified" clothes out of the suitcase and proceed with my morning routine, preparing myself a cup of coffee and settling in the sitting area in my room, next to the open window, looking out on the city at the start of a new day. Suddenly, without any preparation, music starts wafting in through the window. The upbeat tune pervades the entire city; as I come to understand later, it is meant to awaken the laborers, students, pensioners – all the city's inhabitants – to a new day of work and creativity for the sake of the beloved homeland. Citizens of North Korea rate themselves second in the world in the national happiness index – second only to neighboring China. I smile to myself. An alternative reality; only in North Korea.

Breakfast is served at another restaurant in the hotel. It's an interesting breakfast, held in a huge, well-lit hall that is almost empty. When all nine of us are seated at the table designated for our group, we make up about a third of the diners in the hall. There is a buffet offering vegetable salad and East Asian-style dishes, and another with yoghurt, toast, butter, and fried eggs upon request (even two per diner). Further along, there is a coffee table. The coffee, it turns out, is not included in the price. For one euro, one receives a cup of instant granulated coffee, with powdered creamer. There is no milk. (This comes as no surprise; I am reminded of my first visits to China and Vietnam. Cows' milk has no place in the culinary culture of East Asia.) The service is very courteous, displaying a real desire to please, and a seemingly unlimited variety of side dishes, compensating for the rather mediocre menu, together with the morning chatter and exchange of experiences among the group members, make for a pleasant meal. Afterwards we are ready for our second day of touring. But before setting out, as promised, we prepare for "morning inspection." The requirements are that we dress in an outfit that is simple, dignified, and befitting the occasion. Jeans are permitted, but not T-shirts, and no sports shoes; we have to wear "proper" leather shoes. Everyone passes the inspection, but our guide, Li Mi Soon, steals the show: she is wearing a traditional Korean floral satin dress, close-fitting on the top half, a belt at the chest, and then flaring outward as it descends to her feet, forming a tent-like triangular shape. Today is a holiday – April 15th, the most important day on the North Korean calendar. It is the birthday of the Great Leader, President Kim Il-Sung, who was born in 1912. This day marks the beginning of the North Korean calendar; the New Year. Tomorrow will be the start of Juche 105 – the 105th year of the Juche calendar (see box). An alternative reality, only in North Korea.

Juche

Juche is the guiding ideology of North Korea. The ideology was formulated by President Kim Il-Sung in the 1950s – a period when North Korea wasn't an isolated pariah state, but rather

67

was part of the Communist Bloc, with a relatively healthy economy (better than that of South Korea). The ideology combines the idea of a nation-state with Marxist-Leninist teachings, despite the inherent contradiction between a nation-state and "Workers of the World, Unite." The main component of the ideology might be summarized as self-reliance in every area: defense, economy, and culture. The collapse of the Communist Bloc and the isolation of North Korea over the past thirty years have made this ideology ever more relevant, certainly for the regime's internal purposes. It eventually spread to many Third World countries under the name Kimilsungism – in deference to the originator of the teachings.

*

We set off. Close to the hotel is the central train station. The giant square is full of pedestrians and bicycle riders hurrying to their destinations on this holiday. There is no congestion on the roads; the traffic consists mostly of trams and buses, with just a few small cars. My eyes, and the cameras of all the members of the group, are glued to the city gearing up for a day of events and festivities. The sidewalks are fairly full of pedestrians, despite the relatively early hour. Their dress shows that today is a holiday. The men are mostly wearing jackets, but the women look truly festive: most are wearing traditional Korean dresses, all in colorful floral satin. It is a celebration for the eyes; a victory of esthetics and tradition over dull routine. Our journey lasts about half an hour, with the sights along the way a joy to the eyes and the soul.

Before we approach the site, Miss Li Mi-Soon grows serious and appears slightly tense. She addresses us and starts to list the rules of etiquette, which are extremely detailed and strict. Pockets are to be emptied of all contents, including room keys and even Kleenex. Wallets, cameras and cellphones are permitted, but they will be deposited in the locker room. "There is no tolerance for deviation from the rules," she explains. Later, when I return here with groups, I come to understand that any deviation in behavior on the part of a tourist is regarded as the guides' fault. After all, we are about to visit the holy of holies.

Kumsusan Palace of the Sun: In the past, during his lifetime, this was the residence of the President of North Korea, Kim Il-Sung. Kim Il-Sung was the "rising sun" illuminating the sky of the new Korea (if you will, the Korean version of Louis XIV, the French sun-king). After his death, it was converted into a mausoleum. Its status in the North Korean religion is like that of Mecca for Muslims: it is a pilgrimage site to be visited by every citizen, at least once in his lifetime – and the more often, the better. The embalmed body of President Kim Il-Sung, Father of the Nation and founder of North Korea, is on display, along with his embalmed son, the Eternal Chairman Kim Jong-Il, the man who promised to continue the revolution even as the entire Communist world was collapsing around him. The father and the son, along with the present leader, their son/grandson, represent the world's first and only Imperial Communist dynasty.

The parking lot is busy; there are a few tourists, and a crowd of hundreds of locals, all dressed in their finery, of course. Separately from the locals, at the entrance to the building, we arrange ourselves in groups of four. We start walking down a long corridor with granite flooring, in silence. After walking for a few minutes, we pass through a security check and then rearrange ourselves in fours. The corridors are lined with portraits of the leaders; all the pictures on one side show the Father of the Nation, Kim Il-Sung, engaged in his activities on behalf of the homeland. The other side is dedicated to his son, Chairman Kim Jong-Il. Quiet requiem music, composed in memory of the leaders, accompanies us, creating a special atmosphere even for the greatest cynics. We step onto a conveyor belt that cleans the soles of our shoes, and then continue through gates where air is blown through our hair for disinfection – only in North Korea! The atmosphere of "sanctity" envelops the visitors whether they like it or not. I cannot (and perhaps do not wish to) fight it. Only now are we ready to enter the palace – and the palace is huge. It's built mainly of grey granite, decorated with red granite. Red carpets and glorifying pictures adorn the walls. Soldiers are stationed as guards of honor in each of the halls. Their faces are frozen, their eyelids and facial muscles showing no hint of movement – living statues.

It is in the central hall that visitors make a ceremonial bow before the statues of the leaders. It is only now, after about forty-five minutes, that we are standing before the holy of holies – the room in which, in a glass sarcophagus, the embalmed body of President Kim Il-Sung lies in state. I observe the Koreans who enter before us. Their entire appearance projects the tense anticipation and awe of those whose supreme wish is about to be realized.

We enter a room illuminated by a dim red light. In all four corners of the room, of course, live soldier-statues are stationed as a guard of honor. In front of us in the room, Korean woman have come to pay respects to their "god." Suddenly one of the women bursts into cries of anguish and weeping; two of her companions are brought to tears; a few seconds later, they manage to suppress their emotions and to continue with the ritual. After them, it is our turn. Awestruck and respectful of the worshippers and the sanctity that they attach to the place, we approach in rows of four: bows on three sides of the sarcophagus: at the feet, and on each side of the corpse. There is no bowing from the direction of the head. The first stage is over. There is a sense of relief; the test of etiquette is behind me. At the same time, again I have a sense of discomfort at the reverence that has overcome me: I, a Westerner, a man of the free world, am emotionally caught up in in this ritual that is completely foreign to my beliefs.

From here, we proceed to the two exhibition halls: the first documents the travels of the Great Leader throughout the world and all over North Korea; the second shows certificates and medals of honor awarded him by different countries and organizations. On our way out we follow a similar route, with a ceremony honoring the Eternal Chairman, Kim Jong-Il. Again, a room dimly illuminated with red light, bows of respect, and then on to a hall displaying the train carriage in which Kim Jong-Il died, before the age of 70, during a work tour for the sake of the nation and the homeland. This is how the leader is portrayed. The most central dimension of his personality is the myth of his limitless self-sacrifice and giving of himself for the sake of the people.

About two hours pass between our arrival at the Kumsusan Palace of the Sun and the end of our visit. They are quite unlike any two hours that I have ever experienced. I have a sense of having participated in a religious ritual altogether different from any other religion I have encountered; a ritual of a religion that I completely don't believe in, but nevertheless I am extremely emotional. I have participated in seemingly similar ceremonies in Moscow, Beijing, and Hanoi. They were similar in terms of procedure, but very different in their effect on the visitor. Unquestionably, this is unique to North Korea. When we are back on the bus, one of the Americans mutters – perhaps to himself, perhaps to us – something like, "Okay, this visit to Kumsusan completely delivered on all my expectations of the trip to North Korea. I got a full return on my investment. The rest of the tour is a bonus." His brief monologue seemed to reflect what everyone in the group was thinking. It certainly reflected my feeling.

Great Leader Kim Il Sung

(From the official North Korean tourist guidebook, *Panorama of Korea*, 2017)

Entering the modern times, Korea with 5,000-year-long history and brilliant culture gradually weakened in national power owing to the policy of sycophancy and dependence on outside forces of the feudal Joson dynasty and was reduced to a theatre of competition of big powers. Finally it was placed under the Japanese military occupation since 1905.

It was Kim Il Sung who saved the Korean people from the miserable fate of a ruined nation.

Kim Il Sung was born in Mangyongdae, Pyongyang, on April 15, Juche 1 (1912), and embarked on the road of revolutionary struggle for Korea's liberation in his teens. In the course of groping for the road of the Korean revolution, he authored the Juche idea and the Songun idea and commanded the anti-Japanese revolutionary struggle for two decades under the banner of these ideas, finally achieving the historic cause of Korea's liberation on August 15, Juche 34 (1945).

After his triumphal return to the liberated homeland, he founded the Workers' Party of Korea without delay, carried out democratic reforms, including the land reform, nationalization of key industries and enforcement of the Law on Sex Equality, and founded a regular armed force. Based on these achievements, he founded the Democratic People's Republic of Korea, the first people's democratic state in the East, on September 9, Juche 37 (1948).

He creditably safeguarded the sovereignty and dignity of the DPRK in the Korean War (1950-1953) unleashed by the US in its attempt to stifle the two-year-old Republic in its cradle. He carried out the postwar rehabilitation and socialist revolution in a short period and led socialist construction of several stages to victory, thus turning the country into a socialist power, independent in politics, self-sufficient in the economy and self-reliant in defense.

He regarded "The people are my god" as his lifetime motto, and his benevolent politics got a people-centered socialist system deeply rooted in the country.

He advanced the fundamental principles and ways to Korea's reunification, including the three principles of national reunification, the ten-point program of the great unity of the whole nation for the reunification of the country and the plan for the founding of the Democratic Federal Republic of Koryo, and devoted his all for achieving the cause of national reunification until the last moment of his life.

He defined independence, peace and friendship as the basic ideals of the DPRK's foreign policy and enhanced it international prestige through his energetic external activities. Working as head of state and veteran of world politics for nearly half a century, he made immortal contributions to developing the socialist and non-aligned movements.

It is not fortuitous that former US President Jimmy Carter said that President Kim Il Sung was greater than the three American Presidents who had represented the nation building and destiny of the United States – George Washington, Thomas Jefferson and Abraham Lincoln – put together.

The DPRK conferred the title of Generalissimo on him on the occasion of the 80th anniversary of his birth. Though he passed away on July 8, Juche 83 (1994), he is always alive in the hearts of the Korean people and the world progressives as the founding father of socialist Korea, pioneer of the cause of independence of mankind, eternal President of the DPRK and the Sun of Juche.

President Kim Il-Sung (according to Western sources):

Born Kim Song-Ju on April 15th, 1912, near Pyongyang. His father was a Christian pharmacist (!).

In 1925 his family fled the Japanese occupation, heading for northern Manchuria. In 1931 he joined the Chinese Communist Party.

In 1935 he joined the Northeast Anti-Japanese United Army, a Communist guerilla group led by the Chinese Communist Party. About six years later he traveled to the USSR, where he underwent guerilla training, and later enlisted in the Red Army, rising to the rank of Captain. He adopted the name Kim Il-Sung (the name of a hero of the anti-Japanese resistance).

In 1945, he entered Pyongyang with the Red Army and declared Korea's liberation from Japanese occupation. Korea was divided between the American-backed south and the Communist north. The 38th parallel was the demarcation line between them.

On September 9th, 1948, in the wake of the announcement of the establishment of South Korea, the independence of the Democratic People's Republic of Korea was declared.

The Korean War took place between the years 1950-1953, followed by purges and the development of a cult of personality. China became the country's main ally rather than the USSR.

IN 1966, in the wake of the Cultural Revolution in China, ties with the USSR were strengthened.

IN 1972 a new constitution was introduced, declaring Kim Il-Sung "President for life."

In 1989, the Communist Bloc collapsed, and the situation in Korea deteriorated dramatically.

On July 9th, 1994, President Kim Il-Sung died of a heart attack.

Personality and leadership:

Founding father; the "Great Leader."

Liberator, founder, and ideologue of North Korea.

Remained in power for 46 years, longer than all his counterparts in the Communist world (Stalin, Mao Zedong, Ho Chi Minh).

Father of the ideologies guiding North Korea (Juche, Songun, socialism, reunification).

The "sun" bringing a new dawn to North Korea.

Billboard sign – one of many

Great Leader Kim Jong Il
(From the official North Korean tourist guidebook, *Panorama of Korea*, 2017)

The Dear Leader, Chairman Kim Jong-Il, was born in a village on Mount Paektu on February 16, 1941, during the heroic struggle against the Japanese. Already in his childhood and youth he lived the lofty ideologies of his father, President Kim Il-Sung. The first stage of his leadership came in 1960, immediately following his visit to the 105th Guards Seoul Ryu Kyong-Su Armored Division, with the adoption of the idea of Songun ("military first"). The same year, 1960, he was elected Chairman of the Party – a position that he occupied for fifty years, until his death. Fifty years of activity with historical, eternal results. He led the Party with wisdom and practical skill, consolidating his father's ideas into an integrated, comprehensive ideology: Kimilsungism.

His embracing leadership swept along all the key personnel in dedicated work and cooperation, with a recognition of the need for national unity in order to realize the lofty ideas.

With the death of his father (1994), in his modesty and his recognition of his father's eternity and his superlative activity in leadership of the nation and the Revolution, he decided that his late father would bear the title, Eternal President.

At the end of the 20th century, when the country stood alone against an anti-socialist onslaught led by the United States and its imperialist allies, Chairman Kim Jong-Il reformulated and reinforced the Songun ideology as the basis of socialism. Accordingly, development of the army was prioritized to an unprecedented extent, and the country embarked on development of a modern military industry that would allow the army to stand up to the country's many enemies without foreign help. This included leading the country to nuclear capability.

Decade after decade, the flame of the Revolution continued to burn. The industry developed with 21st century technologies, to the point of capability of launching missiles and satellites into space.

Along with development and action, Chairman Kim Jong-Il never relinquished the idea of Korean reunification. Inspired by his father's legacy, he formulated the Three Principles for Reunification in his declaration of July 15th, 2007 – a declaration that was adopted as an operational program at the meeting of leaders of South and North Korea, on October 4th, 2007. This introduced a new era in the relations between South and North Korea – an era that will lead to unity and independence.

Kim Jong-Il's leadership extended friendship and cooperation to independence-seeking countries and encouraged them. This was his decisive contribution to security, peace, and stability in Northeast Asia and throughout the rest of the world.

With the motto, "The nation is my god," he devoted superhuman efforts, day and night, for the sake of the nation. Kim Jong-Il died on a train, on December 17th, 2011, during a work trip. His entire life was devoted to the Korean people. After his death, it was decided that the title "Chairman" would remain his for eternity.

Kim Jong-Il (according to Western sources):

His father was President Kim Il-Sung; his mother was the fighter Kim Jong-Suk. Kim Jong-Il was born in Siberia, in the village of Vyetskoya, on February 16th, 1941.

In August 1945, upon Korea's liberation, he returned with his family to Pyongyang, and studied at an elementary school for children of senior Party members.

In 1964, he completed his studies at Kim Il-Sung University, and commenced his public activity in the Party.

In 1973, he served as Party Secretary for Management and Propaganda; and in 1974, his father, the President, publicly named him as his successor.

In 1978, he ordered the kidnapping of South Korean film director Shin Sang-Ok, and his actress wife, Choi Eun-Hee.

In 1991, he was appointed Commander of the Armed Forces of North Korea.

On July 8th, 1994, with the death of his father, Kim Il-Sung, the Great Leader, he assumed the title "Chairman."

In the years between 1994-1998, famine claimed about 800,000 North Korean lives, according to official North Korean figures; Western sources put the number somewhere between 900,000 and 3,500,000.

In June 2000, the first summit between the leaders of South and North Korea was held; principles for reunification were agreed upon; families separated during the war were reunited, and a joint industrial complex was established.

In 2002, the US halted the supply of crude oil that had been stipulated in the agreement between the countries.

In 2003, North Korea withdrew from the Nuclear Non-Proliferation Treaty.

In 2006, the country conducted its first nuclear test.

In 2007, an agreement was signed with the US for economic

aid in return for halting nuclear activity. Economic reforms were instituted.

In 2009, in the final days of the presidency of George Bush Jr, the agreement was revoked owing to disagreements between the countries. Nuclear activity was renewed, a satellite was launched, and a nuclear test was conducted.

On December 17th, 2011, Kim Jong-Il died during a train journey on official business.

Personality and leadership:

In North Korea, Kim Jong-Il is considered a leader who devoted his entire life to the people and the homeland, even during the most difficult periods (the collapse of the Soviet Bloc and the great famine).

With leadership, determination, perseverance, and maintaining the spirit of the Revolution, he led the country to a better future.

Among his more noteworthy initiatives:
- Development of a nuclear program
- First summit with a South Korean leader
- Chinese-style economic reforms

It turns out that the surprises aren't over. The April 15th holiday also includes a flower exhibition, featuring just two types of flowers: the Kimilsungia and the Kimjongilia (see boxes).

The flower show takes place in a building around 80 meters long and 30 meters wide, with two floors. The exhibition consists of two elements. The first is the flowers themselves – the purple kimilsungia and the red kimjongilia. The second is the pictures: arrangements of flowers decorate an endless series of portraits of the Leaders and other "patriotic" pictures highlighting both father and son. The grandson, the current Leader – Marshal Kim

Jong-Un – is entirely absent from the exhibition. The real celebration is the hordes of visitors: adults, the elderly, families with children – everyone dressed in their finery, the women in their colorful traditional dresses, and a carnival atmosphere. We and other tourist groups are engulfed in the celebratory crowds. With hand gestures, we request permission to photograph the Koreans; approval is granted, and in many instances, the locals ask to be photographed together with us. There is no shortage of interaction based on hand gestures and pantomime, but there is no verbal communication. The language presents an insurmountable barrier. One of the responses that I hear innumerable times when sharing my experiences in North Korea with family, friends, acquaintances, colleagues, and others, is: "You know that it's all a show for tourists," or "The greatest show in the world." If that is the case, then it truly is the greatest production in the world – thousands of people visiting a site just to impress a few dozen tourists.

Kimilsungia

On April 19th, 1965, Kim Il-Sung visited Indonesia. During his visit, he went to see the Botanical Gardens, accompanied by the President of Indonesia, Sukarno. The chief botanist showed him a bright, purple-colored orchid that captivated him. The flower had been cloned in Indonesia at the end of 1964 by orchid breeder, Carl Ludwig C. L. Bundt, who named it after his daughter, Clara Bundt. Final approval of the proposed name had not yet been issued. As a gesture of friendship, since Kim Il-Sung was so taken by the flower, Sukarno decided to name it after him: Kimilsungia.

Kimjongilia

This hybrid cultivar, produced by Japanese botanist Kamo Mototeru, was designed to bloom precisely on February 16th, 1988 – the 46th birthday of Chairman Kim Jong-Il. Mototeru, an admirer of Juche philosophy, dedicated the star-shaped, bright red flower to the North Korean leader as a gesture of appeasement for Japan's crimes during the period of occupation. He asserted that the flower, like the Leader, symbolized justice, wisdom, love, and peace.

*

At noon, Li Mi Soon "suggests" that we go back to the hotel and change into more comfortable clothing, as well as eat lunch. We dine in the largest restaurant in the hotel. Once again, our small group comprises about a third of the diners. This is, in fact, the first typical North Korean meal of the trip, and since I am often asked about food there, I will devote a few words to the subject. In general, the meals are in Asian style – in other words, many different foods served in large bowls, including stir-fried vegetables, vegetable tempura, some chicken or fish, rice or noodles made from buckwheat or white flour, fruit for dessert, and special additions for tourists – French fries and eggs (vegetable omelets or a sort of shakshuka) – at almost every meal. Not an exciting culinary experience, but quite satisfactory and filling.

*

The festive day continues, and we are invited to watch the crowds dancing, and to join them. Hundreds of young people and students fill the broad plaza alongside a museum-like building. The boys are elegantly dressed, and the girls are in brightly colored dresses. About ten buses drop off tourists who have come to watch the festivities. A good-quality amplification system plays cheerful music that sounds a lot like military marching music, and especially Red Army songs. The large plaza, measuring around two thousand square meters, fills with circles of synchronized dancers. The impression I have is that they are groups that gather regularly to dance. We stand on the raised platform at the entrance of the building. It is a captivating sight. After some time, the dancers invite us – the tourists – to join them. Many do so.

*

The Juche Tower (or the Tower of the Juche Idea, as it is formally known) is a hundred and fifty meters tall, topped with a twenty-meter illuminated metal torch.[11] It was built in Juche Year 70 (1982), commemorating seventy years of President Kim Il-Sung's leadership. It consists of 25,550 blocks – one for each day of the President's life (365 x 70). The tower stands on the banks of the Taedong River, at the center of a wide plaza. When one stands facing the river, Kim Il-Sung Square can be seen on the other side – the "Tiananmen Square" of North Korea. The boundaries of the site are marked with huge granite statues bearing patriotic slogans. A few steps lead to the entrance. On the entrance wall are dozens of friendship plaques from universities and institutes around the world, the great majority of them with a socialist orientation, expressing their admiration for President Kim Il-Sung and his philosophy – the Juche idea.

---

11 Reaching 170 meters in total, it is the second-tallest monumental column in the world. The tallest, at 173 meters, is the San Jacinto Monument in San Antonio, Texas. Third in line is the Washington Monument in the US capital, measuring 70.6 meters.

The guide at the site (there is a local guide for every tourist site in North Korea) proudly shows off the two marble gates, weighing several tons, and moving on their hinges with surprising ease. We enter, and the guide continues, giving a brief explanation of the principles of Juche ideology. Then, to our surprise, in a quick shift from ideology to "business," she shows us the books and souvenirs for sale at the Tower store. She then directs those interested in a panoramic view of the city from the top of the Tower to purchase a ticket for five euros, granting the right to ascend the elevator. Of course, we are all interested.

The view of the city is impressive. From this elevated perspective, at the center of the city, on the banks of the river, the city looks marvelous. Wide roads, plazas, and plenty of parks and monuments. The city buildings are lit up in soft shades of pink, brownish-red, pale green, and azure. Upon closer inspection, many of the buildings – especially the residential buildings – aren't in good shape, but the panoramic view is spectacular. Three prominent structures draw one's immediate attention: Rungrado 1st of May Stadium, the largest in the world, with a seating capacity of 150,000; the 330-meter-high Ryugyong Hotel, built in the shape of a pyramid (or perhaps a missile); and the Great People's Study House, which dominates Kim Il-Sung Square. We descend from the top of the Tower, and while we wait for the other members of the group, Yaki lights up a cigarette. Mr. Li approaches him and, with a shy smile, says, "Yaki, we are not allowed to smoke here; we are within the monument precinct. You know how much I like to smoke, too, but I'm holding back." Over the two days that we have toured together, Yaki and Mr. Li have become smoking partners. In North Korea, smoking is almost obligatory for men, and happens everywhere, even in the hotel lobby. I estimate that nine out of every ten men are smokers. (Women do not smoke – or, at least, not in public.) Yaki is slightly alarmed, apologizes, and explains that he wasn't aware of the prohibition. Mr. Li, in the same apologetic tone, tells him, "No, no, it's my fault. It seems I wasn't clear."

It is already evening and we are on our way to dinner – this time, in a restaurant outside of the hotel.

*

The purpose of our trip to North Korea was to open a new tourist destination for Israelis, led by Tarbutu. Yaki, director of the Rimon Group (of which Tarbutu is a subsidiary), was in charge of the commercial aspect, while I was in charge of the tourist aspect. The reason for our joining the trip was obviously known to the managers of the Koryo North Korean tourist company, and we therefore knew that at some stage, it would come up for discussion. On the first day, we had made our intentions clear to our guides, who did not seem surprised. I requested and received permission to sit in the front seat of the bus and to photograph, the purpose of the pictures being to advance tourism to North Korea (as expected, my attempts at photography turned out to be a complete failure, mainly because looking through the video viewfinder interfered with my desire to devour and internalize the sights). In any event, Yaki waited patiently for his opportunity, believing that it would come towards the end of the trip.

Arriving at the restaurant for dinner, a surprise awaited us: while the rest of the group entered the dining room that had been set up for us, Yaki and I were picked out by Mr. Li and led to a different room. This room looked fancier, and a quick glance was enough to show that the table had been set for an upgraded meal, including wine. In the room were two men who looked to

84

be in their late fifties, dignified and formal. They stood to greet us and introduced themselves: Mr. Tang, president of Koryo Tours, and Mr. Cha, the CEO.[12]

We are invited to sit down, together with Mr. Li, who will serve as our interpreter. Both men understand some English; Mr. Tang can speak a rudimentary English, while Mr. Cha speaks a basic French. The small talk surrounding the meal soon gives way to business. As noted, I am not a businessman. I enjoy my occupation as a tour guide, and keep myself completely separate from anything that is not directly connected to my profession. Thus, I find myself once again (and not for the last time) in the position of a spectator. As hard as I try – and as hard as I will try on future visits – to explain to our hosts that in business terms, I personally am not worth wooing, I get nowhere. They understand that Yaki is the boss, but they view me as a central partner in the decision-making. In the future I return seven times to North Korea, with seven tour groups, and the status that I am awarded, against my will, has significant ramifications for my conduct. The conversation follows the style of mutual courting, but it becomes clear at a very early stage that it is the Koreans who are more interested in a partnership.

---

12 The fact that Mr. Tang was a fairly senior executive was apparent even during our first trip. He traveled in a fancy car with a driver. Wherever we met him, everyone present stood when he entered. He is the president of Koryo Tours, the largest and most important tourism company in North Korea. The Koryo Hotel in Pyongyang, along with the splendid hotels at the Masikryong Ski Resort and at the Myohyang Reserve, are also managed by Koryo, along with a bus company and a host of other tourist services. My assumption is that Mr. Tang, Mr. Cha, and all those directly involved with tourists, are more highly placed and more senior than the Westerners who are their professional equals, owing to the caution and sensitivity surrounding them in the eyes of the regime, in view of their direct and intensive contact with foreigners.

As a participant-observer, it is a fascinating experience, and in all such meetings during our trip, and on later trips, I am fascinated and startled by the role into which the Koreans have pushed me – not in the business sense, but certainly in terms of the planning and content of the tours. Firstly, we experience in unmediated fashion the economic revolution that North Korea is undergoing. I had understood already in our meeting in Beijing that the North Korean economy is undergoing a change like the one in China during the 1990s and in Vietnam at the beginning of the 21st century. Our meeting will be continued on almost every day of our trip, and on each of my future visits to North Korea as a tour guide. These meetings bring me into contact with people who listen, think, make notes, and promise responses, quite unlike the apparatchik prototype that I have created in my head.

It seems to me that they do not have much experience in negotiating with representatives of tourists. Their discussions are usually held with a go-between company, such as URI, which organized our trip. I am therefore impressed by their ability to listen and to try to understand our requests and the way in which we run our trips. Mainly, our requests reflect the desire to expose participants to the human element and day-to-day life of North Korea. For example, we request a visit to a supermarket and to a recreational space such as a pub or a Korean show, rather than the circus visit that is offered to us. (On this trip, none of our requests is fulfilled, but later on, when I return with Israeli tourists, I am surprised each time anew by the speed of their response to our requests, and the flexibility of thought that they display – obviously, within their set boundaries).

For their part, all that concerns them is the conduct of the tourists that we will bring in the future. Several times, Mr. Tang turns to me and repeats the same statement or request: "As long as they behave properly." Here I add my small contribution to the conversation, telling them, "That's my responsibility. I will do everything to ensure that there are no problems."

We anticipate that our tourists, in their great desire to take photos, might deviate from the rules, and therefore ask that a photographer representing the Korean company accompany us on our future trips. This will lessen the urgency to take photographs, making things easier all around. Our request is approved, and indeed on our future trips, we will be accompanied by Mr. Kim, who will be responsible for both videos and still photography throughout the trip. Our tourists will happily purchase his pictures.

*

After we finish dinner, there is another surprise to end the day with. There is a fireworks display in honor of the holiday, and we are invited to watch. We travel the short distance to Kim Il-Sung Square, and nearby, on the banks of the river, facing the Juche Tower, we see crowds of people. Among the myths about North Korea, there are two that are especially popular: one is that everything is a show for tourists; the other is that tourists will never find themselves in proximity to regular citizens – except those who have been screened and approved. Even after seeing cracks appear in these myths at the flower show, we still don't expect to come into contact with the local population, and we wonder how the guides will isolate us from the crowds. It turns out that they don't even try. Three staff members accompany us. For this evening, Mr. Cha, CEO of Koryo Tours, is joining our group. As we get off the bus, we are asked to stay close to them. Just in case, we are asked to come back to the bus after the fireworks. Still somewhat uncertain, we try at first to remain close to the guides – but don't stand a chance. All of us, whether intentionally or not, find ourselves in the midst of the crowds with no guide close by.

Mr. Cha attaches himself to Yaki and I, but when the show begins, I find myself alone. Naturally enough, like all the Koreans around us, I look upward, watching the sky. After a moment or two, I turn my gaze towards the crowds of Korean spectators. My thoughts float back in time, to 1958, and the celebration of the 10th anniversary of the establishment of the State of Israel. I was ten years old. Our family, consisting of three adults and two children, had recently moved from a small, cramped, two-room apartment in a subsidized-housing project in Bat Yam to a two-and-a-half room apartment that seemed to me to be positively palatial, near "the Monument" (officially known as Defenders' Square) in the same town. The tenth-anniversary celebrations coincided with my own personal celebration of my first dual-digit birthday. During the Independence Day celebrations, on the stage set up by the municipality, I received a certificate affirming that I, Avraham Zamichkovsky, was born in the year of the establishment of the state. The climax of the festivities, which of course everyone followed with close attention, was a fireworks display. My personal joy merged perfectly with the sense of national pride and jubilation, and the many hues and shapes of the fireworks drew gasps of wonder, joy, and pride from the crowd; pure, wondrous innocence.

I watch the crowd around me and see no fearful glances trying to identify potential threats. The crowds are fixated by the exhilarating sight, proud, joyful, and full of enjoyment. I am almost offended: no-one casts more than a cursory glance in my direction; I am just part of the scene.

*

It is the end of a long day, full of scenes and experiences. Upon reaching the hotel, none of us is looking for any sort of activity. Like everyone else, all I want is the quickest route to my room. Each evening (on this trip and on all future trips) I first call home, to reassure my wife that all is well, and then Chaim, to report on the day's events.

My second night in Pyongyang: short periods of sleep are interrupted by a lot of thinking in between. My thoughts swirl among the sights and experiences of the past two days, which are different from all that I have seen and experienced so far on hundreds of trips around the world, and also completely different from what I had prepared myself for. Slowly I find myself focusing on how unsettling and disconcerting it has all been – especially Mansudae and Kumsusan Mausoleum, but not only. I have a general feeling that everything is different; unreal. I find myself part of the backdrop of a surrealistic film; any moment there will be a "cut," and I will emerge from the film studio and get back to reality. Like mosquitos buzzing around my ear, two central issues are disturbing me: my enthusiasm, on one hand, and on the other hand, the dissonance between my expectations, based on what I (thought I) knew about North Korea, and what I am experiencing.

My thoughts lead me back to my youth; the late 1950s and early 1960s in Bat Yam. The ultimate entertainment experience at the time was going out to a movie. Films came to Bat Yam with some delay in comparison to Tel Aviv, and since Tel Aviv was far away for us, we in the "periphery" had to just wait patiently. Every Saturday night, the neighborhood youth would go to Oren Cinema to watch whatever was showing that week. Westerns were, of course, our favorite, followed by war films. As for historical films, Hollywood produced some epics that were remarkable for their time – *The Ten Commandments, Ben Hur, Quo Vadis*. Now, I am overcome by a sense of déjà vu. As a teenager, I was drawn into the plots and, of course, identified with the heroes, played by Charleston Heston or Robert Taylor. What was common to *Ben Hur* and *Quo Vadis* was the theme of the persecution of Christians by the Roman Empire. I would emerge from these films fired up and full of empathy for the persecuted Christians, and then I would feel shame: how could I, a Jewish, Israeli boy, sympathize with Christianity, which had caused such suffering to the Jewish People? I didn't know enough to understand that the Christians, during the period in question, were, in fact, still Jews. But I soon found a way of resolving the dilemma: It was only a film, and thus I could put Christianity back in its proper place in my consciousness. I am experiencing something similar right now, and my way of coping with it as an adult isn't all that different.

I continue my attempt to analyze my feelings and to address them with clear-headed logic. I think back to religious tourist sites that I have visited and question myself about them. In what way is my enthusiasm about North Korea different from my enthusiasm for hundreds of historical sites I have visited, such as the pyramids and temples in Egypt, the pyramids in Central America, the Terracotta Army guarding the grave of Chinese Emperor Qin Shi Huang, Angkor Wat in Cambodia … the list goes on. All of these are megalomanic sites built by tyrants who repressed their peoples, showing no compassion or consideration. How is the Korean worship of their leaders different from the other forms of worship – no less "unreal" in the eyes of non-believers – that I have watched and even been part of, such as the processions of the sick at Lourdes in France, or at the Shrine of Fatima in Portugal? Visitors to Tibet watch people crawling thousands of meters on their bellies to approach the temple in Lhasa. I attended the Chinese Vegetarian Festival in Phuket, and watched as believers no more than a meter away from me put themselves in a trance and then pushed a pipe ten millimeters wide through one cheek and then through the other. There was even a "regular" Mass at the Chartres Cathedral in France, which the tourists in the group I led – all former Yugoslavian Communist partisans – refused to leave. Perhaps it is the dimension of time that makes the difference. All the sites I am thinking about were built in the distant past, while those in North Korea were constructed in recent years. That is true. Yet the sites, the rituals, and the wonderment make it clear to me that there need not necessarily be any overlap between amazement at a phenomenon and agreement with it. On the contrary, sometimes it is possible to feel wonder at a belief or behavior for which one feels revulsion. And since I have decided in my own mind that I have come to watch the show, and since I have no control over either the plot or the backdrop, I will give myself over to the show and allow myself to be amazed and enjoy, setting aside my own moral position and moral accounting for the time being.

The second insight that comes to me concerns the encounter with people, with human beings. For some reason, in my mental preparation for this trip, I imagined myself watching a film from afar. The script, the plot, and the stage directions were, of course, out of my control, and I had no part to play; thus, when I came out of the film, I would come back to myself. But here I have found myself onstage and in the play – on the fringes, admittedly, as an extra, but nevertheless exposed in conversation and visible to others, not to situations; to human beings with feelings, thoughts, and desires. This was not part of the script that I imagined and upon which I based my expectations. I feel embarrassed and unsettled. Embarrassed – because I understand that prior to my arrival in North Korea, I had prepared myself to see a phenomenon, not people. Unsettled – because not only am I seeing and meeting people, but I am talking with them, joking, and even gently arguing. The frightening entity named "North Korea" looks a little different from how I had pictured it. No, I have no illusions that I have been exposed to the depths of the reality of this regime, but the minimal exposure that I have had thus far is enough to throw me off balance. Later I will be surprised again and again. The second day of the trip is over, full of experiences and features unique to the alternative reality that exists (today) only in North Korea. I identify completely with what a participant in one of my later visits (as a guide) would say: "Thanks for the fantastic week we've had today!"

CHAPTER 5

Comfortable in the Alternative Reality

O ur second morning in Pyongyang. As usual, I am awake early. The wake-up music that I remember from yesterday takes me by surprise all over again, but it's already less strange. I've been in North Korea for a day and a half already. In the flood of experiences and otherness, a day feels like a week, and the mind, apparently, becomes accustomed to surprises.

At noon we will be leaving Pyongyang, but until then, we will spend the morning at a series of sites. We will start at Kim Il-Sung Square – the official North Korean plaza for military marches and celebrations. On the southern side of the square is Taedong River, and on the other side of the river is the Juche Tower. On the northern side is a giant pagoda-shaped building – the Grand People's Study House. The entrance plaza is raised, and it serves as the dais where dignitaries are seated for ceremonies and festivals. To the east and west are administrative buildings, all typical of Communist architecture and devoid of imagination or soul. It is, to put it diplomatically, a large and not particularly impressive square.

We cross the square on foot and soon find ourselves in a foreign-language bookstore. On sale are books, newspapers, stamps, postcards, and other souvenirs. Payment is in foreign currency only, preferably euros, but dollars or Chinese yuan are also acceptable. Later on in our trip, we will discover that the same items, or others very similar, are on sale at almost every site that we visit. Upon entering and leaving the store, one's attention is drawn to "the most photographed policewoman in the country." The policewoman is standing across the road. With sharp, robotic movements, she jerks her head left and right, directing the traffic and the pedestrians crossing the road. Since all the tourists in the country visit this store, usually near the beginning of their trip, the policewoman's exhibition draws attention and invites photographs (preferably after requesting permission from the guide). From Kim Il-Sung Square, we head to the Museum of Victory. As we approach, my gaze is caught by a pyramid-shaped building 330 meters high – 105 floors – looking like a missile ready to launch into the sky. This is the Ryugyong Hotel – a.k.a. the Story of a Colossal Failure.

Construction on the Ryugyong Hotel began in 1987, but in 1992, still under President Kim Il-Sung, it was halted. In 2008, construction was resumed and glass windows were installed throughout the hotel. In 2011, under the leadership of Chairman Kim Jong-Il, the building was supposedly completed, but the opening of the hotel was "temporarily" postponed. The crane that had been used in the construction was left at the tip of the pyramid, as a decorative element. In 2013, under Marshal Kim Jong-Un, the final decision (to date) was that the hotel would not open. In 2018, in honor of the celebrations marking the seventieth anniversary of the country's establishment, an LED display was installed covering one entire side of the building. The non-opening of the hotel is a story of failure relating to severe engineering flaws. Nevertheless, the local guides explain the delay in the inauguration of the hotel as arising from budgetary difficulties resulting from American sanctions.

The Victorious Fatherland Liberation War Museum

Henceforth to be referred to as the Victorious War Museum. Dedicated to the victory over the US in the Korean War (1950-1953) and the clashes that followed.

Following a security check at the entrance, we proceed to a large plaza. At the center is the victory monument, comprising a series of giant statues depicting scenes and victories in various battles in the Korean War. An officer with the rank of captain introduces herself as our guide at the museum, and leads us to an exhibition of weapons and ammunition captured as booty in the war. Slightly bored, I am tagging along at the back of the group, but still listening to her explanations. The officer points to a bomb from an American plane and mentions its weight. With my background in the Air Force, I know that she is mistaken. We move on to see USS Pueblo (see box), a spy ship anchored in in a water channel within the museum grounds connected to the Taedong River. Still not particularly interested, I finish my tour of the ship quickly and as I emerge, my eyes meet those of the captain, our guide. To engage her in conversation, I present myself as a former officer in the Israeli Air Force, and add gently that I am surprised to hear the weight of the bomb, since to the best of my knowledge, bombs of that size weigh double. Meantime, the rest of the group has caught up, and we head for the main building of the museum, which was inaugurated in 2014, under Marshal King Jong-Un. The first exhibition of weapons captured in war was opened in August 1953, about a month after the end of the war. The museum opened in 1974 and has been renovated repeatedly since then.

The entrance hall is extremely imposing: spacious, high, with a curved staircase leading to the second floor. At the center of the hall is a statue of Marshal Kim Jong-Un. "Can that be?" I turn to the guide. She responds with a smile, "This is a statue of President Kim Il-Sung, in his youth."

"He is very similar to the present leader," I nod, and she nods in agreement. Are they really that similar, or has someone made sure that they look similar? I wonder.

Aside from the museum's splendor, its human engineering is visitor-friendly; it is not oppressive. A fifteen-minute film "proves," by means of US documents, that the war was an American plot to seize control of North Korea. Another exhibit, depicting one of the battlefields, has the visitor make his way between the trenches, experiencing what it was like for the soldiers. There are displays of photos and heroic stories, and, in conclusion, a three-dimensional diorama portraying one of the heroic battles of the North Korean army. Throughout the visit, I am in a state of defensive apathy in the face of this display of propaganda.

The "Marine Research" ship _SS Pueblo_ – On January 23rd, 1968, the SS Pueblo, sailing without a flag, was stopped in the territorial waters of North Korea. It was seized by North Korean forces following a brief battle in which ten American crewmen were injured, including one who died. The Koreans reported a total of three casualties from both sides. The ship, 54 meters long with a maximum load of 895 tons, had been launched in 1945. After its capture, it was transferred to the port city of Wonsan on the east coast of North Korea. The official US response declared the ship a marine research vessel that had been sailing in international waters. This claim was disproved by the abundance of intelligence-gathering equipment on board, along with two machine guns. In addition, all the crew members were US soldiers. Upon setting sail on its mission, Admiral Rank Johnson had told Lloyd M. Bucher, the captain, "Remember: you aren't going with the aim of starting another war." Following the capture of the ship, indirect negotiations were held, concluding with a letter of apology from

US President Lyndon Johnson, and the release of the 82 captive crew members. The ship officially remains a commissioned vessel of the US Navy. It is moored alongside the Victorious War Museum in Pyongyang.

Mangyongdae – "A Thousand Beautiful Mirrors" – In the past, a village was located around eight kilometers from the center of Pyongyang. The entire village, with the exception of a single house, disappeared and became a well-tended park within the city boundaries. It was in this house that President Kim Il-Sung was born. The house, carefully preserved and tended, became a "holy site," a place of pilgrimage for North Korean citizens – and, of course, an obligatory item on the tourist itinerary.

From the parking lot, a path winds its way through the park grounds. Koreans – in groups and individuals – have come to show respect to the Kim family. Before reaching the village house, we pass by a wall mural, portraying a mythological scene from the contemporary North Korean ethos. In 1925, the young Kim Song-Ju (who would later change his name to Kim Il-Sung, in memory of a Korean freedom fighter by that name, during the struggle against the Japanese) convinced his parents[13] to leave their home for Manchuria, leaving his grandparents behind, and to join the war against the Japanese occupiers. The child swore that he would return to his homeland only when it was liber-

---

13 According to Western sources, Kim Hyong-Jik, the father of the future president, was a Christian pharmacist. North Korean sources contain no mention of this. There are countless versions of the life stories of the Leaders of North Korea. Obviously, there are contradictions between these and Western sources. Since this book focuses on the North Koreans, I believe that the myth supersedes the (supposed) facts – in other words, the North Korean version is unquestionably more relevant for understanding the reality of North Korea.

ated. On August 15th, 1945, with the liberation of the homeland after a heroic resistance struggle, Kim Il-Sung, who had led the battle, returned to his liberated homeland.[14]

Despite the propaganda aspect, the visit to the site is pleasant, interesting, and important: pleasant, since the well-tended park is simply inviting; interesting, because the small farming house, with its thatched roof, simple furniture, and agricultural implements, is in fact a well-preserved and authentic ethnographic museum. Important – because it contributes to an understanding of the North Korean reality and a glimpse of the mindset of the "faithful" as, full of awe, they make their pilgrimage to the holy site of the birth of the nation's founder.

After the visit to the birthplace of Kim Il-Sung, Yaki and I approach Miss Li and ask where the official residence of the ruler of North Korea is, and whether it would be possible to see it. Miss Li's response is short and simple: "We don't know where his residence is." We prod further: "In every country, visitors to the capital city are shown the splendid official residence of the Leader, along with the Supreme Court building, the Parliament, and so on." Nothing in Miss Li's tone changes: "Not by us." There you have it – North Korea.

*

Our journey back to the hotel for lunch includes, inter alia, the Pyongyang metro. Miss Li leads us into the station and tells us, "The metro system was opened to the public in 1973. There are two train lines, with sixteen stations. Each station is decorated

---

14 Nowhere in North Korean sources is there a word about the Pacific War, led by the US and Britain, nor the bombing of Hiroshima and Nagasaki and the Japanese surrender on August 14th, 1945. Thus, in the Korean narrative, the resistance simply succeeded, all of a sudden, in overcoming the Japanese.

with mosaic motifs relating to the name of the station. The train runs at a depth of 110 meters – deeper than any underground train in the world."

The name of the station we have entered is Puhung, meaning "prosperity" or "flourishing." We descend the escalator into the bowels of the earth. Our eyes are drawn to chandeliers in a range of colors. In the center of the station, on the platform, Koreans are reading newspapers that are spread between glass panes and attached to poles that can be turned on their axes for the readers' convenience. Everything is spotlessly clean. The walls of the station are decorated with mosaics showing happy people in their everyday occupations. We board a train as it enters the station. The carriage is full, but the congestion is bearable. After a few minutes, we arrive at Yonggwang ("Glory") station, even fancier than the previous one. We see chandeliers, mosaics, marble columns, and crowds entering and leaving the station. Anyone who has visited the metro stations in Moscow will doubtlessly understand where the idea originated. As the Soviet rhetoric would boast: "While corrupt leaders built magnificent palaces above ground for themselves, we are building palaces underground, for the benefit of the entire nation." The investment in design and embellishment, aside from the esthetic value, is meant – as in churches – to convey and inculcate a message.

We take a walk around to marvel at the place and to take photographs. On the escalator going back up to the street, Mike comments offhandedly, "Two stations, of course!"[15]

Lunch brings a refreshing change: a typical Korean meal served in a jeongol. The jeongol (hot pot) is a pot containing liquid, with a flame underneath keeping its contents heated. The

---

15 I didn't attach any special importance to his comment at the time, but would later discover its significance.

diners add the ingredients to be cooked – usually meat, mushrooms, and seafood, but any other combination including fish, chicken, and vegetables, is also fine. In general, Korean food is very spicy, but tourists are served a milder version.

Close to the northern exit from Pyongyang is the **Arch of Triumph**, dedicated to the victory over the Japanese. At first glance, its shape recalls the Arc de Triomphe in Paris. It stands 60 meters high (ten meters higher than the Arc de Triomphe), and is the second tallest victory arch in the world (the Monument to the Revolution in the Plaza de la Republica in Mexico City is the tallest, at 67 meters). As in Paris, the Arch stands in the center of a huge square, but there are only three roads leading into the square, as opposed to the twelve in Paris. Of course, there is no comparison in terms of the volume of traffic. Upon further inspection, one notes that the architecture includes some eastern elements. The three levels of the roof resemble a pagoda, and on each side, there is a vaulted gateway 27 meters high. The pillars supporting the archways are decorated with bronze reliefs illustrating the battle against the Japanese and the glory of the Leader of the struggle. The northern side shows the dates of the struggle:

"1925-1945, led by President Kim Il-Sung, born in 1912." The resistance against the Japanese was led by a thirteen-year-old boy! Only in North Korea. Like the Juche Tower, this site, too, was built in 1982, marking the President's 70th birthday, and for this reason it is built out of 25,550 blocks of white granite – each block representing one day of his life, up until the age of 70.

*

After the Arch of Triumph, we set off for Mount Myohyang. For the first time, we are leaving Pyongyang. Mount Myohyang is over a hundred kilometers north of the capital. The drive will take about two and a half hours. We are told before setting out that there are no service stops along the way for a drink; should anyone need the toilet, there is the surrounding countryside... Preparing ourselves for whatever discomforts might await us, we set off. None of us has come to North Korea to enjoy creature comforts. We are all full of curiosity and eager to have our questions answered.

The first thing that catches one's eye is the soldiers working on the roadside. In Pyongyang, too, we saw soldiers occupied with what might be called "non-military" activities, but now, throughout this long drive, the phenomenon of the North Korean army engaged in roadbuilding is especially conspicuous. Obeying the instructions that forbid photographing military personnel and military facilities, we hold back, taking no photographs and asking no questions. The road, wide enough for six to eight lanes, is unmarked, and in really bad shape; it is full of bumps and holes in the asphalt. Certain sections of the road are straight, with no island in the middle and no electricity poles on the sides; clearly, these sections were built with the intention of serving as runways, although in their present condition no jet plane could land or take off on them. Apparently, the idea was abandoned.

Intercity road

Traffic is light, and the further we go from the capital, the sparser it gets. Many long moments pass between one passing vehicle and the next.

We all have our eyes glued to the road; we are eager to see the "real" North Korea, the mountainous countryside – although at this stage there are no tall mountains to be seen. The road runs through a wide, undulating valley; agricultural land. It is the middle of April, and everything is green; there are cultivated fields, cereal crops, and vegetables. The towns are at a distance from the road, so there is no way of seeing the farmers' houses up close, but they don't look particularly inviting. There is no sign of mechanization; the labor is all manual. The towns are distant from one another. The most interesting phenomenon is the great number of people, including soldiers, walking alongside the road.

After about two hours of driving, we leave the main road and turn eastward, towards the grey, granite mountains. The road twists along a stream, and agriculture gives way to woodland. The further we progress, the thicker the growth, ultimately becoming a forest. Finally, we arrive.

Mount Myohyang ("Mysterious Fragrant Mountain") – despite the altitude, at 1,909 meters, the topographical structure and granite cliffs are not suited for winter sports. The entire area has been declared a nature reserve, and is meant for summer recreation. Indeed, this is one of the regions that Pyongyang residents head to for summer vacations. Li Mi -Soon explains that there are gold deposits deep in the ground, but the Leaders have prioritized the natural beauty of the place over the gold. The natural surroundings are indeed beautiful. We bypass Hyang-san county and drive deep into the reserve. The road becomes narrower. At a sharp turn on the way, we come upon a layered, pyramid-shaped building that looks new and inviting. This is the hotel where we will be spending the night. We waste no time and make the most of the remaining hours of daylight to visit Manphok valley ("Manp" – ten thousand; "hok" – waterfalls). After an easy walk of about half a kilometer, we are at the bottom of some waterfalls. Right in front of us is a tiny waterfall, just two or three meters high, with a path leading to it and onwards. Feeling familiar with the situation from my experience as a tour guide, I ask Li Mi-Soon how we will proceed. She points to a chart showing a map of the waterfalls and the path.

"Mr. Li will go first, and I will be at the back," she explains. "As the path climbs, there are more waterfalls, until you reach an observation ledge, with a place to sit."

Mike jumps up and asks, "Can we go on further than that? I see that there are more waterfalls." Miss Li answers, "No problem; Mr. Li will accompany you as far as you wish."

I choose to stay at the back, chatting with Miss Li. From the moment she understands that I am a tour guide and that I plan to come back to North Korea with tourists, something in her rigid demeanor softens and slowly a collegial professional dynamic starts to develop between us. The path, of medium difficulty, leads from one waterfall to the next; it is a pleasant and charming walk. Nature at its best – the complete opposite of the sites and experiences we have had so far. When we reach the observation ledge, we find the entire group waiting for us, except Mike and Mr. Li. After a few minutes of relaxation, Miss Li says, "I suggest that we go down and wait for Mike and Mr. Li at the bottom, since they'll be coming down a different way." Our impression is that her "suggestion" is her gentle way of saying, "This is what we're going to do," and we have no choice but to accept her advice.[16] We walk down the path leading back to the bottom of the waterfalls, and wait patiently for Mr. Li and Mike. The minutes go by, but there is no sign of them. The sun is about to set; it's not dark yet, but it's starting to get late. Miss Li tries to call Mr. Li's cell phone, but there is no reception. She starts to look worried, and we, in turn, become concerned. Suddenly the two of them appear, as promised, from a different path. Mike is beaming; excited about the hike and he shares his enjoyment with us, while Mr. Li – who is at least thirty years younger than him – is puffing and panting, hot and perspiring, and making no attempt to hide his relief at having this torment come to an end.

---

16 Later on, when I came to North Korea with tourists, I discovered very quickly that in many cases these are indeed suggestions, and not decisions. It turns out that there is room to discuss a different course of action in instances where it makes sense.

Hyangsan Hotel in Myohyang deserves some further elaboration. Nestled among the mountains, in the heart of the nature reserve, it is a shiny new luxurious hotel with an eye-catching design. It houses an indoor swimming pool, massage rooms, a gym, a spacious lobby, a bar with a surprising range of drinks, a very tall ceiling over the inner area, a second floor with dining rooms and lecture rooms, and spacious, nicely decorated rooms with luxurious bathrooms, and gracious personnel who go out of their way to accede to one's every request ... in short, everything that a spoiled Western tourist could wish for in a hotel. There's only one thing that's missing, and that's tourists. We have a sense that we are the only visitors, or close to the only ones, in the hotel.

The hotel testifies to the beginning of the realization of the goal set forth by the country's leader, Marshal Kim Jong-Un: the dream of "a million tourists per year," in contrast to the meager few thousand that currently comprise the country's tourism (mostly Chinese businesspeople who come as "tourists" to evade sanctions). Gina, Brian, and Michael – the three members of our group who work for United Airlines, choose to try out a massage before dinner. The meal, served in a medium-sized hall that serves as a dining room, offers typical Asian cuisine. Despite our fatigue, we sit at the bar exchanging experiences.

In the morning, as though agreed among us in advance, most of the group gathers outside the hotel. The morning chill and clear air draw us like a magnet outside, with no guide and no supervision. It is a refreshing change, in all senses.

Our itinerary today starts with **Pohyon-sa**, a Buddhist temple dating back to the 11th century. Located in the midst of the natural surroundings, its religious architecture is typical of eastern cultures. The temple features a lone monk who tries hard to tout the freedom of religion enjoyed by the faithful. For some reason, we feel that he plays his role rather well. We do not see any devotees. Among his explanations about the temple and Buddhist ritual, the "monk" manages to include a description of the damage caused to the temple during the Korean War. The story sounds a little strange: would the US army really invest effort in blowing up this "strategic target" – an isolated Buddhist temple surrounded by nature? This doesn't seem to make sense, but in any case, there is no way of establishing the truth.

The **International Friendship Exhibition** is without doubt the highlight of our visit to the nature reserve. In the heart of the reserve, on a hill overlooking an enchanting valley, stand two large granite buildings that hold a permanent exhibition of gifts awarded to the country's leaders by visiting dignitaries. One building holds the gifts given to President Kim Il-Sung; the other is reserved for gifts to his son, Chairman Kim Jong-Il. In the short time at our disposal, there is no possibility of visiting both exhibitions, and no matter which we choose, we will see only a very small portion of the collection. We end up choosing to view the gifts to the nation's founding father, Kim Il-Sung. As at every other site, information is conveyed in Korean by the local guide, and our group's guide translates into English. The local guide is dressed in the same uniform worn by guides at all the sites we visit. It is a beautiful uniform: a dark blue velvet dress in traditional style with a high belt worn under the armpits, with an understated pattern that adds character. Two soldiers, guarding the entrance, open the two bronze doors with a light push. As at the Juche Tower, the guide invites us to try to move the doors, which clearly weigh a few tons, and indeed they swivel with ease. The guide expresses her amazement at the technological achievement. After passing through a security check and depositing our cameras and cell phones, we are inside the museum.

From our visit to the Kumsusan Mausoleum, we are already familiar with the Korean style – polished grey granite floors, with red granite for variety, and unpolished granite walls. The size and cleanliness convey a sense of stately splendor. We start our visit in the room honoring President Kim Il-Sung. His statue, against the background of the room, creates the illusion of a living being. Over a hundred exhibition rooms are arranged by geographical location, and they house countless objects d'art: gestures of appreciation presented by visiting delegations and gifts from heads of state, associations, political parties, and "ordinary" VIPs from dozens of different countries (even Israel is represented with a gift from the Israeli Communist Party).

The visit is fascinating in two respects. Firstly, there is the historical perspective. The gifts recall some long-forgotten names and faces, including such "friends of Israel" as Muammar Gaddafi, Saddam Hussein, Yasser Arafat, Leonid Brezhnev, Fidel Castro, Hugo Chavez, and more. Some respectable Western leaders are also featured, including former US President Jimmy Carter (not during his term of office); French President Francois Mitterrand, and others. There are countries that have changed their name or status, and countries that have disappeared: East Germany, Czechoslovakia, and of course, the USSR. The collection of artifacts sums up the historical processes of the second half of the twentieth century. Another aspect of the exhibition that captivates the visitor is the artistic, esthetic variety: there are works of carved jade and ivory, drawings and paintings, folklore artifacts, porcelain vessels, goblets, ceremonial plates, and more.

The visitors' route takes us to the top floor of the building. A huge balcony looks out over the valley, and armchairs are set out for the convenience of visitors needing a rest. A souvenir shop is open, and for one euro, one can buy coffee or tea with cookies. The coffee is, of course, instant granulated coffee with powdered creamer, but, tired and enthused by the visit, we relax in the comfortable armchairs, enjoy the scenery, and invite all the tourists for a drink. A fitting conclusion to a unique experience.

The road back to Pyongyang is, presumably, the same road we came on. Nowhere in North Korea are there parallel roads. The low volume of traffic, the mountainous topography, and the limited resources all dictate a minimum of roads – or, at least, paved roads. As usual, I sit at the front of the bus, periodically moving to the tour guide's seat in order to take photographs. Some of the time I sit next to Miss Li, and I find myself chatting with her more and more. At this stage, the conversation is mostly professional – one tour guide to another. The responses I receive to my questions for now all seem to be taken directly from a list of "national responses." Miss Li projects a strict demeanor that accords with my expectations. Among other topics of conversation, I explain to her that Israeli tourists are very curious about the everyday life of ordinary citizens. Again I ask that we visit a local supermarket. Her answer, as in the case of every request, is positive, with the addition: "I'll see what I can do." Just before we reach Pyongyang, I ask Miss Li for permission to photograph the sights along the roadside (I have decided that at every stage, even when it is clear that the answer will be positive, I will ask permission to photograph). In fact, I prepare to photograph the soldiers of the North Korean army, working along the road on tasks that are not even remotely connected with any military purpose. And indeed, as we approach the city, the soldiers are busy with their jobs, and I photograph them (with permission!). In the back of the bus, Mike pulls out his camera and starts photographing them, too. At this stage, Mr. Li, who has been sitting at the back all along, gently asks Mike to stop photographing. Mike ignores him and continues, and Mr. Li repeats his request, this time in a more commanding tone. Mike looks towards me, observes me holding a camera and photographing with approval, and carries on, ignoring Mr. Li. At this stage, Mr. Li starts to look angry and he approaches Mike, demanding emphatically that he stop. Mike smiles, and with a calm smile, closes his camera and holds it up to Mr. Li, as though saying, "Here, all yours; tell me what's the problem." Mr. Li looks through the photos and calms down with impressive speed. He resumes his polite tone and tells him, "If I ask you not to photograph, then please do not photograph." The incident is seemingly over (the continuation is still to come). It is a key incident for me in preparation for running tour groups in the future: Ask permission and act in accordance with the answer; you may be pleasantly surprised.

The North Korean army

To the Western ear, the title sounds frightening – and for good reason. But let's look at the dry facts. A layman seeking to gauge the military might of a certain country will consult sources that refer him to research institutes that rate the military power of different countries in the world. Not surprisingly, the military power of North Korea is the subject of much interest, especially when the Korean dispute is in the news. Global Firepower, an academic research institute based in Hershey, Pennsylvania, tracks and calculates the strength of different armies in terms of the quantitative range and quality of their weaponry. The US, of course, ranks no. 1, followed, predictably enough, by Russia, China, India, and Japan. In sixth place is South Korea. Where is North Korea on the list? It ranks no. 28. In a different ranking, the US World Report, the North Korean army is not included among the thirty strongest armies, as opposed to South Korea, which ranks no. 8. In terms of size, the North Korean army is the fourth largest in the world, with 1.1 million soldiers. The CIA World Factbook says nothing at all about the military strength of the North Korean army; it does however, provide the following facts:
-    1.1 – 1.2 million soldiers
-    Military spending amounts to 22-24% of the Gross Na-

tional Product (!). (By way of comparison, in Saudi Arabia, the figure is 8.78%; in Israel, 5.1%; in Russia, 3.93%; and in the US, 3.16%).

- Mandatory service: Eight years for men; five years for women.

A Wikipedia search for "short-range ballistic missiles (500 kilometers) in North Korea" produces a wealth of estimates ranging from 300 – 600.

A review of the dry facts as to the military might of North Korea in terms of conventional weaponry points to a large army equipped with outdated weapons. This explains why its army is not ranked as one of the world's strongest. However, the picture changes considerably once we turn to the question of its arsenal of nuclear bombs and delivery systems. Western sources agree that North Korea has at its disposal an inventory of thirty to sixty nuclear bombs, as well as possessing delivery capability to strike short and medium-range targets – certainly South Korea and Japan. The ideological basis for this poor country allocating such vast resources to such advanced and expensive weaponry is to be found in the concepts of Juche and Songon.

In light of the above, along with the fact that the North Korean leadership is regarded as "unpredictable" and devoid of restraints, it is clear why the average Westerner is struck with fear upon hearing the words "North Korean army." The impression I got from my conversations with the Koreans is that that is precisely their aim. Deterrence is their strategy: "Unlike the past, when we were conquered over and over again because we were weak, now we are strong, and we are unpredictable; beware!" I do not pretend to speak for the leadership, but this is the message as projected by North Korean people, and the feeling is that this is indeed their truth.

Moreover, their "truth" is based on the fact that Korea has never attacked any foreign country. The Koreans view themselves as seekers of peace, and as such embrace the well-known adage, "If you want peace, prepare for war." This teaching of the 4th century Roman historian Publius Flavius Vegetius Renatus, erroneously attributed to Plato, Klausowitz, Napoleon and many other leaders, is the security mantra of North Korea – or, at least, so it is presented to visitors.

In the tourist-oriented publication *Panorama of North Korea* (2017), in which the regime tries to portray the wonders of North Korea, a series of texts and photos describe the scenery, culture, heritage, leadership (focused solely on the welfare of the citizens), and history of the country – all within fourteen pages, under the heading "Tourism." Another fourteen pages (!) are devoted to the topic of defense, with some brief text and a few photos of soldiers, and a great many more showing advanced weaponry that includes missiles, planes, and landing craft. Again, this is a book that aims to have tourists take the story of North Korea home with them. I peruse my library and rack my brains in an attempt to find a tourist publication even remotely like this one, from any country I have visited. There is none. Only in North Korea.

Songun

Songun is based on the idea of self-reliance – Juche. The state is, of course, an essential condition for the realization of socialist national and cultural ideology, and thus simple logic leads to the concept of Songun, which dictates that priority be given to the defense of the state. In other words, the army takes precedence over the revolution – and, in fact, over everything.

Songun ideology was originally formulated in the first years of North Korean independence, under the leadership of President Kim Il-Sung. In 1994, with the reins of power moving to the hands of Chairman Kim Jong-Il, it was awarded a central place, second only to the ideology of Juche and, in essence, an integral part of it.

Soldiers in the fields

CHAPTER 6

Back to Earth

T he road heading from Pyongyang southwards, towards the border and the demilitarized zone, is of course also the road to Seoul, the capital of South Korea. As such it is the most important highway in Korea, linking three historical capital cities: the two capitals that are today the most important cities in the Korean peninsula – Seoul and Pyongyang, and in between them the most important city in Korean tradition: the city of Kaesong. The road is called Reunification Highway. Immediately after the last buildings of Pyongyang, heading south, one encounters the **Arch of Reunification**. Inaugurated in 2001, it is a concrete structure straddling the road in the form of two Korean women – one representing North Korea, the other South Korea – in national Korean dress. The women lean towards each other, jointly holding a globe, at the center of which is a map of unified Korea. As noted already, every monument is first and foremost a manifesto, and thus there is no room for coincidence. Every detail is planned so as to convey the message. The two women form an archway 30 meters high and 61.5 meters wide, spanning the road. These measurements are symbolic: the death of the president of North Korea on July 8th, 1994, delayed – but did not cancel – the summit meeting that eventually took place in June 2000, concluding on June 15th with a joint statement. The gateway formed by the two women of concrete also bridges over the conflict. The 61.5-meter width symbolizes June 15th (6/15), the date of publication of the joint statement. As to the height – at every opportunity when North Koreans talk about the population of Korea, they refer to three groups: inhabitants of North Korea; inhabitants of South Korea; and Koreans in the diaspora. The number '3' in the thirty meters represents these three groups.

If there is any topic that vexes North and South Koreans alike, it is the division of their country. The Arch of Reunification leading to the DMZ and connecting Pyongyang with Seoul, along with many billboards promoting the dream of reunification, are testimony to the official aspiration, and in every conversation, one senses the sincere longing on the part of the population, along with a sober awareness that it will be a long and complex process. They emphasize the differences in worldview and the difficulty of the task, but mention the reunification program formulated by President Kim Il-Sung, based on three principles: direct negotiations with no foreign interference; peaceful reunification; and ratification through referendums for the citizens of both countries.

I sit next to Miss Li, lost in thoughts about the division of Korea. Having grown up in the West, with an awareness of the reality of a Korea that was divided – just as other countries were divided – I had never given much thought to the question of whether things had to be this way, nor to those affected. The visit to North Korea and the encounter with the victims of this reality are thought-provoking.

It must be remembered that the Koreans (North and South) are a single, homogeneous people in every respect: ethnic origin, founding myths, language, folklore, and food. The Korean nation was conquered and trampled in the Second World War. As though that was not enough, it continues to pay the price of the Cold War struggle in the form of the arbitrary division of its homeland into north and south, as determined in the compromise between the Great Powers, which completely ignored the Koreans and their suffering. The 38th Parallel is an imaginary line creating an arbitrary separation of Korea and dividing villages and families. The struggle between the Blocs has undergone a transformation. Germany and Austria, which were punished for being the aggressors in WWII, have been reunited. Japan paid for its war crimes immediately after the war, and within a short time, resumed its respectable place among the nations. The Korean people, in the meantime, continue to pay for their previous weakness and for being pawns in the hands of the World Powers.

In the present reality, reunification seems far off. But perhaps the joint appearance at the Winter Olympics in Seoul in 2018, the North-South summit meetings, and the change in rhetoric that led to meetings between the US President and the Leader of North Korea could all be signaling the start of a long, convoluted process with ups and downs that will finally end in reunification.

*

The drive to the DMZ takes about three hours. The scenery is similar to what we saw on our trip to the north: a wide road in bad condition, with farmers and soldiers along the roadside, but the mountains here are not as tall and dramatic. As I sit at Miss Li's side, deep in thought about the division of Korea, I address her, and a conversation develops between us. I say, as though to myself, "The division of Korea is an injustice and an anomaly. The injustice has to be righted, and anomalies eventually disappear." I emphasize that I am ignoring completely the political aspects of the conflict, focusing only on the human perspective and natural justice. I tell her, "I believe that in your lifetime, you will see Korea reunified."

Miss Li turns inward in silence, offering no response. After a few moments, she says, "You know, when I was younger, I dreamed that there would be a war and that within a few days, we could reunify the country. But now I have children, and I don't want war."

Her answer astounds me. I have already discovered that Li Mi-Soon comes from a family that is part of North Korea's administrative and intellectual elite. Her father spoke, in addition to Korean, fluent Chinese, English, Spanish and Russian. He was the chief interpreter for President Kim Il-Sung and for Chairman Kim Jong-Il. As an interpreter, he would presumably have been party to the country's most closely guarded secrets. After that, he served as North Korea's ambassador to Cuba, where Miss Li completed her university studies. Her mother was a very popular professor at Kim Il-Sung University. I would not have expected to hear such words from Li Mi-Soon, who thus far has projected an image of such rigidity and "religious fanaticism."

Our conversation continues, and in light of the fact that she has traveled outside of her homeland, I try to ascertain whether she has met South Koreans and talked with them. She challenges me, her contempt towards the South Koreans clear in her voice, "Yes, I met some, but what do I have to discuss with them?" (North Koreans regard South Koreans as collaborators with the American Satan.) I gently prod, "Yes, but you all belong to the same people. They, like you, are also victims of circumstance."

Again she astonishes me – this time, not with her answer, but rather with her silence. She sits thinking. Perhaps I am mistaken, but her facial expression suddenly seems to have softened. Silent, side by side, each of us is lost in thought.

*

After about an hour and a half of driving, surprise! Thanks to lessons learned from the journey to Mount Myohyang, we are making a road stop. We get off the bus, and there are kiosks selling fruit, candies, coffee, ice-cream, t-shirts with inscriptions about North Korea, and other souvenirs. In the building where the toilets are located, there is no running water. There are containers of water, and a brush to use for cleaning the bowl. Not wonderful, but almost reasonable. The kiosk sellers here, as at all other souvenir shops we have seen so far, make an active effort to sell – not aggressively, but in a pleasant manner.

Again I recall my first encounter with Communist Bloc countries and the culture of selling that I found there, characterized by disregard tinged with contempt. Here, in North Korea, although everything is owned and run by the government, the attitude of the shopkeepers is completely different. It is quite clear that they enjoy the incentives that are linked to their results – the beginnings of a type of private commerce.

About half an hour after the stop, Miss Li takes the microphone. She tells us that we are close to the border – in other words, the region where the enemy is located, and hence we are forbidden to take photographs. She asks that we put our cameras and cellphones away in our bags. At a spot where the road is raised, there are some strange concrete pillars at its sides, like pillars lining an avenue, about six meters tall and about a meter wide. In response to my question, Miss Li mumbles something about bridges. We have already learned not to push too hard for answers, and the vague, mumbled response goes unchallenged. On our next stop, one of the members of the group explains that the pillars have been placed there for the purpose of being toppled onto the road, thus serving as a barrier against tanks. Indeed, we are nearing the border with the enemy.

As we draw closer to the DMZ, we stop at four checkpoints. Before each stop, Miss Li emphasizes that we are not to photograph. We pass by Kaesong, the historical capital of the Korean kingdom (more on this below). A few minutes later, we see lettering – in English, too – indicating that we have arrived at the entrance to the Demilitarized Zone. The bus passes through the gate, and we are in a facility around eighty meters long and forty meters wide. On the right is a propaganda poster in two parts: one shows two children, the other shows a forefinger pointing upwards, as though showing "one": two children from two countries that are one and the same. The bus comes to a stop in front of a white stripe painted on the ground, and about thirty meters ahead, there is another white stripe. The bus is boarded by an officer who exchanges a few words with our guides. Miss Li tells us: "On the right is a building with a tourist shop; an instruction room with a model of the area, in which guides address tourist groups; and the offices of the facility. On the left are toilets." Miss Li, her body language and intonation serious and somewhat tense, adds, "You must remain between the two white lines; do not cross them. You are free to enjoy the facilities; please wait patiently for further instructions."

I turn to Mr. Li and ask his permission to cross the white line in order to take a photo of the poster, which has captured my attention. Mr. Li deliberates for a moment and then says, "Come with me." We cross the line. I take a photo, turn slightly, and then walk towards the toilets. On my way, I see Mr. Li receiving a loud rebuke from the officer. I keep moving, but after I come out of the toilet, I apologize to Mr. Li for getting him into trouble. He waves his hand dismissively and gives a shy smile, insisting that everything's fine and it certainly wasn't my fault.

We wait for about half an hour. The shop is selling the same products we have seen before, with an important addition: ginseng! It is on sale in every possible form: natural root, liquid, cream, cakes, candies... It is clear that Kaesong is the ginseng capital of the world – at least, as far as the Koreans are concerned.[17]

We are delayed longer than expected. It turns out that the scheduled time for our visit has been changed, owing to the April 15th celebrations. In order to deal with this problem, a phone call has to be made to the company in Pyongyang, but at the border there is no phone reception (by design). So our guides, with the approval of the commander of the facility, travel about two kilometers north, and call from there. The "complication" is sorted out after a few rounds backwards and forwards to the area of telephone reception. Only then are we invited into the instruction room. As we stand there, we are shown – with the help of the model and some maps – the route for our visit, and what awaits us. We are entering the DMZ, a four-kilometer-wide strip – two kilometers on each side; the ceasefire border. Korea was divided along the 38th parallel. At the end of the Korean War, the ceasefire lines were slightly different from the arbitrary division imposed by the Great Powers. They are more reminiscent of a natural border. In the east of the country, the border is north of the 38th parallel, while in the west it lies more to the south, such that the city of Kaesong is located within the borders of North Korea. We arc in the western region of the border, which follows the Sacheon River.

---

17 *Ginseng* is the root of plants of the genus Panax. It grows mainly in northern Asia and North America. In Chinese, "ginseng" means "manroot," owing to its humanlike form. In Chinese medicine, ginseng occupies a place of honor and is said to boost energy and the immune system, improve liver health, bestow inner calm, and – most of all – enhance male virility.

A small village named **Panmunjom**[18] is "trapped" at the heart of the DMZ, on the northern side of the border. The homes in the village have disappeared – its inhabitants were evacuated to Kaesong – but its location, right on the highway between Pyongyang and Seoul, made it the ideal location for the ceasefire talks that brought the Korean War to an end. Over the course of nearly two years, some six hundred meetings were held between the sides, concluding with the signing of the ceasefire agreement on July 25th, 1953. The huts in which the talks took place have remained in place. On each side of the border, by mutual consent, structures serving tourists have been built. For tourists visiting either South or North Korea, a stop here is almost obligatory. The collection of buildings at Panmunjom serves as a meeting point between the two sides. A summit meeting between the leaders of the two states, held on April 27th, 2018, ended with a joint declaration of the start of a new era (the Panmunjom Declaration). Following the guide's explanation, we go out to the center of the facility and arrange ourselves in a line behind the white line. Our bus approaches and crosses the line, and then we are invited by the officer to cross the line and climb aboard the bus. Once we are seated again, the Koreans join us on the bus: first our guides, then the officer and the site guide, and finally an armed soldier, who sits right in front. With a serious expression and tone of voice, Li Mi-Soon tells us that we are in close proximity to the dangerous enemy. She points to the armed soldier and adds, "He is joining us in order to keep us safe in the vicinity of the hostile border." These words give us some relief, the tension that has

18 The village has become symbolic of Korean division, on the one hand, and of talks and reconciliation, on the other. In Billy Joel's protest song, "We Didn't Start the Fire" (1989), listing significant historical events of the 20th century, Panmunjom is invoked as a symbol of the conflict in the Korean peninsula and its tragic consequences.

built up is released, and we are ready to continue our visit. The enemy is unquestionably close by and dangerous – this is apparent in light of the barbed wire fences and the cylindrical concrete blocks that can be rolled quickly and easily onto the road to block tanks. For a moment, we forget that we are in the second decade of the 21st century, and that North Korea has demonstrated possession not only of nuclear weapons, but also of missiles with impressive ranges that can deliver them. But then we all realize that we are watching a show – a show in which North Korea is ready for war – at the precise spot where the war ended more than seventy years ago. Five minutes later we are at the hut that was constructed for the ceasefire agreement signing ceremony. On one side of the table is the North Korean flag; on the other side, the flag of the UN. It must be remembered that the Western forces, led by the US and South Korea, fought as part of a UN force together with another twenty-three countries, including Britain, Canada, France, Australia, Turkey, New Zealand, the Philippines, Thailand, Colombia, Greece, Ethiopia, South Africa, Belgium, Holland, and even... Luxemburg. Our guide, the officer, points to the faded UN flag, presenting it as a symbol of the fearfulness of the American enemy, which hid behind it, and which, despite the assistance of many other countries, was not able to overcome the Korean people (for some reason, China's aid in the war is not mentioned). After spending a few moments in the hut, we head for the border itself – a modern, concrete building with the North Korean flag fluttering above it. Opposite us is almost a mirror image – a concrete building with the South Korean flag. In between are six huts; three white and three blue, with a concrete marker indicating the border in between.

We get off the bus and our first stop is a large stone inscribed with a short text written by President Kim Il-Sung, together with his signature, taken from the last document that he signed – a paper dealing with Korean reunification, in anticipation of the summit meeting with the leader of South Korea. Owing to his death, on July 8th, 1994, the summit that had been planned for a few days later never happened. We move on to see one of the huts that serves to this day as a location for talks whenever necessary for the maintenance of the ceasefire agreement. Throughout our visit to the DMZ, we are permitted to photograph to our hearts' content, even photos of the soldiers and the officer accompanying us. Our last stop is the building looking out towards South Korea. Everyone takes photos of the view and of themselves, including the officer. Yaki and I ask to be photographed together with him, and we ask Miss Li to tell him that we are from Israel. The officer hears this, and nothing in his expression changes. Afterwards, I have a photo taken of just myself together with him, and again I ask Miss Li to tell him that I am from Israel and was an officer in the Israeli Air Force. I cannot be certain, but it seems that this time his handshake is a little warmer. (In the future, his positive attitude will become more apparent.)

Arch of Reunification – at the southern exit from the capital of North Korea, Pyongyang, on the main highway leading to the capital of South Korea, Seoul.

Entering the DMZ – a poster expressing the longing for reunification. There is no differentiation between the two children, one from each side of the border; Korea is one.

At the border with South Korea, the DMZ.
The armed soldier is protecting us from the "dangerous enemy."

Kaesong (in Korean: "Breaking through the fortress")

The city of Kaesong has a population of over 300,000. It is located south of the 38th parallel but north of the ceasefire line. Its strategic location on the highway between Pyongyang and Seoul would be enough to give it special importance, but it is all the more important as the capital of Korea for more than four hundred years, during the Koryo Dynasty (936 – 1392). In Korean history, the Koryo period is regarded as a golden age. It was during this time that Korea was consolidated as a single country and a single people. The same emperor ruled over the entire peninsula, with a uniform legal system, a lesser status for soldiers, and greater esteem for enlightenment – in other words, Confucian philosophy – as the basis for running the country. At the same time, the Buddhist faith was introduced by the Koryo dynastic rulers. The centrality of Kaesong in the

Korean myth indicates the enormity of the achievement of having Kaesong included in the territory of North Korea despite lying south of the 38th parallel. As a city with such a significant historical and cultural legacy, Kaesong and the surrounding areas boast a great number of UNESCO heritage sites. Our visit included several of them.

The city of Kaesong allows a glimpse of a more provincial Korean town, quite different – to put it mildly – and less exciting than the façade that awaits visitors to Pyongyang, although there, too, some neighborhoods are quite run down. The way people dress here – especially the women – is very different. Their simple clothing is more reminiscent of youth movement uniforms. There are few vehicles on the road, but plenty of bicycles and pedestrians. On the road leading into the town, of course, there are statues of the two leaders – the President and the Chairman – and further on, some fairly nice-looking public buildings. In contrast, the main road in the center of the town has dirt margins instead of pavements. It reminds me of provincial towns in China in the 1990s. Nevertheless, everything is clean, and some level of effort to enhance the esthetic aspect of the public space is evident. There is no question – this is not Pyongyang. The difference between them is glaring. I have to say, though, that the situation looks better than in many of the peripheral towns or even outskirts of capital cities in countries in Asia, Latin America, and certainly in Africa. On my future visits to North Korea I would have the good fortune of passing through rural areas, and my impressions are described further on.

*

Miss Li makes use of the short journey from the DMZ to Kaesong to prepare us for lunch, which will be held at Tungil restaurant. "This restaurant serves a meal in royal style," she tells us. "The top culinary dish in Kaesong in general, and at this restaurant in particular, is chicken cooked in ginseng. Unfortunately, this meal is not included in the standard tour fare; whoever wishes to, may order it for an additional twenty euro." Yaki and I exchange a few words and arrive at our decision: we will order one portion for both of us. We are not about to miss out on the local delicacy. The entrance floor at the restaurant houses a souvenir shop, where ginseng maintains a strong presence. On the second floor, a beautiful table has been prepared for us. At each place setting there are seven covered bowls. The bowls and their lids are made of gold-colored pewter – indeed, a royal meal. They contain a range of foods: spinach, rice, kimchi (see box); some are unfamiliar to the Western palate. It seems doubtful that these portions will satisfy anyone's hunger. After a few moments, the delightful waitresses appear with the chicken cooked in ginseng, for those who have ordered it. Yaki and I turn to the business of eating the special dish. In short, it is chicken soup made with boiled chicken. Somehow, along with the other dishes, the meal manages to be filling. "How did the chicken taste to you?" Yaki asks, and I answer, "Reminds me of the chicken my grandmother used to cook." Yaki is surprised: "So good?" I tell him, "I come from a Polish background; a working-class family. My mother sewed; my father was a textile worker who earned a daily wage. As I see it, my family was the archetype that inspired Karl Marx to write the Communist Manifesto. While my parents were at work, my grandmother ran the household, and, along with everything else, she was in charge of cooking. The kitchen was her kingdom. Generations of poverty and evolution had their effect. Not only was my grandmother's cooking devoid of any taste; it seemed to us (my late sister, Yehudit, and I) that grandmother had no awareness of the concept that food could or should be tasty. From a single chicken she prepared soup to last for a period that no-one really knew how to gauge, but it certainly could have been listed in the Guinness Book of Records. In the "tasteless" stakes, her boiled chicken rated well. My sister and I shared a memory that we would often discuss over the years: we would laugh as we remembered how, when we wouldn't eat the chicken, grandmother, with a loving rebuke, would try to persuade us, using her own unique brand of logic: "Eat, eat, it's good; there's no salt, no pepper. Why aren't you eating it?" The taste of the chicken here reminds me of my childhood."

Although the lunch (unlike the other meals so far, which had been altogether satisfying) was barely enough and quite unexciting, it had been a cultural and culinary experience. Later on, on my future trips, we would come back for this same meal, since its added value – despite its deficiencies – was far greater than just another meal of eggs, chips, and rice.

Kimchi

Kimchi is the Korean "national food." It is first and foremost a side dish or appetizer, made from fermented and pickled vegetables. The most widely used ingredient is cabbage, although almost any vegetable in season can be used in preparing kimchi. During the fermentation process, spices and hot peppers are added. The versions of this national food are infinite in number. In the past, kimchi was kept in clay vessels that were buried in the ground.

Kimchi is an indispensable element in any Korean meal. Its importance in Korean folklore is evidenced by the fact that in

Seoul there is a Kimchi Museum, and also the fact that for the first space flight that included a Korean astronaut, a special kimchi adapted to conditions in space was developed. (Cynics, on the other hand, like to comment that once kimchi is divested of myth and tradition, all that is left is sour pickles...)

*

Opposite the restaurant is a UNESCO heritage site: **Sonjuk (Bamboo) Bridge**. It is a small, unimpressive bridge – 8.35 meters long and 3.35 meters wide, built in 1216 during the Koryo era. For UNESCO, its importance lies in its perfect state of preservation. For the Koreans, its importance relates to the end of the Koryo dynasty, in 1392. The change of regime came when General Yi Seong-gye, of the house of Joseon, conspired against the Koryo emperor. In order to ensure the success of his scheme, he enlisted the senior members of the administration and the emperor's advisors. All these senior personnel supported Yi Seong-gye, except for the emperor's close confidant, Mong Ju, who declared that loyalty was a supreme value and that he would not be part of the plot. Obviously, Mong-Ju was going to reveal the scheme, and on his way home, while crossing the bridge, he was attacked by five warriors and beaten to death. The coup d'etat succeeded, and Yi Seong-gye became the first emperor of the Joseon dynasty, which went on to rule for five hundred years, until Korea's conquest at the hands of Japan in the early 20th century. Mong-Ju became a symbol of boundless, unconditional loyalty. His faithfulness to the ruling emperor was admired even by the rulers of the Joseon dynasty. Officially, no one drew any connection to the loyalty owed to the new leadership, but the message to the Koreans – and not only to them – was clear. Originally, the bridge was named after Emperor Yi Seong-gye, but the myth of loyalty was (and still is) so powerful that by popular demand its name was changed to mark the bamboo bush growing at the spot where Mong-Ju was murdered. There is a brown patch on the bridge, and legend has it that when there is rain, its color changes to blood-red – the blood of Mong-Ju.

Another UNESCO heritage site is the **Songgyungwan Confucian Temple**, founded in 1089, under the rule of the eleventh emperor of the Koryo dynasty. The structure burned down and was rebuilt in 1592.

Chinese civilization is the basis of Far-Eastern culture. China's neighbors – Vietnam to the south, Japan to the east, and Korea to the north – draw central cultural elements such as their script, silk, tea, gardens, and more, from its example. Confucianism (see box) is one of the belief systems that passed from China to its neighbors, and in Korean culture, as in Chinese culture, too, it forms the basis of government and public administration. The Confucian temple served as a home for the preservation of this belief system and for the inculcation of teachings in the realms of governance. Most importantly, it was at the temple that public servants received their training to serve at all levels of administration. The Confucian temple was the Eastern equivalent of the Faculty of Public Administration at a Western university. In these countries, success in the studies and exams at the Confucian temple was an essential condition for climbing the hierarchy of government systems.

In 1992, a university was established in Kaesong, and the decision was made to locate it adjacent to the temple. The idea was, of course, to connect the present with the legacy of the past. The temple had served as the central institution of learning in the time of the Koryo dynasty. The Joseon dynasty had made its seat in Seoul, and the central temple of learning was relocated accordingly.

The temple that we now visited in Kaesong, and which is recognized as a UNESCO World Heritage site, is built in classical Chinese architectural style: a wooden structure with pagoda roofs turned upwards at the corners, several layers high. A courtyard leads to additional courtyards until one reaches the central building. Separating the courtyards are gates on raised sills. The temple houses the historical and anthropological Koryo Museum. In addition to the buildings, which are interesting in and of themselves, some of the notable exhibits include a collection of weapons and fighting styles from the Koryo period, and an impressive collection of celadon pottery. The clay is thick and coarse, while the glazing lends a delicate, smooth coating in mixed shades of blue, green, and grey, lending the vessels a jade-like appearance. There is also the world's earliest example of movable metal type, which might be regarded as the real source of modern printing. Most impressive of all, perhaps, is a perfect replica of the tomb of King Kongmin (1330-1374). In his great love for his wife, the king ordered that a mausoleum be prepared for himself and his beloved queen, with an above-ground tunnel linking the two chambers.

The Teachings of Confucius

Confucianism is a Chinese philosophy dating back to the sixth century B.C.E., as transmitted by Kung Fu Tse (Confucius) and recorded by his disciples. Confucianism is not so much a religion as an accumulation of wisdom meant to serve as a guide to life. The foundation of this philosophy is a mythical past when people lived in peace and tranquility; hence, this tradition is a tool for problem-solving. One of its central pillars is the principle of "Ren," meaning benevolence, consideration, and uprightness in human relations. "Li" is another principle, expressed in rites – not just ceremonies, in the national or religious sense, but also propriety and manners in everyday interaction (a bow is an example of a rite in both senses). The principle of "Xiao" refers to filial respect, which is expanded to include loyalty and respect for anyone above oneself in the social hierarchy.

"Every person has to know his place in society!" Confucianism defines very clearly a set of hierarchical relationships in which obedience, discipline, and loyalty are supreme values. There are five different areas in which these relationships are set forth: between a son and his father; between a wife and her husband; between a brother and an older brother; between someone younger and someone older; and – most importantly (for the regime) – between a subject and the ruler (or his representative at any level of the administration). The supreme ruler (the emperor) rules by divine mandate. His position is the embodiment of wisdom and benevolence. In keeping with the principle of "Ren," his mandate is conditional upon his rule being directed for the benefit of his subjects. If the ruler misuses his power, the heavens send indications of displeasure, in the form of natural disasters. In such cases, the people have the right to rebel. In any event, the signs from heaven bring about the proper result. If the rebellion fails, it is a sign that the disaster was merely a warning to the ruler. If the rebellion succeeds, it is the new ruler who has the divine mandate to rule. The embodiment of wisdom and benevolence in the persona of the ruler, along with absolute loyalty and obedience, thus became the basis of public administration in eastern Asia, China, Vietnam, Japan, and Korea. Even today, these countries are "imperial" regimes for all intents and purposes (less so in the case of Japan), in keeping with Confucian tradition.

Religions in Korea

The religious belief system and worship in Korea are similar to those of the Chinese religious culture. In Eastern Asia (China, Japan, Vietnam, and Korea) religion is not organized and dogmatic, as in monotheistic Western culture, but rather comprises an assortment of beliefs, myths, rituals, and customs. In China, this totality is based on three philosophies. Two of them – Confucianism and Taoism – are Chinese in origin; the third – Buddhism – comes from India, having been introduced by the leaders of China as well as the leaders of Japan, Korea, and Vietnam. The Oriental parallel of religion in the Western sense is faith and personal devotion, with each devotee finding his own place among the three philosophies.

Taoism (in China) addresses man's relationship with Nature, and with himself and his health. In Korea, this niche is filled by Shamanism/Animism – a system of beliefs that appeals to the mighty powers of Nature and natural phenomena, and worship of the spirits of ancestors, both immediate and mythological.

Confucianism defines the relations between the individual and others, at all levels of society, including the supreme ruler. The problem with Confucianism, from the point of view of the regime, is that if the ruler is the embodiment of wisdom and benevolence, then responsibility for any difficult situation facing the country or society as a whole, or even just an individual, rests solely with him. Oriental rulers handled this problem by importing Buddhism into their countries.

Buddhism is wholly directed towards the individual. One of the fundamental principles of this philosophy is the idea of reincarnation. This concept solves two central problems of human existence: the finality of death (which turns out to be just the end of a certain stage), and the suffering of the righteous (which turns out to be the result of deeds committed in a previous life). Thus, Buddhism transfers responsibility for the state of the individual from the ruler back to the individual himself. It is indeed no wonder that eastern Asian rulers adopted this philosophy.

The "religions" of the East are not institutionalized and do not threaten the ruler, but rather help and support him; there is therefore no tension between the administration and religion. In South Korea, where there is freedom of religion, 28% of citizens define themselves as Christians; just 16% identify as Buddhists. Under Japanese rule, Pyongyang served as the center of missionary activity in Korea, coming to be known as "Jerusalem of East Asia." The war waged on missionary activity and the prohibition on bringing Western religious literature into North Korea is therefore understandable. With that, when it comes to religion, the Korean leadership suffices with the Confucian tradition that is inborn in Koreans, including the principles of discipline and hierarchy. In practice, the personality cult surrounding the Leaders is the main "religious" ritual defining this society, along with traditions of the past which guide the conduct of family life.

*

The city boasts additional historical heritage sites, especially the graves of the Koryo dynasty leaders, some of which were ransacked by the Japanese occupiers. The spoils were taken to Japan, and then returned to South Korea after Japan's defeat. Of special importance are the double tomb of King Kongmin and his wife, and, more importantly, the **mausoleum of King Wang Kon** (877-943). This site, too, was granted the status of a UNESCO World Heritage site. The mausoleum was renovated and officially opened on the king's 1,117th birthday, on January 31st, 1994. The ceremony was attended by North Korean President Kim Il-Sung, once again with the aim of cementing the connection between the contemporary leadership and the ancient Korean heritage. The mausoleum stretches over 5.5 hectares (fifty-five thousand square meters). The burial chamber that was not ransacked is open to visitors, by prior booking and at a cost of two hundred euros per person (!).

*

It is the last day of our tour in North Korea. We are on the road, covering the almost hour-long drive from Pyongyang in a south-westerly direction, towards Nampo – a large port city and important industrial center. Fifteen kilometers to the west of Nampo is our actual destination: the **Western Sea Barrier**. (The city and the sea barrier will be discussed in a later chapter.) The road is like any other in the country, perhaps a little wider. The scenery is unremarkable, with the same agricultural activity that we have seen elsewhere. We had asked to visit an agricultural collective, and our wish was granted. It turns out to be a great disappointment, because we are not given the chance to see the cultivated fields. Instead, we have a local guide who recites the page of messages that she has clearly learned by heart.[19] However, the initiative is not a total failure, because the local guide's recitation confirms what I have already begun to understand on this tour, and what Western sources that I consult upon my return to Israel will confirm over and over: North Korea is undergoing a quiet revolution in the economic sphere. It finds expression in the sale of agricultural produce on the open market; small-scale commerce (souvenirs, snacks, drinks); the development of industrial areas based on the Chinese model; competition between government (tourist) businesses, and more.

---

19 The explanations given by the guide (the guides were all women; in all eight of my visits to North Korea, I never encountered a single male guide at any tourist site) illustrate and highlight the difference between the local guides and the guides who accompany our tour groups. Our guides are more flexible in their thinking and less dogmatic, and there is a notable difference in their approach – in relation to me in particular, in view of my multiple visits.

*

On the way to Nampo, I request, as usual, to sit in the guide's seat in the front of the bus, and the guides agree. The highlight of this journey, for me, is two conversations. In the double seat behind me sit Li Mi-Soon and Mike.[20] While my eyes are on the road, my ears prick up as I overhear them talking. What starts

---

20 Michael A. Hoer is a Colorado-born member of the Church of Jesus Christ of Latter-day Saints, a B.A. graduate (cum laude) in Chinese and Journalism from Brigham Young University (BYU), and an outstanding sportsman. In 1979 he was chosen as one of the first eighteen American students to study in China, where he completed his studies in the Chinese language. In 1982, he completed an M.B.A. degree in International Trade at BYU.

For the past thirty years, his main occupation has been managing agricultural projects in Asia. Throughout these years, he has lived and worked in China, Taiwan, Singapore, Japan, and Hong Kong. In Hong Kong, he was awarded permanent resident status, which allowed him to receive a Hong Kong identity number and a Chinese name: Huo Ting Chang. Mike speaks fluent Chinese (Mandarin and Cantonese). From 1989-1992, he was a senior director of Continental Grain Asia, the USA grain company that was the first foreign company to take up premises in the Guangdong Free-Trade Zone in Shenzhen. He was also a consultant to several Western companies that began operating in China, including McDonald's. For most of his career in Asia, he served as CEO and President of Continental Grain Asia. At the same time, he was active in the humanitarian projects undertaken by the institutions of the Church of Jesus Christ of Latter-day Saints in Asia. In 2007, he retired from his full-time job but continued to serve on the Board of Directors of a number of commercial companies, as well as on the National Advisory Council of the Business School at Brigham Young. Currently, he devotes most of his time and energy to humanitarian work for Latter-day Saint Charities of the Church of Jesus Christ of Latter-day Saints. In recent years he has been living in Egypt and Sudan. Mike's commercial and humanitarian activity, along with his curiosity, have taken him to more than a hundred and thirty different countries.

out as a mundane conversation turns to the subject of Otto Warmbier.[21] The story of his indictment in a North Korean court and his sentence – fifteen years of imprisonment and hard labor – had been publicized just before our arrival in the country, arousing horror the world over.

The conversation is engraved in my memory; it went more or less as follows:

Li Mi-Soon asked, "What do you say about the action of the American student and his punishment?"

Mike thought a bit and then answered, in a measured and dignified tone, "We were all young once, and as youngsters we all did silly things. Silly actions are deserving of punishment, but the purpose of the punishment is to teach a lesson, so that when we get older, we will behave properly. From what I have experienced during my tour of your country, as you have said, Marshal Kim Jong-Un, provides the DPRK people with everything – their homes, food, and clothing – and protects the country. We also

---

21 Otto Warmbier (1994-2015) was a member of an American student group on a tour of North Korea in December 2015. Towards the end of his tour, he decided to take a picture of the North Korean leader that decorated the wall of his room, and keep it as a souvenir. It seems that he did, in fact, take down the picture, and left it face-down on the floor. His action was captured by the cameras installed in the hallways of the hotel. At the end of the tour, on January 2nd, 2016, upon reaching the airport, Otto was separated from the group and arrested. He was accused of a "hostile act against the Korean people," an offense for which he was sentenced to fifteen years' imprisonment with hard labor. On June 13th, 2017, Otto was released "on humanitarian grounds" and was returned home, in a coma. Six days later, on June 19th, he died. The North Korean authorities claimed that the coma was the result of botulism and the fact that he had taken sleeping pills. An autopsy found no trace of botulism, nor any evidence of beatings or physical abuse. According to the doctors, his state was consistent with a lack of oxygen to the brain, the reason for which was unknown.

know that Kim Jong Un is wise, benevolent and loves all the people of the world, so that is why many foreigners are confused. Why doesn't Grand Marshal forgive this young man? It is therefore clear to me that in his wisdom, your leader will lessen his punishment when he understands that Otto has learned his lesson and mends his ways; Otto has also already apologized to the Korean people for offending them."

Li was silent for a moment and then asked, "But the student Otto Warmbier acknowledged that the purpose of his coming here was to offend the Korean people."

Mike answered without hesitation: "Otto was under harsh interrogation, and everyone knows that in an interrogation, a person can be led to confess to anything. I still believe, and anyone who thinks logically will agree with me, that his actions were silly mischief and not a pre-planned scheme. He clearly came to your country to learn more about the DPRK, not to offend anybody."

Li continued to challenge him in a manner that reflected deeply rooted conviction: "But he confessed that he was sent here by President Obama."

Mike's voice remained steady, answering in a fatherly tone: "Mi Soon, you are very intelligent, you know many foreign tourists, you are experienced, you know people and you know the world -- so let me ask, do you really believe the president of the United States would hold a special meeting with a young boy and send him to another country to steal a poster? If a Korean student was arrested in the US and confessed in an interrogation to having been sent by the Leader of North Korea to carry out some offensive action – and again, it has to be remembered that under interrogation people confess even to things that they didn't do; all they want is some relief – would you believe it?"

There was silence. Li gave no answer. Mike, in his wisdom, turned the conversation to some element of the scenery that we were passing.

I sat, tense in my seat, amazed at Mike's courage and his astuteness, and trying to digest what I had heard. At the first opportunity I approached him and said, "Mike, I'm dumbstruck at the courage and wisdom you revealed in that conversation." He answered, "I have a lot of experience in talking with people from regimes like this in Asia. Avraham, remember – after all, you're planning to come back here: in your conversations with local people, don't ever offend the Leader. It doesn't matter what you say, the main thing is that you remember to speak of the Leader in positive terms."

More than five years have passed since that incident in two parts. Not only haven't I forgotten, but Mike's advice became my motto, the "compass" directing my conduct and my exchanges in North Korea.

On the return journey, I sat next to Miss Li. As we neared Pyongyang, I suddenly decided to try out Mike's advice. The western entry, like all the entries to the capital, is quite impressive. I looked at the buildings as we passed them. They weren't new, but they didn't look like they had been standing for twenty-five years or more, meaning that they were built under Kim Jong-Il. I looked at the city, then turned towards Miss Li and said, "The buildings are so beautiful. It looks to me like they were built by Chairman Kim Jong-Il, the father of the present leader. Now I understand why you love him so much." I went on, repeating things I had heard from her a few days previously, when we visited the Kumsusan Palace (the mausoleum where the mummified remains of the previous leaders lie in state): "I know that throughout his whole life, he worked hard for the sake of the people; I believe he didn't live a long life. How old was he when he died?"

"Less than seventy," she told me, and I was completely honest when I commented, "So young! Just a little older than I am now." Once again, I was astounded by her response. With a sad face, almost in tears, her voice choked and full of admiration, she said, "During the last year of his life, I saw him twice. When our leader Kim Jong-Il died, we felt orphaned and alone; we didn't know who would lead us. It was only after his death that his successor, Marshal Kim Jong-Un, was presented to us. When our leader Kim Il-Sung had died, it was clear that the heir apparent was his son, Kim Jong-Il, and despite the heavy mourning, we knew that we were in safe hands."

Trying to maintain empathy, I went on, "I remember that his mother died while giving birth to him." This was a mistake, understandable in light of my inexperience. Miss Li turned to me angrily: "Who told you that? It's not true!" She continued adamantly, "We don't talk about the lives of our Leaders." Here our conversation ended. Western sources indicate that Kim Jong-Il's mother did indeed die of complications in childbirth, but it was later on, with the birth of another child. The official Korean version of the story is that Kim Jong-Suk died of complications following an injury sustained in fighting the Japanese.

*

It is the last day of our tour. I awaken to the morning "routine" in my room at the hotel, with a cup of coffee, waiting for the national wake-up melody, and thinking to myself. This is not just another tour coming to an end; I feel as though I've arrived at the Everest of tourism. I am filled with joy and satisfaction; I did it! The next moment I have reservations and try to see things from a different angle. I take a good, hard look at myself and my experiences. My friends always complain that I'm an incurable optimist. My guiding principle in life in general, and on tours in particular, is that "the real achievement isn't being in a place that you enjoy, but rather enjoying the place that you're in." I think to myself, Am I getting carried away? Maybe all my enthusiasm here is just because of an unrealistically positive approach? I decide to check with the other participants in the group at breakfast.

Our flight is at 8:30, and we have been asked to be ready to leave for the airport at 7:00. How can this possibly give us enough time? Responding to our concerns, the guides and Mr. Cha, the CEO of the tour company, are reassuring. As usual, I am the first to arrive for breakfast. A few minutes later, Mike appears. As he drinks, he asks me, "Did you have a night-time visit?" I assume that he's joking, and respond with some silly comment. But his face is serious as he tells me, "At around 23:00 last night, I heard knocking and opened the door. There stood Mr. Cha, the CEO, and Mr. Li. They came in, and Mr. Cha told me, 'Mike, you have a big problem.'"

As I tensed up, Mike continued in his calm tone, "I asked what the problem was, and Mr. Cha told me: 'You take many pictures, and you take many videos, and you ask many questions... Admit the truth! You're a journalist!' I told him, 'I'm not a journalist; where did you get that idea from?' Mr. Li interrupted, asking, 'Why did you take photos of the road?' I answered, 'Firstly, I'm not the only one who took photos. Secondly, you know that I was among the first Americans to go to China. When I was in China, I took photos of the roads and the infrastructure. You also know – I showed you pictures – that I was close to many high-ranking Chinese officials, including the President of China, Yang Shangkun, who visited one of our factories in Shenzhen. When I visit China now, and show my Chinese official friends the pictures of China from the 1980s, they are full of joy and pride at how their homeland has developed.' Then I went on to tell them, 'When I see the remarkable development of Korea under the leadership of King Jong-Un, I know that when I come back in a few years' time and show you the photos, you, too, will be full of pride.' They were surprised by my confidence and my response, and seemed less suspicious, but nonetheless viewed every one of my photos and videos. If they did not like a photo, they deleted it."

Mike said that fortunately he had been backing up his photos as they entered the room, and used a sleight of hand to remove the back-up scandisk without them seeing, so he still had a second copy of all the deleted material. This review of the pictures and videos took an hour or more. At the end of the review, Mr. Cha and Mr. Li told him that he was guilty of gathering information to harm the DPRK.

By now, Charles had moved over to listen to Mike's story. He gasped and told Mike, "If they accused you of harming the DPRK, that is almost as bad as being an enemy of the State. The punishment for both of these offenses is imprisonment! I really hope they let you out of the country." (We found out later that Charles knew what he was talking about, because he was a member of Amnesty International.)

Mike said he had felt the conversation was going very poorly, so he had to change his approach. "I could not just deny the accusations," he said, "so I reminded them that my company had been invited to invest in the DPRK and I had helped bring 200,000 tons of corn into the DPRK during the famine of the 1990s. I told them, 'I am a friend of the DPRK!' I thought they would accept this, but they said, 'You have a second big problem.' I couldn't believe it. I asked them, 'What's the second problem?' Mr. Cha responded, 'Once, when you went up to your room on the twelfth floor, you used the stairway.' I started to tell him, 'That's absolutely not true!' but before I could continue, Mr. Cha said, 'We have footage of you running on the stairs.' I explained, 'That's correct, you have photos of me on the stairs, but not just once: I ran up the stairs every day.' Mr. Li looked shocked: 'Every day?!' Mike replied, 'Yes, I run marathons, and I like to maintain my level of fitness. Since you didn't allow us out of the hotel at night, and the hotel gym is closed, that was the only means of exercise I had.' I turned to Mr. Li and said, 'You know that I'm in good shape; we climbed the waterfalls together.' Mr. Cha turned to Mr. Li, and he recounted, with an embarrassed smile, the challenging climb we did together through the waterfalls in the Myohyang mountains."

Mike added with a smile, "I thought my answer satisfied them, but they said quietly, 'Otto Warmbier stole the poster on those stairs. Did you take any posters off the walls?' I was shocked at this accusation because Otto Warmbier was now in a prison camp for this offense. I offered for them to check all of my luggage, but after a glance around they said, 'You must write a self-criticism.' Of course, I knew better than to write my own words; I asked Mr. Cha and Mr. Li to tell me exactly what to write. After writing the self-criticism they became strangely friendly and asked, 'So, did you enjoy your stay in the DPRK?' I replied, 'I did enjoy it – up to now.'"

Mike added, "I tried to remain calm but don't think I wasn't sweating; by the end my hands were shaking and I was drenched in a cold sweat. It was past 1:00am when they left, and I couldn't sleep for hours!"

I listened, frozen, trying to take in what he was telling me. I said to him, "I am more grateful to you than you can imagine. This story you just told me was a real wake-up call; maybe a warning alarm, for my future visits."

Mike nodded, and added, "Never forget that you have no idea what's going on behind the screen. I hope they let me out of the country today."

In the meantime, the other members of the group had joined us. Mike asked me not to tell them what had happened the previous night. Everyone was in a jovial mood. This was a good time to check whether they, too, had experienced this tour as powerfully as I had. I addressed them all: "Well, how would you sum up the experience of our visit to North Korea?"

It was Gina who answered first, reflexively and without thought or hesitation: "Overwhelming!"

A second later, everyone (so it seemed to me) concurred. Even Mike and I, despite our conversation, felt that the experience had been overwhelming. So – no, this hadn't been just my own personal feeling. The visit to North Korea had been a powerful experience for everyone (in the future I would discover just how powerful).

At 7:00, we left the hotel, heading for the airport. The drive would take about twenty minutes. We would arrive just one hour before our flight. But on the way, as we reached the Arch of Triumph, the bus suddenly came to a stop. Miss Li explained that the president of the company, Mr. Tang, wanted to say goodbye, so we would wait for him. About ten minutes later, he appeared, wished us well and expressed his hope to see us back again. At these last words, he looked towards Yaki and I. Owing to the wait and the speech, we would now arrive at the airport only fifty minutes before takeoff (!). Our flight was the only one listed; all the other passengers, it seemed, had gone through check-in already. Mis Li returned our passports, and we approached the check-in counters: nine tourists; five counters. There was no security check. The boarding passes were ready. We handed in our luggage and headed for passport control, with a final goodbye to Miss Li and Mr. Li. I promised to come back, and they promised that they would be waiting. After a one-minute stop at passport control, we found ourselves in the departures hall. A small duty-free store was right next to us. Incredibly, we still had time to sit and wait. Such speed and efficiency at **a country's only international airport, with just one international flight per day**... an alternative reality. Precisely at the scheduled hour, 8:30, the plane took off. **Only in North Korea!**

*

An hour and a half later, we were back in Beijing. We said goodbye to the rest of the group, and smiled with relief. We had done it; we were back in the free world. Strange, no? In the 1970s, under Mao's regime, during the Cultural Revolution, China had seemed like the furthest place from Planet Earth. Now, arriving in China, we felt as though we had returned to Planet Earth **from North Korea – the furthest place on earth from Planet Earth.**

CHAPTER 7
Getting Started

Y aki and I spend the day in Beijing, waiting for our flight back home. The last of the tension, strain, and worry melts away, and the awesome experience stands out in all its clarity. North Korea – at least, as it appears to me now, immediately after our departure – comes with three surprises.

The first is the reality that we encountered, which is altogether different from what we had imagined prior to the trip. It turns out that the picture portrayed by Western media reports is out of sync with what the tourist actually sees and experiences. At the same time, though, it is a reality in which innumerable fundamental habits that are integral to our daily routine are absent: direct access to information – even personal information (bank account, medical records, email); immediate and direct communication with anyone, anywhere in the world; unlimited access to unlimited knowledge; direct access to the press, social media, advertisements, billboards – and all this in a modern country, not some God-forsaken backwater. It is truly a journey backwards in time.

The second surprise is the encounter with life in Korea, as we observed it. I searched for the frightened faces that I had seen in Romania in 1988, but found none. I found a functioning country – not up to Western standards in many respects, but I have been to a great many places in the world where the poverty level was similar or even more acute. I found people busy with the most basic occupation – living. Of course, our guides showed us only what they wanted us to see, but the exposure also included, in some small measure, aspects that they did not intend for us to see.

The third surprise is the manner in which the Korean experience enveloped us. All at once, we found ourselves in a completely different, unfamiliar reality – an alternative reality to which, to our surprise, we adapted quite quickly, easily, and naturally. Clearly, what we saw was mostly a show for tourists, but equally clearly, it could not all have been a show.

Obviously, in addition to processing the experience, we were preoccupied with planning and organization. Yaki's thoughts were focused on attracting groups of tourists to this new destination, while I was thinking about guiding them in North Korea.

Yaki, a successful and very experienced former tour guide, and I, a practicing guide with considerable experience, discussed and analyzed the differentness of North Korea and the challenges of future tours to the country. We concluded that the main difficulty would be preparing the group to behave properly, but the potential participants, at least for the first few tours, would be curious and eager to see the country, and they would be well aware that the rules of etiquette there were different from anywhere else. Moreover, participants might feel disappointed if they were not exposed to special rules of behavior (this estimation was fully realized in our first few tours). We also agreed that North Korea would be "the easiest tour for the guide," since the infrastructure – the itinerary, buses, meals, entertainment, purchases, and entry into sites – was entirely under the control of the local tourist infrastructure, and none of our participants was likely to expect us to start giving orders in North Korea. As for hotels, we chose the best. All that remained was for our guide to be at optimal levels of functioning; in any case, he would not be allowed to lecture or explain anything; at most, he could translate. Of course, there was no possibility of anyone getting lost, since we could have no influence whatsoever on the content of the tour. All the tour leader really needed to do was to ensure that the group behaved properly. And in this regard, we had already agreed that good preparation would neutralize most potential problems. (Only later would I discover that this was an oversimplified estimate.)

*

At home, among friends and acquaintances, and of course in the Rimon-Tarbutu offices, we were welcomed back like returning heroes; all that was missing were laurel wreaths. As we walked in, everyone dropped whatever they were doing and rushed over, surrounding us and peppering us with questions, eager to hear about our experiences. In fact, wherever we went, the moment people heard we had been to North Korea, the reaction was the same: disbelief mixed with astonishment at our courage (or stupidity), eagerness to hear details, and skepticism in relation to our stories and explanations.

Celebrations are all very well and good, but it was time to get to work. The first stage was the experiment. On the first Friday after our return, Tarbutu placed a small ad in *Haaretz* newspaper:

Bombshell of a Tour

Seeking 20 courageous men and women to join a fascinating and challenging 9-day organized tour to North Korea

While the office waited for responses, I got back to my routine. As on every Monday morning, my wife and I met with some friends for coffee on the beachfront. Obviously, the main topic of conversation at this stage was North Korea. I told my stories – apparently with a lot of enthusiasm, because by the end, one couple had made their decision: "We're going. Where do we sign up?"

"No problem," I answered, and called up Tarbutu. "It seems we've made a start. I have a couple that wants to sign up for the tour to North Korea."

Hagit, on the other end, sounded surprised: "What? You're joking. Impossible. The tour is already full."

"Come on, Hagit," I protested. "Please take these names…"

"Tashach," she interrupted me, "What is it that you're not understanding? There's no room. The tour is sold out."

Embarrassed, I turned to my friends and said, "She's just fooling around. Tomorrow I'll be in the office and I'll arrange everything."

The next day I met with Chaim. He got straight to the point: "I don't know what to do. The tour is sold out, and we're having trouble turning people away."

I was sure that Chaim was joking, but before uttering the cynical response that was on the tip of my tongue, I looked at him. He was serious. There were a few seconds of silence, and then I suggested, "Let's duplicate it. In other words, two groups at once."

"No," he said, "I'm not sending a group with a guide who's never been there."

"Then let's do the two groups back-to-back, with the second departing as the first returns."

And that's what happened. From the original idea of a group of 20 participants, we ended up with three groups, numbering 26, 28, and 26 participants respectively. Altogether, eighty tourists over September and October.

*

It was early May, four months before the first tour was scheduled to depart, with a busy spring and summer ahead, full of
tours to other destinations. I felt that I was proficient in the material I needed for these tours, but every tour demands preparation time, study, refreshing one's memory, and deepening one's
knowledge, in order to be properly ready. I didn't have much
time, and I needed to start preparing for the task that I regarded
as the climax of my career.

As a first stage, I decided to watch films and clips made by
visitors to North Korea. I found several specimens; they all described something similar to our experience, but from a different perspective: they noted that their rooms were bugged and
that that they were being filmed; we had somehow failed to
notice this. We made eye contact with local people (at the fireworks and at the flower exhibition), and danced with them,
but admittedly there had been no intensive interpersonal
contact. We did not walk around freely in the streets, and we
traveled between just two subway stations; nevertheless, we
didn't feel that we were at the center of a show that was being performed especially for us, as other people described it. I
was feeling less sure of my sensations and memories, and yet
I was supposed to be leading tours there... Eventually I called
Yaki and asked him, "Tell me, could it be...?" and started listing
all my doubts and hesitations. Yaki cut me short rather angrily. "What's come over you? We were there together just two
weeks ago!"

"Yes," I replied, "but in the clip I just watched, the narrator is
talking about the policewoman at the entrance to the bookshop;
he says that she almost arrested him when he photographed
her, but we were filming freely!"

"Have you completely lost it?" he asked drily.

149

I breathed a little easier and decided that maybe it was the other visitors who were mistaken, but at the same time, I thought that perhaps the culture shock of the first encounter had given me a distorted picture of reality. Since I was going to be returning to North Korea, I would give special attention to some specific issues, and would also be able to rely on the responses of my tour participants.

*

During our tour in April, over the course of several days we had repeatedly seen rehearsals for some sort of event at Kim Il-Sung Square. When we asked our guide what it was all about, we were told that they were practicing for some sort of ceremony, but they didn't know any more than that.

Naturally, in view of the culture shock that I had experienced during my first visit, along with my need to be well-prepared to lead the tour, I paid close attention to any mention of North Korea in the news, no matter how insignificant. But in May 2016, there was an event in North Korea that was covered extensively by media throughout the world, including in Israel: the seventh Congress of the Workers' Party of Korea. The sixth Congress had been held in 1980. In other words, throughout the term of Kim Jong-Il, father of Kim Jong-Un, no Congress had been convened!

From the pictures in the media, I understood that the rehearsals that we had watched in the Square in April were in anticipation of the Congress in May (the citizens of North Korea, including our guides, were indeed unaware of the planned event). Of course, the ceremonies are not the essence, but rather just the backdrop. The gathering of the Central Committee of the Party – for the first time in 36 years, out of a total of 68 years of the country's existence – was more than just a formal gathering. This was to be a declaration of recognition of the leadership of Marshal

Kim Jong-Un. His father, Chairman Kim Jong-Il, had needed no such endorsement. His assumption of the country's leadership was a natural step that was taken for granted. From his youth, he had been destined to succeed his father, and at the previous Congress, in 1980, at the age of 38, this intention had been made official. In 1991 he had been appointed Supreme Commander of the army. His name and picture were familiar to every citizen of the country. Hence, when his father, Kim Il-Sung, passed away, his status entailed no struggle and needed no confirmation.

"When Chairman Kim Jong-Il passed away," Miss Li Mi-Soon told me, "We felt lost; orphaned.[22] We, the citizens of the country, knew nothing about the Leader's private life, who he was married to, or who his children were." The general sense of being left without any direction, protection, or authority was thus quite understandable, as was the supreme joy when, just two days (!) after the death of Kim Jong-Il, his successor was confirmed: the twenty-seven-year-old Kim Jong-Un, whose greatest asset was the similarity of his facial features to those of his deceased grandfather, Kim Il-Sung. Under any form of government, a leader's power and authority are established with the help of a circle of loyal followers. In democratic regimes, potential opponents are distanced by means of the accepted legal political processes. In dictatorial regimes, there is a life-or-death struggle between groups of cronies. Kim Jong-Un, still in his twenties, apparently had a hard time consolidating his leadership. Ridding himself of adversaries and potential rivals was a drawn-out process that took almost five years, concluding in May 2016.

---

22 It must be emphasized that anything positive in North Korea is viewed as having its source in the wisdom, benevolence, efforts, and great love of the Leader for the people. Anything negative is the result of the evil US administration and the sanctions imposed by it.

*

I was immersed in study and preparation. Yaki and I already knew that, owing to the rules and regulations in North Korea, which included the exclusive appointment of local staff, I would not be able to guide the group, but old habits die hard. Israeli travelers are curious and interested, requiring that guides always be ready and well-prepared. Hence, I busied myself learning and summarizing the material which, as a tour guide, I had to know, hoping that somehow I might still have an opportunity to share it.

*

As part of the preparation for any tour, there is a preliminary meeting of the group where I convey some practical information about the destination: climate, dress, food, communications, and so on. This tour would be different, because the destination was altogether different from any other, and the emphasis would be on behavior and etiquette. There would be no room for mistakes.

My work schedule between May and September offers very little downtime. One tour follows another, and of course, each comes with its own demands and challenges. Thoughts about North Korea gave way to more immediate concerns, but they remained in the background of my mind. Somewhere in the recesses of my brain, the upcoming trips to North Korea remained an item of relevance. On my calendar, I set aside the second half of August to plan what I viewed as the most exciting challenge of my career as a tour guide abroad.

Group meetings were scheduled, and they lasted twice as long as for any regular tour. In addition to the usual practical information and tips, participants listened to a lecture I had prepared about North Korea: geography, history, leadership, form of government, and – most importantly – rules of behavior, what to do, and what not to do.

North Korea – Basic Facts for Tourists

1. Koreans are a single, homogenous people sharing the same language and culture.
2. Korea is a single country. It is currently divided, temporarily, for political reasons.
3. The Leaders of North Korea are:
4. (Eternal) President Kim Il-Sung (15.4.1912 – 8.7.1994)
5. His son, (eternal) Chairman Kim Jong-Il (16.2.1941 – 17.12.2011)
6. His son, (current) Marshal Kim Jong-Un (8.1.1983)
7. The birthday of President Kim Il-Sung is a national holiday, and the North Korean calendar is counted from April 15th, 1912 (thus, April 15th, 2016, was the start of the Juche year 105).
8. The Juche ideology, developed by President Kim Il-Sung, is the basis for all that happens in North Korea. In essence: Korea can depend on no one but itself, in every area – economy, agriculture, industry, science, defense, etc.
9. The principle of Songun means that the military takes preference over the revolution.
10. Korea suffered oppressive Japanese occupation and was liberated from this occupation in a heroic war led by President Kim Il-Sung.
11. Following Korea's liberation, the US and its allies conspired to seize control of the country. Another heroic war led by President Kim Il-Sung concluded with another victory, but the southern part of the country remains under occupation.

Rules of Behavior for Visitors to North Korea

Remember that the reality of North Korea is different from anything that we are used to. It is therefore important to take care to adhere strictly to the following rules:

1. Take as given that throughout our stay in North Korea, we will be monitored: Big Brother sees everything!

2. In North Korea, anything that is not expressly permitted, is forbidden!

3. The Korean people regard their leaders as supremely holy. Therefore:

- Do not point towards statues or pictures of them, nor towards the pins that the locals wear on their lapels, showing portraits of their leaders.

- Do not tear, cut, crumple, throw into the trash, or paste into your trip journal any picture of the Leaders.

- In conversations with the locals, speak of their leaders in positive terms.

- When discussing the Leaders, it is preferable that their titles be used (President Kim Il-Sung; Chairman Kim Jong-Il; Marshal Kim Jong-Un).

- At some of the sites we visit, we will be asked to participate in a ceremony of bowing, out of respect, to the Leaders' portraits or statues.

4. Photography:

- When photographing statues or pictures of the Leaders, make sure that the frame includes the entire body.

- Do not photograph military facilities or soldiers.

- Do not photograph people close up without their permission.

- When in doubt, request permission from the tour guides.

5. Do not leave the hotel or go about without an escort. Also, do not remove anything from the hotel room without permission.
6. Interactions: Do not talk angrily; maintain a positive approach; avoid judgmental terminology ("dictatorship," "tyrant," "worship," and so forth). You may talk freely with the tour guides.
7. Praise of the Leaders is permitted (and encouraged).
8. When filling in arrival forms, make sure that your declarations are true.
9. Do not bring maps, travel guides, articles, newspapers, newspaper cuttings, or Bibles with you.
10. Do not wear clothes bearing political inscriptions.
11. You are advised not to bring a laptop, tablet, or disk-on-key.
12. In summary: We will not be able to change North Korea, but our trip offers a unique and enjoyable mind-broadening experience, so long as we respect our hosts and abide by the rules of etiquette expected of us.

The participants I met at these meetings were not the typical tourists. Using sports terminology, I would call them the "national league." Some had already "been everywhere and seen everything;" North Korea was the last remaining country for them to mark off on their maps. Others were full of curiosity, enthusiasm, and adventure. Meeting all of them raised my level of alertness, my sense of responsibility, my excitement, and also my concerns. I was eagerly awaiting the first Israeli group tour to the most insular country in the world – North Korea.

A Brief History of Korea
(As viewed by North Korea)

We, the Korean people, have a 5,000-year-long history and magnificent culture in our land.

During the periods when we were strong, we enjoyed freedom, peace, and prosperity, and our culture flourished.

During the times when we were weak, we were attacked and occupied over and over by neighboring peoples: Chinese, Khitans, Mongols, and Manchurians.

In the late 19th century, our weakness allowed the Japanese to conquer our country, imposing an occupation and oppression unprecedented in its cruelty.

The most elementary human rights were denied to us, and terrible crimes were perpetrated. We were forbidden to speak our language, to perform our religious rites, and to give our children Korean names. Our national treasures were stolen by the occupiers.

Our sons were taken away to perform forced labor and were compelled to serve in the Japanese army. Hundreds of thousands of our daughters were forced to serve as "comfort women" – sex slaves – for Japanese soldiers.

The Japanese occupation cost over a million Korean lives!

In 1945, after a heroic struggle led by President Kim Il-Sung, we succeeded in liberating our homeland and restoring our independence.

Then, however, through the interference of the World Powers, our country was divided in half, with no consideration for the will of the Korean people.

Attempts at reunification were obstructed by a multinational force led by the US, which invaded our country. In another heroic war, led by President Kim Il-Sung, we managed to maintain our independence in the northern part of our homeland.

The struggle for independence cost over two and a half million Korean lives!

By virtue of our determination, under our Leaders' direction, we have maintained our independence. We will not rest until the terrible injustice – the division of our single homeland – is set right. We will not cease to act, in peaceful ways (in accordance with the roadmap set forth by our Leader, President Kim Il-Sung, and adopted by his successors), to bring about reunification of the people and the beloved homeland.

CHAPTER 8

First Tour – September 2016
(The Nuclear Explosion)

As the tour drew closer, the Chinese Uri tourism company forwarded us the program that had been conveyed to them by Koryo. I reviewed the details and was surprised to discover that almost all my requests had been integrated into the itinerary. In our work conversations with Mr. Tang and Mr. Cha, we had asked for greater exposure to everyday life in North Korea, and indeed, the program now included a visit to a supermarket, an evening at a pub, and an option of attending a Korean performance rather than a performance for tourists. In addition, we had requested a dedicated photographer throughout the trip, and Miss Li Mi-Soon as our local guide, and in view of the acquiescence to the other requests, I understood that we could count on these, too.

As noted, during our group meeting, I encountered people with extensive tourist experience, including some for whom North Korea was more or less the last spot on Earth that they had not yet visited. The composition of the group gave me a sense of confidence, while my concerns – still on the radar of my mind despite the meticulous preparation – engendered a positive tension.

*

On September 4th, 2017, the first ever group of Israeli tourists to North Korea set off. There were twenty-six participants, and I was their leader. We arrived in Beijing early the next morning, and spent two days sightseeing there.

On September 7th, we headed for the Beijing airport. As we drove, I reviewed the rules of conduct for North Korea. Inter alia, I reminded the group that we would be asked to show any electronic equipment and books that we had brought with us. I noted again the specific prohibition on religious literature and travel guides. We arrived at Terminal 3, next to Café Loi, and waited for Mrs. Yuan, the representative of Uri Tours. She arrived a few minutes early. We received our visas, passed through the security check and passport control, and soon found ourselves in the departures hall. What followed was the usual routine for international flights, and then, with just over an hour in the air, some refreshments, and forms to fill in ... the excitement was growing.

We are in North Korea. Admittedly, it's my second time, but I'm feeling no less excitement and tension; maybe even more than before. After all, for the first time, a group of tourists from Israel is visiting this hermit kingdom, and the responsibility weighs on me heavily. I deliberately wait at the back of the line, to be available to help as needed, but my travelers pass quickly through passport control and move on to wait for their baggage. Once everyone has their bags, I guide them towards customs control. As instructed, they are holding packets in which they have placed all their photography and communications equipment, as well as books and newspapers. As soon as I see that they are all in line for customs control, I join the back of the line. Here, too, everything goes smoothly – or so I think.

In the arrivals hall, as I walk towards the members of the group, the round figure of Mr. Li, from my previous trip, materializes in front of my eyes. It is a happy reunion; we embrace and exchange greetings and questions, and then he presents another guide: another Mr. Li. This Mr. Li is slightly taller, with handsome and intelligent features. With a smile, I say, "Well, we'll have a team of Miss Li and the two Messrs. Li," still convinced that our head guide will be Miss Li Mi-Soon, as per my request. All of a sudden Mr. Cha appears, and the friendly reunion scene repeats itself all over again. After a lively conversation, I turn away for a moment to check that all the members of the group are with us. One of the participants tells me that his friend hasn't come out of customs yet, and that a woman guide is dealing with him there. Slightly worried, I turn to Mr. Cha and ask if he knows what is happening. He answers, "Nothing serious. They'll join you any minute now." Indeed, two or three minutes later, the tour participant and a North Korean official appear. "What happened?" I ask the traveler. With a reassuring smile he replies, "I had a *Lonely Planet* travel guide on me..."

"But that was one of the things I specifically asked not to bring," I cut him short.

"I know," he acknowledges; "I wanted to see what would happen. They found the book in the packet, with all the other items for inspection. They explained politely that I could not bring the book into the country, and they took it."

Two lessons immediately impress themselves in my mind: firstly, I will need to repeat the rules and regulations over and over again, and to remain vigilant at all times. Secondly, and more importantly: transparency in dealing with the North Korean authorities is of supreme importance in preventing embarrassing situations.

I breathe easier and turn to the guide, who immediately introduces herself: "My name is Kim On-Hee."

"Great," I answer hesitantly, "I look forward to us working together."

Kim is relatively tall; she has pleasant features and a friendly expression. She exudes calmness and affability, in complete contrast to Miss Li Mi-Soon, who I have been expecting all along. It turns out that she is also sensitive to unspoken messages. "Disappointed?" she asks me. "You wanted to work with Miss Li?"

"I asked to work with her," I answer honestly, "because I thought that for my first time here as a guide, it would be easier to work with someone I already know. But I'm sure that if the company chose you, they have good reason, and I have full confidence in their choice and in you."

Only later on do I discover how right I am. And it turns out that even in North Korea, interpersonal chemistry makes a significant difference.

*

We head for the bus. Mr. Cha and Miss Kim On-Hee walk in front of the group, and I walk alongside them. On the way, I ask Miss Kim's permission to translate what she says into Hebrew. She agrees readily. Twenty-six tourists are walking behind us, with the two Messrs. Li at the back. Waiting for us is the bus driver, Mr. Jong, and, as per our request, also the photographer – Mr. Kim. Our team now includes three tour guides, a photographer, and a driver. (The same photographer and driver would accompany us also on our future trips, along with a total of twelve guides, in different combinations, three at a time.) We all board the bus. I look at the international airport, which, at this mid-afternoon hour is preparing to close down, and once again am astonished. Miss Kim takes the microphone, introduces all the staff members, and launches into instructions for proper conduct. Unlike Miss Li, she keeps her explanations short, and her tone is softer, even apologetic. She soon shifts to a businesslike tone and pres-

161

ents some geographical data and a short history of the country, focusing on the twentieth century: the Japanese occupation; liberation in 1945 thanks to the heroic war led by President Kim Il-Sung; the division of the country by the Great Powers led by the US; and the attempt at reunification which failed owing to the desire of the US to conquer all of Korea – an aspiration foiled by another heroic war, once again led by President Kim Il-Sung. Kim On-Hee looks towards me, passes me the microphone, and sits down, as though saying, "I'm done; your turn."

In the short time remaining before we enter Pyongyang, I emphasize the rules of behavior, especially in view of the lesson learned from the case of the confiscated travel guide. Naturally, the participants divide their attention between listening to me and watching the passing scenery, photographing (with permission, of course) as we go.

Pyongyang

The name means a "plain" – metaphorically, a place of calm. Pyongyang is the capital of North Korea and the largest city, with a population of over three million. Pyongyang is the political, cultural, and industrial center of the country. Also known as the "capital of the revolution," Pyongyang is situated on both sides of the Taedong River, about a hundred kilometers east of the estuary. Pyongyang occupies a central place in Korean history as a capital city:

- In the second century B.C.E., it was the capital under the rule of the Gojoseon (ancient Joseon) Dynasty.
- From the fifth century until the seventh century (427 -676), it served as the capital of the Goguryeo (ancient Goryeo) dynasty.
- During the Sino-Japanese War, the city was almost completely destroyed. After the war, it was rebuilt by the Jap-

anese, who turned it into an industrial center. The city opened up to Europeans, and became a base for Protestant missionary activity. It was eventually home to more than a hundred churches, and was called "Jerusalem of the East."

- With the defeat of the Japanese in the Second World War and the division of Korea, Pyongyang was declared the capital of North Korea.
- During the Korean war, the city was once again almost completely flattened by bombardment from the air. (On a single night, July 11th, 1952, there were 1,254 bombing sorties over the city. On August 29th, there were more than 1,400.) The city was rebuilt from the foundations after the war was over.

*

The tourists have their first encounter with Pyongyang. The cameras are working non-stop; the guides are fairly relaxed and are allowing everyone to photograph freely. The travelers are all in good spirits, and curious; for me, it is an especially exciting moment, and I am bursting with anticipation. Before we disembark the guide provides a concise overview of the Arch of Triumph and its significance. The enormous, open square, with the adjacent Kim Il-Sung Stadium and the huge painting thrill the group. Miss Kim On-Hee speaks, and Mr. Kim, the photographer, documents everything. The two Messrs. Li mingle casually among the participants, photograph them at their request, provide directions, and help at the stairs leading to the tunnel to the Arch of Triumph. I stand next to the new Mr. Li and ask him the meaning of the inscription of the years "1925 – 1945." He explains what I already know well: "Those were the years of struggle against the Japanese."

I ask again, "And throughout all those years, President Kim Il-Sung led the struggle?"

Without hesitation, he replies in the affirmative. I have to admit that he gives the impression of being very smart (later on I will discover that he is indeed, and that he has served abroad as an emissary of his country). Nevertheless, he fails to detect the skepticism implied in my question: how could a thirteen-year-old lead such a heroic struggle? Not for a moment does he question the truth of this axiom. When we reach the Arch, I ask Miss Kim if I might translate into Hebrew what she has explained in English. She replies: "Feel free." I start talking. This must be the first time that a tour has ever been guided in Hebrew in North Korea. I review the essential facts concerning Kim Il-Sung Stadium and the giant mural showing the victory speech of the Leader of the struggle against the Japanese – President Kim Il-Sung. I go on to point out that the Arch of Triumph is ten meters taller than the Arc de Triomphe in Paris, and draw attention to the legend of the thirteen-year-old's leadership. The guides are attentive, enjoying the novelty of a language they have never heard, and following the names and data which I take care to repeat also in English. When I mention Kim Il-Sung, I take care to refer to him with his title. It seems that they are impressed by three aspects of my monologue: firstly, I have spoken non-stop for five minutes, and as far as they are able to judge, I have demonstrated proficiency in the material. Secondly, they are gratified that I refer to President Kim Il-Sung by his title every time his name comes up. Before starting to speak I asked their permission to instruct the group and told them what I intended to say; after I finish, I let them know what I have said. I follow the same procedure on each of the seven tours that I will lead to North Korea. The bonus is that I earn the trust of the local guides, beyond my expectations. An important note: already in my first hour as a tour guide in North Korea, I discover that my assumption that

I would not be allowed to guide the group was completely mistaken, and it is therefore clear that my investment in study and preparation was not only justified but even more essential than it would be for a "regular" destination.

From the Arch of Triumph, we proceed to Mansudae. This is really where the tour starts. True, we have already seen some sights, but the bow in deference to the Leaders is an essential introduction, and represents a first test of the behavior of the tourists and their sensitivity towards the feelings of the locals. I ask Miss Kim to instruct us, and she does so, her manner conveying a request rather than an order. She requests their cooperation more out of respect for the Korean people than out of the expectation that they respect the Leaders. "If someone prefers not to bow," she continues, "we understand. In that case, please stand aside until the others complete the bow." As agreed, I follow her monologue with a Hebrew version. It seems to me that I sound a lot less tolerant than she does: I set forth the rules and emphasize the importance of adhering to them. I ask that there be no jokes; everyone should please leave their sense of humor on the bus. (I fear that someone will compare the leader-worship to the political situation in Israel, which will make everyone laugh, possibly insulting the locals.) While we were still in Israel, we had decided that in order to avoid embarrassment, we would buy flowers to honor the Leaders. I ask Miss Kim to buy six wreaths, and distribute them to some of the participants, who will represent the group and lay them at the feet of the Leaders' statues. Two big questions percolate in my mind: How will the group behave? And no less important for me – will the impact of the experience for this group be anything like what it was for me? I am torn between keeping an eye on their behavior and the need to guide.

The visit to Mansudae ends without incident. The participants cooperate fully with the rules and regulations. Everyone chooses to bow; more of them than expected want to lay wreaths. And yes, each of them, without exception, is moved by the experience of the ritual and its power. If I had any suspicion, after my first tour, that the enthusiasm that enveloped the entire group, myself included, had emerged from some unique, one-time dynamic, it now turns out that deeply held beliefs and new experiences can co-exist even among educated, liberal adults who are far from subscribing to any cult of personality.

*

We are at the hotel. The reception procedure is quick and efficient, and we meet in the lobby for dinner. I still remember our first meal from my previous trip, and I prepare the group accordingly. When everyone is ready, I lead them to the restaurant that I remember, but the guides stop me and lead us towards the elevators. Surprise! We ascend to the rotating restaurant on the 45th floor; the entire city is spread out below. But it is already dark, and lighting isn't one of Pyongyang's strong points. From time to time, as the restaurant makes its slow circuit, we catch a glimpse of some lit-up monument, but for the most part, everything is dark.

The meal, on the other hand, is altogether different from those that I remember: there are eight individual, modestly sized servings including rice (of course), fish in aluminum foil, some meat, chips, omelet, kimchi, and soup. A little of everything. With beer and water. Smiling waitresses, polite and efficient service – altogether a nice, esthetic meal. Six diners at a table, five tables for the group, and another table nearby where the President of Koryo Travel Company, Mr. Tang, is seated, along with the CEO, Mr. Cha, and the three guides. I am invited to join their table, but I decline apologetically, explaining that I have to sit with my group. They accept this understandingly and suggest that I join them towards the end of the meal. Before the meal begins, Mr.

Tang stands up and welcomes us, assuring us that he and his team will do everything to ensure our satisfaction and enjoyment of the experience. The guides have almost no time to sit and eat; they are constantly busy with different requests, fulfilling them as much as reasonably possible.

As the meal starts drawing to a close, I join the staff table. At first, we exchange pleasantries, and I express thanks for the meal and for the successful first day of the tour. I compliment the guides (they certainly deserve it) for their positive, pleasant demeanor, and thank Mr. Tang for joining us and for his interest in our group. When the pleasantries are over, Mr. Tang apologizes and takes his leave of us; only then does the work discussion with Mr. Cha begin. Since his English is not fluent, Mr. Li translates his words. I am very surprised when Mr. Cha opens the tour itinerary and starts reviewing it with me. We discuss it from beginning to end, site by site, hour by hour. I am not prepared for this. Yaki and I had assumed that this tour would be easy for the guide insofar as there would be little planning left to do, and that in any case, it would not be possible to change anything on the itinerary. Yet now, on this first day of the tour, here I am with Mr. Cha, discussing the tour content. He listens to me, consults the guides, gets back to me, and together we make some adjustments. I have two important requests: firstly, a visit to a pub that is not just a show for tourists. His response is that he will show me two or three, and I can decide. The other request is that we be permitted to attend a performance for a Korean audience – an opera, ballet, even a children's performance – rather than the circus that is meant for tourists. He tells me, "I'll see what I can do."

Then I say to him, "In two days' time, September 9th, it's your Independence Day. Is it like April 15th, with fireworks and dancing in the streets?"

His answer comes as a surprise: "We don't know." I assume that he is evading the question, but later I find out that they truly don't know. The Leader knows what is best for them; he will decide, and they will find out when the time is right. There is no need to invest thought in something you have no control over. Towards the end of the conversation Mr. Che drops his biggest bombshell. He asks, "There is a beer festival going on this week on the banks of the river. Would you like to participate?"

I can't see my own face, but I am certain that I appear very surprised. A second later, I am smiling broadly and telling him, "Yes, of course! What a question! Of course we want to go!"

The evening comes to an end. Back in my room, I call home to reassure my family that all is well. My next call is to Yaki; I tell him all about our first day; he insists on hearing every detail. Upon hearing that the guides allowed me to speak, and about the consultation regarding the itinerary, he murmurs, "I can't believe it ... I didn't expect that."

Afterwards, alone with my thoughts, I try to digest and internalize all that has happened on my first day as a guide in North Korea. My thoughts jump from one event to the next: the conduct of the participants and the conduct of the staff; the relationship that I am building with the guides; the surprising discussion with Mr. Cha about the itinerary. Many "truths" have been disproved; others have been eroded. The most important preconception that has been laid to rest is the image of North Koreans as cold and depressed. Apparently, my first trip to Romania left a strong impression. What I have discovered is that the "scary" North Koreans are actually just people, who become acquaintances, almost friends, who really want to succeed in their endeavors and to please their clients. While this is only our first tour, the next two are already lined up and closed for applications; three groups with eighty tourists, as a start, is not a trifling matter. My thoughts wander to the material I must prepare for tomorrow, and how I will conduct myself with the participants, on one hand; and with the guides, on the other. Our destination will be the holy of holies – the Kumsusan, and the DMZ. Based on this first day, I believe that I will be able – even requested – to guide, and I prepare myself for the challenge.

I generally don't sleep well on tours, especially not for the first few nights, but somehow some wondrous mechanism in my brain puts me in a deep sleep.

*

Breakfast. The company made the decision to pay for beverages at breakfast for all participants. We have made an arrangement with our guides, according to which members of our group will tell the waiters the magic word – "Israel" – and they will receive coffee. At our first breakfast, the concept gets off to a rocky start. Our tourists forget to say the magic word, and the waiters aren't altogether prepared, but from the second meal onwards, until the end of our stay, it works well.

I come to a happy agreement with the two people in charge of receiving payment, based on two principles. The first is that I will make a lump-sum payment at the end of the tour for all the beverages for all the meals; the second is that I will not double-check the figures, but will rely on their calculations. This arrangement ends up causing the waiters some headaches. Tourists from elsewhere are unhappy at times about the "preferential treatment" that our group receives, and the waiters, with their patchy English, have trouble explaining the details of our arrangement and the reason why "Israel" is a magic word that affords "free" tea or coffee.[23]

---

23 Some of the other guests learned to use the magic code word and thereby save themselves the one-euro fee. For my part, I didn't really care. What I liked about this was that "Israel" was a magic word for them.

After breakfast, before we set out, there is a "dress inspection." Since the tourists were told about this visit at the group meeting both before the tour departed as well as last night, and also received written guidelines, they are all ready for the "holy" day and the Kumsusan, the Sun Palace. They all pass the inspection with flying colors. In truth, all that our hosts asked of us is that we dress in a dignified way. It was a request that made sense and was not a great imposition. We climbed aboard the bus. This would be the main test of our behavior. As the tour leader, I felt committed to my promise to Mr. Tang. This promise – that our group would behave properly – made me feel as stressed as if I was about to take a major examination.

As we approach the Central Station Hotel, there is another surprise. In the main plaza is a group of about a hundred "cheerleaders." These women are dressed in a uniform of red and green, holding colorful flags, and moving in coordinated steps that combine dance movements and military exercises, all accompanies by drums and music. During our first trip, I had not seen these cheerleaders. I turn questioningly to Miss Kim and she explains: "At the Party conference in May, our leader, Marshal Kim Jong-Un, announced that we are shifting from Chollima to Malima. Chollima is the monument of the horse galloping 400 kilometers per day. But now we need to move faster, at the speed of Malima – 4,000 kilometers per day. North Korea needs to whoosh into the future. That will be possible only if everyone commits to that supreme objective. A two-hundred-day period of encouragement has therefore been declared, during which we will commit to our Leader's request. Retired women[24] are contributing their share by encouraging the working population to hurry to their places of employment, for the sake of the homeland, of course." Throughout our journey, similar scenes

---

24 In Korea, women retire at the age of fifty-five.

replay themselves at other central plazas and squares. Each spot is characterized by a different costume, and different choreography. Only in North Korea![25]

As we draw closer to Kumsusan, the tension among the staff members is easy to see. For them, this is indeed a holy site; furthermore, it is a most significant test. Miss Kim addresses the group, listing all the rules. I add my own comments, clarifying, emphasizing, pleading. Two questions bother me: the first, of course, is how we will get through the ritual. The second is whether our Israeli group, like the multinational group on my first trip, would regard this visit as a one-of-a-kind experience. The next hour and a half pass, fortunately for all of us, with zero hitches. As we leave the palace, I see a stand holding a visitors' book. I ask Mr. Li if I might write my feelings in Hebrew. He approaches the stand and asks the officer in charge. His response is, "Of course, but please translate it into English, and I will translate it into Korean."

"That's fair," I tell him. I sit down next to the stand and deliberate how I might write the truth without offending the Koreans. Eventually, I write in Hebrew, "I am amazed at how the Korean people respect their Leaders." I then write it in English, adding my name and the name of my country, also in English. Mr. Li reads what I have written and thinks for a moment. He isn't stupid. He understands how I have chosen to bypass the potential landmine, by expressing admiration for the people rather than the worship. A slight smile of understanding lights up his face, and he translates what I have written into Korean.

I hurry off to meet my tourists, who have moved on to the courtyard for photographs, curious to hear their comments on the visit to the "pantheon of the gods." They are all, without

---

25 Or maybe not: cheerleaders are also a feature of sporting events in the US...

exception, excitedly taking photographs, exchanging exclamations, and expressing their wonderment. It would be difficult to overstate the intensity of the experience as expressed by the tourists at the end of the visit, and even more difficult to overstate my sense of satisfaction. Two of my main fears have been laid to rest. The visit to the "holy of holies" has passed uneventfully, and, more importantly, it has been a supremely powerful experience.

*

At the southern exit from Pyongyang, we come to the Unification Arch. It is late, considering how long the drive will be, and so we do not stop. Our guide, Kim, promises that we will stop for photos on the way back. This is the group's first intercity drive, and their eyes are glued to the road, which is potholed and empty. There are farming plots cultivated by hand, and soldiers are working on the sides of the road. Of course, everyone wants to photograph what we are seeing, and they ask permission. Miss Kim agrees, but then it turns out that a similar request from the back of the bus was turned down by Mr. Li. There is a moment of bewilderment. I draw Miss Kim's attention to Mr. Li's veto. She is unfazed, and in her quiet way, she repeats her approval, but emphasizes that we may not photograph soldiers. Incidents in which there is a lack of uniformity in the instructions by the staff will recur in the area of etiquette, too, and this reinforces my conviction that at the end of the day, there is no way of setting down rules that are absolutely airtight. There will always be different interpretations of the same situation. It is clear to me that the fact that there are always at least two staff members on duty creates a situation of structural supervision and control in the lives of North Koreans. I assume that a lifestyle of constant supervision must create tension between people – and certainly between guides who are working with foreigners. Nevertheless, never, on any of my eight visits to the country, do I sense any unpleasant tension among the staff. Moreover, although I have read, in articles written by people who have visited North Korea once or twice, that even the slightest deviation from official rules brings severe punishment, I will return again and again, and meet the same personnel, although there must surely be some slight deviations here and there during our trips.

As we head south, I ask Kim's permission to play music and to guide during the drive. Miss Kim, in a positive tone and without hesitation, answers, "Do whatever you're used to doing on your other tours." I start with some music, taking care to play only instrumental music with no lyrics, so there will be no suspicion of forbidden "propaganda." After a few minutes I say, "I think it's a good idea that I provide some background on the Korean War, since it's relevant to where we're headed." Kim gives a friendly hand gesture indicating that I should go ahead, as though telling me, "We already agreed on that."

This is the first time that I have attempted an approximately hour-long lecture. I proceed from the assumption that my words are being recorded, and that someone will be translating them.[26] I decide that it is better for both my group and myself that they hear me telling them, first, the North Korean "truth" – obviously, only with regard to the issues that are a matter of controversy – and then, briefly, the Western position, always introduced with the words, "Western sources claim that...," noting that the Western sources are freely available. I tell myself that my lecture has to earn me the confidence of the staff, and – as at the Unification Arch – I will achieve this by tweaking what I say

---

26 I never had this assumption confirmed, but it nevertheless governed the way I spoke to each group that I led in North Korea.

as I go along. Finally, I must show respect for their Leaders, and therefore every time I mention their names, it will be along with the appropriate title: President, Chairman, or Marshal.

I start by talking about the principles of colonialism, and then Japanese colonialism. I continue with the conquest of Korea by Japan and the Second World War, and the division of Korea along the 38th parallel. I notice that all three guides are listening to what I am saying. Before each sub-topic, I tell them what I am going to talk about, and after concluding the topic I sum up what I have said. To keep them connected along the way, I take care to name all countries in English as well as in Hebrew. The guides are no less enthralled by my speech than the participants. It is clear that they have never heard a topic reviewed in Hebrew; perhaps they have never heard this sort of historical review of their country by any foreigner. I steer away from discussing the Korean War and talk only about the background to it, preferring that the group first hear the North Korean "truth" from the local guides at the border and at the War Museum, and afterward we'll compare that with the Western version. As we draw closer to Kaesong, Kim prepares the group for the checkpoints that we will cross. She asks that we refrain from taking photographs. I go even further, asking – as did our guide on my first trip – that cameras and cellphones be put away in bags.

We are at the entrance to the DMZ. Following some technical arrangements, we board the bus, and the officer serving as our guide is the same one I met on my first trip, in April. He looks at me, smiles, and starts his monologue, which consists mostly of rules of behavior. Kim translates and explains that during this visit, we can photograph freely, including the soldiers, except during the first section of the drive on the bus. We receive the identical preparation as the one I remember from the previous trip. When we reach the building overlooking South Korea, where everyone takes photographs of themselves, inter alia, with the officer, I ask Kim to ask him if he remembers me. He nods and smiles, and adds the words, "Israel Air Force." He remembers! His name is Wang Ryong Chu. When the tour is just about to end, Kim asks me, "What about cigarettes?"

"What cigarettes?" I ask.

She explains that it is customary to bring cigarettes as a gift for the soldiers at the border. I am surprised, and decide, of course, to note this for future trips.

Our visit to Kaesong includes the "royal" meal (including the chicken soup described in the previous chapter), along with the UNESCO World Heritage sites – Sonjuk Bridge, the Confucian temple, and the adjacent Koryo Museum.

*

Today is September 9th, 2016 – the North Korean Independence Day. On August 15th, 1948, the leader of South Korea, Syngman Rhee[27], declared the establishment of the Republic of Korea. This represented official confirmation of what was already manifestly clear – that the agreement for the establishment of a united Korea, following the country's temporary division, was not feasible in light of the inter-Bloc struggle (the Cold War), which had developed immediately upon the conclusion of the Second World War. In response, on September 9th, 1948, President Kim Il-Sung declared the establishment of the Democratic People's Republic of Korea – or simply, North Korea.

Our day starts at Kim Il-Sung Square, and continues to the foreign-language bookshop. Of course, the policewoman outside with her robotic movements steals the show – at least in the photography department. From there, we move on to the Grand

---

27 In Korean pronunciation, his first name sounds more like "Lee."

People's Study House, whose breadth fills the entire northern side of the square. The structure is built in classic Eastern architectural style, like a sort of pagoda, its dimensions belying its height. A local guide is standing at the entrance. He doesn't speak English, but does speak fluent Spanish. Miss Kim hands over to the new Mr. Li, who will translate the guide's words for us. The tour starts, of course, with an expression of appreciation to the Leader, President Kim Il-Sung. We are led to an entrance hall, where a surprise awaits us: a white carrara marble statue, about four meters tall, of the President – seated against a background of Mount Paektu, of course. (If you think you've seen this statue, or one like it, you're probably thinking of the Lincoln Monument in Washington.)

I ask the group to pass by and to bow, without any jokes or superfluous comments. Whoever doesn't wish to bow can wait aside until the bowing ceremony is over. No one stands aside. The local guide seems to have heard the name "Lincoln" from other tourists in the past, and without our prompting, he notes that he has heard that the statues are similar. At that moment, I am reminded of a quote that I read in one of the books I purchased in North Korea, documenting former US President Jimmy Carter's words during his visit to North Korea after the end of his term in office. I ask the group not to laugh, and tell them: "President Jimmy Carter said, 'The leadership of President Kim Il-Sung is comparable to that of Presidents George Washington, Thomas Jefferson, and Abraham Lincoln all in one."[28] I add, "George Washington led the struggle for American independence; Thomas Jefferson is the father of the American Constitution, and Abraham Lincoln

---

28 American sources quote Carter as having said: "The North Koreans view the leadership of President Kim Il-Sung the way we [Americans] view the leadership of Washington, Jefferson, and Lincoln all in one."

fought for the unity of the United States. As the North Koreans see it, President Kim Il-Sung led the nation in all three of these essential areas."

If only I could photograph the faces of the Korean guides around me who, hearing the names of the presidents, understand what I am saying. In real time I don't understand why they are so amazed and impressed. After I talk with them, I understand that their lifestyle has no culture of research, self-study, and comparison of different sources. The level of education in North Korea is very high, but when it comes to anything involving society, and certainly the country's leadership, they are exposed to one single truth – a sole, absolute truth – while for us in the West, studying, researching, and questioning are integral to the way we live our lives. Their astonishment only grows when I tell them quite simply that I read all this in a book that I purchased in North Korea during my first trip. It seems that they have never read the literature that is sold to tourists, and thus it has never occurred to them that any stranger could know all this. Looking back, I think this was a formative event in the relations between myself and the Koreans. I gained a reputation as someone who "knows everything about North Korea" and who, unlike other Westerners, understands them. The advantages of this status would become apparent later on.

The **Grand People's Study House** offers adult education classes in languages, music, and other areas of enrichment. With the help of the guide, we visit lecture halls and rooms for consultation with university professors – all in all a rather propaganda-oriented visit in which we are exposed to the wondrous ideas inculcated by the Leader. The guide at the site is around fifty years old, relaxed, friendly, and smiling. As the tour progresses, we ask about each other's personal life and talk a little Spanish (which he speaks well, and I speak badly). When I ask his name, he answers with a wink, "Jorge." "Done," I smile back. Just when I feel that we've run out of conversation, we reach the exciting part of the visit – the library. Jorge boasts, "We have books in every language." I challenge him right away to find a book in Hebrew. Jorge stops for a moment and then, without blinking, continues, "We have no books in Hebrew, but if you bring some, they'll be in the library." Then he says, "Hold on, I'll bring you a book." He approaches the librarian, they exchange a few words, and then she goes to fetch two books. Jorge presents them to us. They have similar bindings; one is in Korean, the other in Spanish: "Diaro de Ana Frank" – the Diary of Anna Frank. Seemingly East – there are many people who know nothing about the connection between Israel and Judaism. And they've never heard of the Holocaust, either. Jorge's intelligent connection between these concepts indicates that North Koreans know about Israel and the Holocaust. On future trips, this fact would be proven over and over again., it is not surprising that a book that has been translated into seventy-five languages and has sold thirty-three million copies, would feature in the country's central library. Indeed, anywhere else in the world, this would make sense. But North Korea isn't like any other country. It is an insular country with tight control over everything; there is no book that passes under the radar – certainly not a book like this one, whose very presence makes a statement. Jorge doesn't know in advance where the groups of tourists that will be visiting are from. In our conversation, he asked what language we were speaking, and the speed with which he connected Hebrew with the diary of a Jewish Dutch girl indicates that he connects the language with Judaism and the Holocaust. This connection is not self-evident. As strange as it might seem to Israelis, in many places in the world – certainly in the Far East.

Our visit to the Grand People's Study House ends with the souvenir shop and a marvelous lookout over Kim Il-Sung Square, the river, and the Juche Tower. While I stand there pointing out the various sites to the group, I point to the symbol of the Party. Mr. Li reminds me gently that we are not to point to pictures of the Leaders. Instead, I should indicate with the hand open, fingers pointing forward. A simple and less threatening gesture.

At the Grand People's Study House – the statute of President Kim Il-Sung, whose leadership, supposedly according to President Carter, was "equal to the leadership of Washington, Jefferson and Lincoln all in one."

*

As appropriate for the holiday, we visit Mangyongdae, the birth-place of President Kim Il-Sung. Unlike my previous visit, when we had arrived at the site in the cool evening hours, this time we are here in the afternoon; the weather is perfect and a festive atmosphere prevails. Group after group of "pilgrims" visits the president's home. Once again, the women in their brightly colored dresses are a captivating sight.

Among the other sites that we visit over the course of the day is Mirae Road, which was inaugurated in 2015. The word "inaugurated" may not make sense to someone who is unfamiliar with North Korean tradition. (When was Jabotinsky Road in Jerusalem inaugurated? Or Oxford Street in London?) Never, on any of my trips, had I encountered a local guide who noted the date of the inauguration of a road. Mirae Road – the "Road of the Future," or Road of the Scientists, is one of the pretentious projects led by Marshal Kim Jong-Un. Having consolidated his rule, the young leader decided that his task was to lead North Korea into the future – meaning science, technology, and hi-tech. At the Leader's instruction, work began on the project in 2014, and was completed within a year. The street is very wide, with six lanes – three in each direction, separated by a traffic island. On either side of the road are cycling paths, sidewalks, and lawn strips. In addition to the nearby Kim Chaek[29] Technologi-

---

29 Kim Chaek was born in 1903. From 1927, he was among Kim Il-Sung's comrades-in-arms in fighting the Japanese, first from Manchuria and, later from the Soviet Union. He returned to Korea with the Soviet forces at the end of the Second World War. After the establishment of North Korea, he served as the country's Minister of Industry and, at the same time, as Kim Il-Sung's Deputy Prime Minister and Party Chairman. In the Korean War, he was commander of the fighting forces on the frontlines. As such, he was blamed for the failure of the North Korean army to halt the American invasion at Inchun, but was later exonerat-

cal University, there are hi-tech companies, multi-story residential buildings in pastel shades of green, blue, and mocha, and the flagship fifty-three-story futuristic Unha Tower. The road is flanked by stores and restaurants (for locals only). Across the river, on an island, is the Sci-Tech Complex housing an interactive science museum for children. The residential buildings are meant for scientists and university staff.

We disembark and walk about five hundred meters. Four staff members – three guides and the photographer – along with a large group of tourists, spread out over the road. Along the sides of the road there are Koreans who are also walking – families, couples, youngsters, and elderly people. We exchange looks, full of curiosity. Towards the end of the walk, we see a store selling sports clothing. Some members of the group want to go inside; I convey this request and also ask that they be permitted to purchase goods there. Kim's response surprises me: "Let me check," she says, and steps inside the store with the new Mr. Li. They emerge a short time later and she tells us, "You may go in. This store has the best in Western sports brands. Clothing, shoes, balls, weights, and more. The prices are high, but to you they'll sound reasonable. Here and there, you'll find some very low prices." I question why this is so, and she clarifies: "Items manufactured in North Korea."

I am elated: entering a store that is not meant for tourists, and certainly the possibility of making purchases there, is to my mind the breaking of a barrier. Moreover, it offers an opportunity to strike up conversations with the salesladies. Language is an issue, but with their garbled English and the excellent English of

---

ed. He was killed in 1951 in an American bombardment; some believe that he was deliberately targeted. After his death, the city of his birth was named after him, and the Pyongyang Technology University was likewise given his name.

the guides, there is conversation and discourse. At the payment counter, there are North Korean-made pens on sale. I decide to buy some as gifts. For thirty dollars, I buy thirty-three pens. When the saleslady hands them to me, I look at her and hold out one of them as a gift. She gives a shy smile, hesitating. The original Mr. Li encourages her to accept the pen. Now I notice that all the ladies are watching, so I go on to present each of them with a pen. With the remaining pens, with the approval of the guides, I step out onto the sidewalk. Children are walking home from school. I offer a pen to a schoolgirl, and again there is hesitation and a shy smile. Miss Kim's encouraging gesture breaks the ice, and the girl holds out her hand, takes the pen, and bows in thanks. After that it's easier: the other children smile shyly, then hold out their hands, and bow. Seemingly, a rather mundane exchange. But the behavior of the locals, adults, and children alike, shatters myths: "It's all just a show for tourists;" "They show you only what they want you to see;" and – more than anything else – "You can't make any sort of contact with the locals because they don't dare look at you, for fear of being punished by the authorities."

*

After my conversation with Mr. Cha yesterday, I was left with two big questions: would there be dancing in the streets? And would there be fireworks? Well, at four in the afternoon, we find ourselves in the midst of a dance gathering. Once again, people are dancing in circles and in pairs, the men in boring, formal suits, and the women in festive dresses that flare out into a bell shape as they twirl, like colorful spinning tops. Once again, towards the end of the dancing, they invite tourist onlookers to join. After the dancing and dinner, we enjoy the best treat of the day: although there are no fireworks, we are led by Mr. Cha to the beer festival. It is held in a venue covering a few hundred meters on the bank of the Taedong River, close to Kim Il-Sung Square, where we had watched the fireworks in April. Entrance to the event costs two dollars per person. There are dozens of beer counters, fast food stands, and stages for live performers. With no possibility of retaining our group formation, we agree on a time to meet back at the entrance, reminding the tourists that they may photograph the locals only with their permission. Everyone starts wandering about, buying beer (payment is in euros, dollars, or Chinese yuan), drinking, and enjoying themselves – in short, feeling part of the celebration. There is no need for detailed instructions: a moment after my short "speech," the tourists start disappearing, in ones or twos, into the crowd. I decide to invite our staff for a beer, and then simply go with the flow. I find myself sitting at a beer counter with some Koreans. Language barriers prevent us from engaging in conversation, but there are plenty of glasses clinking, smiles, and photographs. About an hour and a half later, when the members of the group meet up again, there is great merriment. Each participant boasts of his or her photographs and encounters with local people. Did I already mention the shattering of myths?

*

In my hotel room, as usual, I make a phone call to my wife, to reassure her that all is well. But this time the conversation is different from usual. Before I can say a word, Drora asks, in a frightened tone, "Did you feel the tremor?"

"What are you talking about?" I ask. "I didn't feel anything. Was there an earthquake?"

"No," she tells me, "North Korea carried out a nuclear test."

"We didn't hear anything over here," I finish the discussion, and go on to describe the day's experiences. Inside I am agitated, and immediately after hanging up, I call Yaki. Of course, he also starts the conversation with the story of the nuclear test, and tells me, "Ask your guide to tell the group about it tomorrow morning."

"I'm a bit hesitant," I reply. "Here, people don't know anything about it."

"What do you mean, they don't know?" he asks. "That irritating woman[30] announced it."

Although I am still agitated, I tell Yaki about the day's events, managing to elicit his wonderment tinged with envy. Afterwards, alone with my thoughts, I turn on the TV. Indeed, the "irritating woman" is reporting proudly on a successful nuclear test. The story of the nuclear explosion rattles me, and I try to think of a cautious way of approaching the subject with the guides. Once again, I review this second day of the tour in my head. I recall the videos made by Israelis who have visited North Korea, which I watched after my first trip, and wonder: how is it possible that we were able to deviate from the itinerary, meet local people, and communicate with them? How is it that I haven't yet had any sense that I'm being spied on (although it's possible that I am), while others felt it with such certainty? I asked the group if anyone had detected any sign of listening devices or cameras, and the answer was a resounding 'no.' Is it any wonder, then, that all twenty-six participants in the group are in such great spirits, and completely relaxed? Finding no answer to my questions, I turn my thoughts to tomorrow, and our scheduled drive eastward, to the port city of Wonsan, which I did not see on my first visit.

---

30 Ri Chun-Hee, the chief news presenter on Korean Central Television from the mid-1980s onwards, became known around the world as the "pink lady" for her bright traditional Korean attire. She announced her retirement in 2012, but in recent years has still occasionally been entrusted with announcing major developments.

*

On the way to breakfast I meet Miss Kim. Every morning she stands at the entrance to the dining room, greeting and directing the tour participants and offering assistance where necessary. I approach her, and after a "Good morning" and some pleasantries, I ask her hesitantly, "I understand that there was a nuclear explosion yesterday. Could you possibly talk about it when we are on the bus?" Miss Kim answers in her usual, relaxed style: "No problem, but the men know better than I do; ask them."

"She's evading," I think to myself. At breakfast, conversation among the tour participants turns, naturally enough, to the nuclear tear and its potential ramifications for our tour. When we climb aboard the bus, as per Miss Kim's recommendation, I approach the two Messrs. Li and repeat my request. I don't even have time to finish my sentence and the new Mr. Li says, "I'd be glad to talk about it." After the usual preliminaries for a day of touring, Mr. Li takes the microphone and says the following (more or less): "I am proud that on our sixty-eighth national anniversary, we succeeded in the nuclear test that was carried out yesterday. We are lovers of peace. We have never attacked a foreign country, and will never start a war. Now all our enemies know our might and it is clear to them that if they start a war against us, they will pay a heavy price. The aim of the nuclear explosion is to deter our enemies; we thereby reduce the danger of war."

I look at this man – young, handsome, and intelligent – and I see someone who is speaking with utter conviction. I am very surprised. I had expected an apologetic justification; instead, what I have just heard is an adamant, completely unapologetic declaration. I have heard the essence of the North Korean truth. I glance away from Mr. Li towards the tourists, and see them sitting silently, holding themselves back from bursting into applause, their faces showing amazement and surprise: amazement at the patriotism and conviction with which Mr. Li has presented the case, and surprise since this was not the speech that they had expected.

*

The drive to Wonsan is supposed to take about four hours. As we leave the city, and after Miss Kim and I have each given our talks about the sites awaiting us today, I propose that we all take a few moments to look out at the road and at what is happening on its sides. Mr. Li's words are still echoing in my head, and I am trying to understand why they have made such an impact on me. My thoughts wander to a time when I was a soldier performing mandatory military service, and I remember the slogan, "Know thine enemy!" It is a slogan that represents the basis for intelligence work, and entails far more than just collecting data. It requires understanding the enemy, whose actions are the product of wants, aspirations, and capabilities. North Korea is defined as the enemy of the free world, and in order to act against it wisely, it is necessary to understand the way in which North Korea perceives reality. I think some more: in what way is one country that maintains an inconceivably extensive arsenal of nuclear weapons better than another? What is the measure of legitimacy? Is it objective? Who decides? What makes Pakistan, India, or France – all of which are perceived quite naturally as legitimately possessing nuclear weapons – better than North Korea? Would Russia have adopted the same aggressive approach against Ukraine had the latter not given up the nuclear weapons at its disposal with the dissolution of the Soviet Union?

Prof. Bruce Cumings, an American historian and a leading expert on Korea, writes: "For 25 years now, the world has been treated to scaremongering about North Korean nuclear weap-

ons, but hardly anyone points out that it was the US that introduced nuclear weapons into the Korean peninsula, in 1958." ("A
Murderous History of Korea," *London Review of Books*, Vol. 39 No.
10, 18 May 2017)

I am left with many questions that have no answers.

CHAPTER 9

A Fortunate Accident

The port city of Wonsan is situated approximately two hundred kilometers east of Pyongyang. You exit the capital heading south, and then turn eastward immediately after the Reunification Arch. Like everyone else in the group, I am still under the powerful impression of Mr. Li's words, but slowly we immerse ourselves in taking in the view outside the window. It's not substantially different from the other intercity roads we've seen so far: a potholed road that winds between fields, against a wider background of hills and valleys. As we leave Pyongyang, the tourists look out of the window with interest, but naturally enough, as the journey goes on, their level of attention wanes. This is the stage where they sink into their own thoughts, with soft music playing in the background. After some quiet time for reflection, we start talking about life in North Korea. I do this on every tour to every destination, and where there is a local guide present, I like it when he or she participates. Understanding the data on any destination is difficult. As an example, let's think of the Seychelles Islands. Statistics show that the GNP in the Seychelles is almost thirty thousand dollars per person. Seemingly, this should indicate a relatively high standard of living, in comparison, let's say, to Portugal. But when visiting the Seychelles, one immediately notices that something is amiss: the standard of living doesn't look anything like Portugal; it looks closer to countries like Thailand or Sri Lanka. In the case of the Seychelles, the distorted impression created by the statistical data arises from the fact that the population numbers only about a hundred thousand, such that just one single multi-billionaire is enough to ensure that the GNP won't accurately reflect the standard of living. In the same way, in the absence of study, analysis, and understanding, any other statistical datum may be absolutely true and accurate, while still giving rise to a distorted picture. For this reason, I prefer my groups to hear talks that describe a reality, rather than heaps of statistical data. The statistics are meaningful only after a few days of touring, during which time the tourist experiences the place and sees the people, their clothing, the roads, sidewalks, vehicles, homes, stores, and products.

All this takes on special importance in North Korea. As an insular country with its own closed, separate economy, the usual universal economic indicators seem to be valid only up to a certain point. Moreover, although I encourage tourists in my groups to talk with local people and to ask them questions, in North Korea this is a sensitive issue, and it's better that such conversations take place after some of the barriers have fallen and some of the initial strangeness has worn off.

It's the fourth day of our tour, and there is a friendly group vibe, that includes the five staff members: the three guides, the driver, and the photographer. In preparing the group in Israel, we had recommended bringing along snacks, in view of the limited possibility of buying any during long road trips. In typical Israeli style, everyone shares whatever they have brought with the local guides, who respond with gratitude. A similar scene is repeated on each of the future trips, too, creating a pleasant atmosphere that allows participants to ask questions and guides to answer. Now, this first discussion certainly doesn't expose a full picture of the unique reality of North Korea, but it certainly does tell us something about the lives of the people there, and they don't know any other reality. The congenial atmosphere and the conversations will continue throughout the rest of the tour, within the larger group framework as well as in exchanges between individual participants and the guides. The picture arising from these discussions is, for the most part, not surprising.

Like all Communist countries, North Korea commits to take care of all of the citizen's basic needs: housing, health, education, culture and sports, employment, pension, clothing (school uniform, work clothes), and food (each family receives a basic food basket). Thus, salaries translate mainly into standards of living. I discovered something surprising during one of these discussions: the fact that salaries are not standard across the board but rather differential, depending first and foremost on achievement. One's place in the Party hierarchy matters, but less so.

Anywhere in the world, information that one obtains from conversing with local people and asking them questions is subjective. In North Korea, this basic starting point comes with an entire collection of specific biases. In addition to the closed economy and the fact that the usual economic indicators have little relevance, North Korea is an insular, highly regulated country, and our guides have to adhere to the official Party line. Our conversation partners are enveloped in the Korean reality (as they would be even if they were sitting with us outside of their country), and in describing their way of life, they lack the exposure that would allow them to compare with life elsewhere. In the realm of health, for example, they describe a system that provides a complete health basket. But it is clear that they aren't familiar with medicine in the developed world, and have no way of comparing what they have to what others have. The same applies in the areas of housing, clothing, and even food. In a country where the collective memory is seared with the horror of death from starvation, a reality in which no one starves to death is perceived as the pinnacle of material abundance.

At the same time, I have the impression that the educational system, at least, is indeed impressive and well-developed. Of course, it is focused on the sciences and on consciousness-engineering – as attested to by the guides' descriptions, Western sources, the appearance of the children on their way to school and back, and our impressions from visiting schools, a children's camp, and a "children's palace" with its extracurricular activities.[31]

*

Upon arrival in Masikryong, we see, near the junction, a gas station under construction. We are about thirty kilometers away from Wonsan, and to our right is a turn to the ski resort. This is the first gas station that I've seen in North Korea! Miss Kim points to it proudly. "Pornography is a question of geography," declares Sakini in *The Teahouse of the August Moon* (1956), but it seems that the same might be said of tourist sites, too. Only in North Korea: a gas station is considered an attraction worthy of a visit.

Wonsan

Wonsan is a port city with around three hundred and fifty thousand inhabitants. The port, on the southern part of the eastern coast of North Korea, serves both commercial and military purposes. The port and factories were opened here under the Japanese occupation. For two months at the end of 1950, during the Korean War, the city was controlled by UN forces. Retaken by the North Korean army, Wonsan was under blockade from February 1951

---

31 These visits will be described further on.

until the end of the war, on July 27th, 1953 – the longest blockade in modern history. During the war, the city suffered heavy bombardment and was almost completely destroyed. In 2015, Marshal Kim Jong-Un announced a plan to turn it into a major recreational tourist destination. To this end, some six hundred million dollars were invested in urban renewal and the development of tourist sites, such as beaches, therapeutic baths, historical artifacts, and of course, the ski resort, which we will get to presently.

At the entrance to Wonsan, we stop for a visit to the country's main **Agricultural University,** located on hilly terrain in a forested area. The parking lot is in a well-tended park, with a short, steep path leading to the main building. The architectural style of the building is unlike that of the other buildings we have seen so far. A review of the history of the university reveals that it used to serve as a German Benedictine monastery, which explains the neo-Romanesque style. Upon the declaration of North Korean independence, the monastery was closed and its monks expelled from the country. (The locals will not tell you about the building's Christian history.) In 1952, the Faculty for Wonsan Region Agriculture was moved here, and it was decided that this would serve as the central Agricultural University of North Korea. A second building, which had served as a residential building for the monks, was converted into student dormitories, which housed a great number of Third World foreign students up until the collapse of the Soviet Union. The explanations by the local guide are a perfect illustration of propaganda and its results (and, of course, a show for tourists). We are told about the amazing, genius initiatives of the country's Leaders in agricultural developments, such as the modern hothouse adjacent to the main building; the number of times that one or other of the Leaders visited the university, and all the places where he stood, sat, and was photographed. As we return to the parking lot, our eyes are drawn to a picture on the notice board that illustrates perfectly the expression, 'Only in North Korea': the poster shows four permissible hairstyles, two for women and two for men. Another three pictures show the proper etiquette for walking at the university. Students are shown wearing a uniform – black pants and a light blue or grey jacket – and walking along the hallways, keeping to the right. Another picture shows the same principle of keeping to the right as applied on the stairways, and a third picture shows an encounter between a student and a lecturer. Each one bows to the other, but the younger figure – i.e., the student – bows much lower.

For my future trips, I will start the tour of the university at this noticeboard. At first, the locals have trouble understanding why we are so amazed by the poster. I imagine that they are unhappy about the enthusiasm with which the tourists photograph it. On the tour in September 2017, the poster had disappeared.

선군시대 청년대학생의 면모

표 준 머 리 형 태

학 습 기 풍   인 사 례 절   복 도 에 서
통 행 질 서

"This way and no other." "Recommended" hairstyles, etiquette for hallways and stairways and for encounters between student and lecturer, at the entrance to the Agricultural University in Wonsan.

*

Our tour of the city starts with a disappointing visit to the fishermen's wharf, about a kilometer in length and sparsely populated with fishermen who avoid all eye contact. On the other hand, the lunch that we are served at a restaurant nearby is a culinary delight for seafood enthusiasts. The simple, fresh food makes a change from the other meals we have had on the tour.

After lunch, we head for the children's camp, located about five kilometers from the unimpressive center of town, at the heart of some woodlands near the sea. At the center of the campus is a roll-call square, with some buildings around it. The main building holds the dormitories, dining hall, computer rooms, and more; another building is for informal activities: it includes a room for performances, and activity rooms. A third building houses a natural museum and an aquarium, along with a tiny, delightful pond, with some small rowing boats. At the front of the roll-call square is a huge bronze statue, showing the two previous Leaders embracing some children. We already know the procedure, and we bow before the Leaders. Our tour starts in the residential building. The cleanliness of the place is striking. The beds are tidy, and ready for inspection; the kitchen is sparkling, and so is the dining hall. We move on to the computer room, and there is not a fingerprint to be seen on any of the computers. Everything is beautiful and gleaming. Most astonishing of all are the children's toilets, which are cleaner than many kitchens I have seen. There is only one element missing in all this perfection ... children. Not a single child is to be seen. The same is true for all the other camp buildings. In response to our question in this regard, we are told that the camp operates in the summer, not during the school year. The local guide on site and our tour guide both insist that it is an active camp. Among ourselves, we in the group are convinced that it is nothing more than a show. In the future I will learn the truth.

*

From the impressive, curious children's camp we move on to the train station, which was built by the Japanese in 1914, and later destroyed during the blockade of Wonsan during the Korean War. In 1975 it was restored and opened as the Museum of the Revolution. Its main attraction is a train carriage in which President Kim Il-Sung traveled to Pyongyang from Wonsan, at the end of the Second World War, following the Japanese defeat. A granite stone stands at the entrance to the station, engraved with a poem written by the President during the war against the Japanese, while he was at a guerilla stronghold near Mount Paektu. Our visit to the museum focuses, of course, on the train carriage – or, more precisely, on the unbreakable bond between the President and the seat he occupied in the train. In short – a fascinating lesson on the propaganda and personality cult industry.

Having covered all our stops for today, we head back west, to the Masikryong Ski Resort and the hotel where we will be spending the night. The hotel opened in January 2014, as part of Marshal Kim Jong-Un's vision of bringing the number of tourists to North Korea to a million per year. The Trip Advisor website awards the hotel a rating of four and a half to five stars. Essentially the hotel is a ski resort, offering visitors all the necessary infrastructure for a stay during the winter – or any other time of the year. The hotel is beautiful, luxurious, and inviting.

This all-year tourist site sits within a mountainous natural reserve that covers some 2,430 square kilometers and climbs to 1,360 meters. It was built to international standards, with the intention that a portion of the 2018 Winter Olympics, scheduled to take place in South Korea, could be held here. (Ultimately, the International Olympics Committee rejected the request, despite South Korean support for the idea.) The winter infrastructure includes a cable car, ski elevator, ski slopes and ice rink. In summer, the reserve is a good place for hiking and enjoying nature. We sample the attractions, taking the ski elevator for a hike at the top of the mountain, a cable car ride, and a walk.

Our visit to Wonsan is finished; we now head back to Pyongyang, but more relaxing, natural sites await us on the way.

*

After about an hour's drive, we take a turn southward and follow a winding road leading to a parking lot. Following a pleasant ten-minute walk in a gorge, we come to the Ulim Waterfall ("ulim" meaning "echo" in Korean), a hundred and fifty meters tall. Two steps of almost equal height create a breathtaking sight. Since both foreign and domestic tourism in North Korea is rather sparse, when arriving at the waterfall, one has the sense of discovering the place for the first time (on each of my visits to the site, there is no one there other than my group). Even here, a tribute to the Leaders somehow has to be included. According to the official story, in 1999, Chairman Kim Jong-Il saw the waterfall from the helicopter he was traveling in, on a work trip. Observing that there was no way of reaching the site on foot, he ordered that a path be cleared in order that the citizens could enjoy its beauty. The path to the waterfall was opened in 2001.

The enjoyable and relaxing visit to the Ulim Waterfall and the gorge leading to it, along with the refreshing overnight stay at the Masikryong Reserve, are a welcome breather in the midst of the dense, intense, unique experience of North Korea.

*

The rest of the drive back to Pyongyang is spent learning some basic vocabulary in Korean with the help of Miss Kim, hearing the story of the "Arirang" song (see box), and learning to sing it (or at least part of it). "Arirang" is the name of a popular performance that we are due to attend, at our request, when we get back to Pyongyang.

Ulim Waterfall

*

Arirang

Arirang might be described as a song, a fable, an anthem, a myth, and a cultural asset – all this and more. Essentially it is a three-part folk song about the three components of the nation: the south, the north, and the diaspora. Estimates as to its origins range between the years 1600 and 1750. There are at least sixty main versions of the song, and some 3,600 secondary versions. All of them recount a love story with a tragic ending. One version describes a pair of lovers who find themselves on opposite sides of the raging Aoraji River. The boy is unable to bear the separation, and in his efforts to cross the river, he drowns. The version that we hear from our guide adds elements with a social message: the lovers are serfs to a wicked landowner. The boy rebels against his master and is forced to flee to the mountains. While hiding there, he receives a (false) message that his lover was forced to submit to their master. In his great sorrow, the boy is ready to take his life. When the girl hears of his intention, she goes off to search for him in the mountains. As she searches, she calls to him, and the sound of her cry sounds like "Arirang." Miss Kim adds that the story is an allegory for the story of Korea, a country with a single nation that is torn apart into two states. In all its versions, the song has become the unofficial anthem of re-unification, in both South and North Korea – ironically enough, in no small part thanks to the Japanese. Among other decrees under their occupation, the Koreans were forbidden from singing their national anthem, so instead they sang this folksong, which became a resistance anthem against Imperial Japanese rule. But the irony doesn't stop there: many Japanese soldiers took a liking to the song, which is very pleasant to the ear, and thus the song made its way to Japan, where there were eventually at least fifty versions of it.

In 2012, Arirang was included on the UNESCO Intangible Cultural Heritage list as a South Korean submission; in 2014, it was also added as a North Korean submission. The symbolism is remarkable: the same nation, and the same song, but representing two states and hence requiring two separate decisions by UNESCO as to its status as a cultural asset.

*

We are in a theater where the Arirang performance will be taking place; the show is scheduled for 16:00. We sit in the first row after the aisle, in the best seats. The performance is meant for a local crowd, especially children and youth, but not only. The time is 15:50. A meager audience is seated in the large hall. I wonder, with some degree of embarrassment, why this is so. Is it because I insisted on a Korean performance that a decision was taken to punish us with this bizarre spectacle? I'm still focused on my perplexity when the show begins. Not the show onstage. A stream of children and adolescents start entering the hall. Quietly, with muffled giggles and whispering, boys and girls appear as though out of nowhere. Most are of high school age, but some are younger. Dressed in uniform (white shirts and blue pants or skirts), they follow their teachers inside, casting inquisitive glances in our direction and quickly filling the rows until there is not an empty seat to be seen. Within five minutes, the hall is completely full. The performance has not yet begun, but for the tourists – certainly for me – this has been a fascinating demonstration of a different set of cultural norms, at least in everything relating to discipline and order.

At precisely the appointed time, the show begins. Sixty minutes of pure pleasure. A large number of participants have invested much effort in the production. The subject is ostensibly the Arirang story, but it is interwoven with Korean national heritage themes, in song and dance of the highest stage quality. The youthful audience responds with enthusiasm, while still maintaining restraint and order. When the performance is over, there is a brief announcement in Korean. The audience remains seated, and our group is invited to exit first. Only afterwards does the rest of the audience leave the hall, in order of seating. Each teacher leads her students out; within ten minutes the hall is empty, and the children are all in the plaza in front of the theater. A demonstration of children's behavior – only in North Korea!

*

A pub in North Korea – There is an empty window of time before dinner, and Miss Kim suggests that we spend it visiting a local pub. I jump at the suggestion: of all our conclusions from our preparatory tour, the most important one was to try as hard as we could to feel the day-to-day life of the population. Still, the Western concept of recreation doesn't sit well with the idea of arriving at a pub at six in the evening, and so I suggest to Kim that we start with dinner, and then visit the pub afterwards. She explains that the pubs close at nine, and thus it would be better to use the time before dinner for this purpose. I am somewhat doubtful, but in my tours around the Far East – and certainly here in North Korea – I have learned to go along with the local guide wherever the difference of opinion is not over something serious. And so we happily head for the pub. (On my future tours, I would have opportunities to try out two other pubs, on my own, and discover that the one Kim On-Hee recommended was in fact the best one for us.) The pub is near the river, opposite the Juche Tower, on the second floor of a "commercial" building. We climb the stairs, passing two stores along the way: one is a pharmacy, and the other is a liquor store. It doesn't look as though we are headed for a recreational establishment, but when we arrive, our doubts give way to cautious optimism. The place looks like a pub, having a long counter adorned with six beer taps; it turns out that the pub is also a brewery. Each beer is identified with a number. Behind the counter, on the wall, a range of alcoholic beverages is on display. The tables, with seating for around seventy patrons, are made of roughly hewn wood, and the general dimness and décor are typical of a pub. When we walk in, there are about twenty locals seated inside. They glance at us with curiosity, but only for a moment. A pint of beer costs two euros; payment is only in foreign currency, and is covered by the sum allotted by Rimon Tours for recreational activities. All the group participants, along with the guides, enjoy a drink. I am in a good mood, and the beneficiaries are the bartenders and waiters, whom I invite to join the party. As we are drinking and talking, a dialogue of glances and glasses raised in toasts develops with the locals. And thus another one of our requests – to visit a local pub – has been realized. I realize that the patrons of the pub aren't representative of the general public, and the experience belongs to a rather limited elite, but that elite is not a small number of citizens. Later on, with each successive visit to North Korea, I will be increasingly exposed to the way of life in the country, and especially in Pyongyang. Obviously, the picture I have is only a partial one, and what I know about the place is less than what I do not know, but at the same time, it is completely different from what I expected.

After dinner, the drive back to the hotel presents the opportunity for a night-time tour. Darkness in Pyongyang serves to highlight the city's contrasts. By early evening, the traffic – both human and vehicular – is rather sparse. The streets are gloomy and lack charm, but the brightly lit monuments and national buildings stand out clearly even from afar: the Juche Tower, the Grand People's Study House, the Chollima Monument, theaters, the Party Monument, and more. The night lighting has a magical effect, serving like make-up to emphasize the beauty of the place and to conceal its warts. The effect is especially marked in view of the cheerless surroundings. We choose to stop at two sites for a visit.

Arch of Triumph. As we disembark from the bus, we catch a glance of the Kaesong Amusement Park. The place is alive: children, youth, and adults are enjoying the lit-up attractions. The mural depicting the declaration of victory over the Japanese, on the walls of the Kim Il-Sung Stadium – which we have seen already by day – stands out more starkly at night, as does the monumental Arch of Triumph, which seems to have grown even bigger in the dark.

Mansudae Hill. This is unquestionably the most impressive and photogenic site in North Korea. At night, against the background of the painting of Mount Paektu, the two colossal bronze statues of the Leaders of North Korea create an extraordinary, powerful picture that arouses a certain level of discomfort within me. Once again, my liberal conscience objects to the amazement at this display of dictator-worship. A dramatic "only in North Korea" moment catches my eye: three local women are silently cleaning the steps and the path leading to the platform upon which the statues rest. Conscientiously sweeping their twig brooms from side to side, they are working here late at night, keeping the site clean. The new Mr. Li is beside me. Talking quietly so that the rest of the group will not hear, I ask him to explain. Mr. Li, with no embarrassment, tells me that this is a common way for Koreans to express thanks to their leaders. I accept his explanation with no further questions, accepting – at least outwardly – his explanation as the plain truth.

The hill looks out on the city, the well-lit national monuments contrasting with the minimal lighting everywhere else. At the foot of the hill are dozens of fountains, sprouting in a range of colors and forms that change to the beat of cheerful music – a happy, pleasant sight that is incongruous with the city's image in the mind of anyone who has not visited it. What does match the city's image is the absence of local inhabitants enjoying the fountains. This is yet another riddle in the confusing, contradictory reality facing the Western visitor.

Arch of Triumph

*

After the night tour, we return to the hotel. When we left the hotel for Wonsan, I asked that our group be permitted to leave our belongings in the rooms, since the experience of my previous trip had indicated that this should not be a problem, based on the occupancy level of the hotel. My request was refused. But now, everyone is assigned the same room that he or she was in before, and the keys are in the same envelopes we received the last time. When I enter the room, I see that it has been cleaned, but nothing has been moved; a note that I wrote for myself is still lying next to my bed in exactly the same spot where I left it. Since tomorrow we will be leaving the hotel for the night once again, I decide to try requesting once again that we be allowed to leave most of our baggage in the room, so we can take only what is necessary for a single night. I hurry to the lobby, where the three guides are sitting with Mr. Cha. I repeat the same request as last night, and receive the same response: "That will be possible at a cost of sixty percent of the price of each room for a night." After some tiresome negotiations, we arrive at a compromise: five dollars per room for a night. It turns out that even in North Korea, it's worth trying to bargain.

In my room, I find myself once again immersed in philosophical thoughts. I recall a similar feeling from my first visit to India, but for some reason that I can't quite understand, this time it seems far more intense. I find myself once again wrestling with my wonder at a site of worship – worship that goes against everything that defines me in my own eyes. The image of the women sweeping the statues comes back to me, and I decide that they are performing a sort of "constructive punishment" that has been meted out to them by some committee or organization. A moment later I reject this explanation, since it makes no sense that the authorities would allow foreigners to view such a scenario at a central tourist site. The question marks pile up, and more and more exclamation marks curl at the ends and lose their certainty. And why are there no locals around the beautiful fountains? Clearly, I will not find answers to every one of my questions.

I am back to my evening routine in the hotel. After a call to my wife and a call to Chaim, I turn my attention to the itinerary for tomorrow. In the afternoon, we will be leaving the city again, heading for the Myohyang mountains. Reviewing the activities planned for tomorrow morning in Pyongyang, it doesn't seem possible that we'll manage all of them, and I write a note to myself to discuss this with Miss Kim On-Hee in the morning.

When we meet up before breakfast, I share my doubts as to the possibility of fitting in the full program for the day. Miss Kim looks over her papers and says simply, "That's the program that we need to get through." As always in Eastern Asia, I don't argue; I just express my hope that we will indeed manage to cover it all, while muttering to myself in Hebrew, "We'll see."

Our tour starts at the Korean War Museum – officially, the Victorious Fatherland Liberation War Museum. On my first visit to the museum, I hadn't been particularly interested. I simply don't like military museums, and I hadn't paid much attention.

After we get through the strict inspection at the entrance to the museum's giant courtyard, the officer who will be guiding us around the museum approaches. As she reaches us, she looks at me and declares, "You've been here before!"

Without hesitation I reply, "No, this is the first time I've brought a group here."

She insists, "You've been here before."

I start to answer and then suddenly remember the previous visit. I pull out my cellphone, open my photos from my previous visit and scroll through them and – sure enough – there she is! With some embarrassment I answer, "That's correct; here is a photo of you. I was here." To assuage some of my embarrassment I explain, "But I came as a tourist. You can't possibly remember the faces of all the tourists you've ever guided here at the museum."

The officer gives a friendly smile and says, "But you see, I remembered!"

At some point during the tour we take a break for refreshments. I invite all the guides for a drink, including the guide from the museum and the two salesladies. While we are all sitting together, I turn to the officer and ask her name and her rank. "Che Un-Jong," she replies. "I'm a captain." I introduce myself and mention my past as an officer in the IAF (this is something that I do only in North Korea, as a sort of preventive measure to avoid potential problems). She smiles and tells me, "I know." Seeing my look of surprise, she reminds me, "Last time, you corrected a mistake I made regarding the weight of the bombs. I checked, and you were correct. Thank you!"

"That's right," I recall. "I had forgotten that completely."

In all my future visits, I request that she be our guide at the museum, and each time, she is indeed assigned to us, except for once when she was on maternity leave. We become friends, as much as circumstances allow, and I make sure to bring her a small gift on each visit. Her openness in our chats is always a pleasant surprise for me. (I will discuss further on about our most surprising discussion, on my last visit, in September 2018, when she was already Major Che Un-Jong.)

Our tour continues: production studios, an art gallery, and the 1st of May Stadium. After our lunch break, we are supposed to visit the Workers' Party Monument, a supermarket, and the Pyongyang Underground. After that, we are scheduled to take a two-and-a-half-hour drive, arriving at the Myohyang Hotel for dinner. Clearly, we are not going to have time for everything. Once again, I turn to Miss Kim: "If we end up short of time, I suggest that we leave the visit to the underground station for when we get back to Pyongyang." Miss Kim listens, and thinks, and this time her response is less decisive: "We'll see."

*

Supermarket in North Korea – The store is more than a supermarket. On the ground level, to the left, is a well-stocked supermarket with brand-name foods and hygiene products, wine, Italian olive oil, Russian vodka, and of course, Chinese products of all types. On the right of the entrance, there are kitchen utensils on sale, along with work tools and a range of accessories. On the second floor to the left is a clothing and footwear store. To the right are home appliances: washing machines, televisions, and once again international brands – Siemens and more. The third floor is all about food. To the right is a large cafeteria; to the left is ice-cream and children's snacks. Purchases can be made at the store only in local currency. At the entrance is a currency exchange counter, and one can convert whatever local currency is left over into foreign currency. I come to an agreement with our guides as to how long we can spend in the store, and after instructions have been given, we are free to walk around the facility as we choose. We are asked not to take photographs.

I convert ten euros and set off with eighty thousand won[32] to explore the place. I take a quick walk through each of the branches of the store to see who is buying and what they are buying. Then I stand in line at the food counter, buy myself a typical Korean meal of Ryomyong (noodles made of buckwheat, served in cold soup), and take my tray to sit among some locals. My appearance arouses curiosity. Many shoppers look in my direction, and I look back at them. Once I am ready to start eating, I discover that I have no chopsticks. I look around, catch the glance of one of the diners, and with hand movements express my predicament. The Korean stands up and brings me chopsticks. Many eyes are still on me. I choose to ignore them, and start eating. From the moment I pass the chopsticks test, the interest in me dissipates. When I am finished, I take another walk around, this time focusing on the character of the shoppers and on the dynamics between the shoppers and the salespeople. As our allotted time comes to an end, I sit down alone on a bench outside the store, watching people walking in and out. As usual, I am lost in thought: how strange it is that we are visiting a supermarket as part of an organized tour, and even that only

_____

32 Korean currency

after repeated requests – a fact that testifies to the uniqueness of tourism to North Korea. Even stranger is that the visit is duly noted as an item on the tour itinerary. Once again, I conclude: only in North Korea.

Moreover, it is very strange how everything about this store is very similar to anywhere else, and yet so different from one's prior expectations. This is almost certainly not a store that reflects the reality of the country as a whole, but it is also not a store catering only to the ruling elite. Members of the ruling elite do not come to a store on a bike, or with shopping baskets on wheels and with children in tow. Of course, we can always come back to the ever-useful catch-all: "You know that it's all a show for tourists." But seriously – is it possible that these hundreds of people are all actors in an Oscar-worthy production, and that the store is filled with products merely for the sake of the show? At the same time, I find myself wondering: all the locals who are showing up at the currency exchange counter at the entrance – how do they come to have foreign currency? From the purchases that we make at the souvenir shops? From Koreans living abroad, who send contributions to family members? This is just one of many mysteries that I am unable to solve. The explanations provided by the guides provide no satisfactory answers.

Our group has finished exploring the store. Our bus has shifted out of its parking spot, but is still standing in a prominent spot where it can easily be seen from afar. We board the bus and prepare to leave. An Israeli guide will never set off without first checking that all the group's participants are on the bus. I stand up to count, but Mr. Li tells me, "It's okay, they're all here." As I am counting, one of the participants notices that another is missing. The guides decide to check for themselves, and after a quick count, go running off to look for the missing tourist in the store. I follow them off the bus – heading not into the store, but rather to the spot where we got off the bus when

209

we arrived. Indeed, the missing participant is standing there patiently, waiting for us. Another assumption has been shattered: it is indeed necessary to check and make sure that the entire group is present and accounted for. The time is now a lot later than the hour noted on Kim On-Hee's itinerary. Kim glances at her watch and tells me, "We'll leave out the visit to the subway for today. Let's head directly for the Myohyang mountains, and we'll take the subway when we come back to Pyongyang."

*

As the tour progresses, the dialogue between Kim and me becomes increasingly informal and friendly. Her personality, the way in which she listens to requests, and her intuition all project an easygoing calmness that in no way conforms with one's expectations of a representative of a totalitarian regime. As is my custom when dealing with guides in the Far East, I compliment her. Once we are a few minutes into our drive northward, I look at my watch and mumble, "I think our idea of leaving out the Pyongyang underground station was a good one." Kim casts me an amused glance and says, "What do you mean, 'our idea?' It was your idea all along!"

The camaraderie that has developed over the course of our intercity trips between us (the Israeli tourists) and the five staff members (the three guides, the driver, and the photographer) continues in discussions in small groups with the guides, focusing mainly on the way of life in North Korea – and also in Israel. As a rule, the guides avoid asking questions that might lead in the direction of topics which they are apparently forbidden to discuss with foreigners. The members of the group have already learned to steer the discussion around potential landmines. And thus a friendly discourse has developed, surprising in its openness. What we have learned, inter alia, is that all our guides have been overseas within the framework of their professional roles, or as children with their parents. The hypothesis that at first had seemed logical is reinforced over and over: the guides come from families belonging to the ruling elite. I learn that Kim's husband works as a state-appointed dealer in China, purchasing various raw materials and consumer goods. Kim has joined him more than once on his trips there. Against this background, I am very surprised when in one of our conversations she asks, in a tone of incredulity, "Is it true that in your country, too, you have to pay for your apartments?" Kim is a very smart woman, she has visited China several times, and yet her worldview is still one in which the government provides its citizens with all their basic needs – including, of course, housing. It seems that even though she has been exposed to the "capitalist communism" of China, she is still captive to the reality in which she was born and in which she lives her life. It is important to emphasize here that with some very rare exceptions, the citizens of North Korea know no other reality; those that do, remember Korea of the twentieth century. In fact, every adult Korean has heard the stories told by his parents and grandparents. In other words, the image of life in Korea, as they have heard it from first-hand accounts, relates to the previous hundred years, starting from the Japanese occupation, through the Second World War (resulting, from their point of view, in liberation from occupation, but at the cost of the division of their country), the Korean War, and the end of the twentieth century – a period of hardship and deprivation following the collapse of the Communist Bloc and the famine that resulted in widespread death.

These periods of hardship are the basis for comparison with the present. Western intelligence sources note that the economic reforms instituted in recent decades, recalling similar reforms that were undertaken in China and then in Vietnam, are bearing fruit, and today there is no more starvation in North Korea. Korean society remembers that thirty years ago, hundreds of thousands died of starvation; at the same time, the population has no experience of societies of abundance. Hence, as strange as it may sound to the Western ear, the way Koreans perceive their reality today is that things have never been better. (This also explains why, on the basis of their own reporting, North Koreans are ranked as the second happiest society in the world, after China.)

*

Further on in the journey we make a toilet stop in the open, since nowhere along the two-and-a-half-hour drive is there a proper facility. (This was the case in 2016; however, in September 2018, a reasonable highway stop opened.) The wonders of North Korea! Admittedly, a similar reality exists in many countries of the world, but North Korea is a nuclear power, a hi-tech country. One leaves Pyongyang, a city of millions of inhabitants which, despite its peculiarities and differentness, projects vitality and power, and then one encounters an astonishing contrast. What is even more astonishing is how one quickly becomes accustomed to the strangeness and the alternative reality on the road to the Myohyang mountains. Once again, diverse conversations are struck up between members of the group and the guides, and then Kim and I decide to channel the positive dynamic into a continuation of the group discussion with the panel of guides. Once again, the questions veer towards everyday life. As the discussion goes on, it seems to become freer and starts sounding less like texts recited from a page of messages. These conversations give rise to some interesting and surprising insights about Korea, Korean life in general, and the way in which the Koreans perceive their reality, with no awareness of its uniqueness.

The media in North Korea is, of course, run by the government and under its full control. There are a few television channels, including one meant for children and youth. Listening to the locals describe it, the picture that emerges – or that would emerge, if you didn't know where you were – is something like television in Israel in the early 1970s. But when you ask a few more questions (as I did in a personal conversation) you hear confirmation of the rumors that there are speakers in every home that broadcast twenty-four hours a day: news, stories, and ... propaganda. There is no possibility of turning them off; all that one can do is control the volume, which is lower at night in any case. An alternative reality – only in North Korea!

We ask about marriage, divorce, sex outside of marriage, and more. It turns out that Korean society is quite extreme in its conservatism. When we ask about unmarried couples living together and engaging in sexual relations, the answer we receive, after an embarrassed pause, is that there's no such thing in North Korea. Such behavior would be a violation of all social norms. Moreover, in rural areas, matches are still largely made by the parents. Even in Pyongyang, and amongst the elite, it is very rare for a wedding to take place without the parents' approval. When we prod some more and ask what happens if the parents do not approve but the couple wants to marry, the response we get is, "They keep trying to persuade them, until they agree." Kim goes on to describe the continuation of the process, including the meeting of the families, the wedding ceremony, and the celebration. After the ceremony, she tells us that the parents and elders of the family sit down at the table of honor, and the bride and groom come to thank them, with a bow, for agreeing to the marriage. "Hold on," I interrupt her, "What do you mean when you say, 'a bow?'" She replies, "A bow – like the way we honor our Leaders." Only then does it dawn on me that in the East in general, and in Korea in particular, bowing is a gesture of respect and honor. It acknowledges the status of the older or more senior party, but it is not an act of self-abnegation. Wherever we go in Korea, the locals bow to honor us. The depth of the bow expresses the attitude towards the person who is being honored. Unquestionably, there is leader-worship in North Korea, but its expression is not the bow itself, but rather its depth, and the air of awed sanctity with which it is performed.

The other side of the same coin is divorce. In conservative Korean society, divorce is a disgrace that affects the whole family. Conjugal relationships outside of marriage are completely unacceptable. If divorce is a stain, a woman's betrayal of her husband is an unforgiveable sin. Of course, there is no symmetrical opprobrium concerning men; for some reason, unfaithful husbands are shown a certain degree of tolerance. One has to remember that in addition to the conservative foundations of their society, South and North Koreans alike still carry the trauma of the "comfort women." Under Japanese occupation, hundreds of thousands of Korean women were forced to serve as sex slaves to Japanese soldiers. This is still an open wound that reinforces the conservative orientation.

When we ask how North Korea deals with homosexuality, the response is, "There is no homosexuality here." Simple and convenient...

*

These conversations add to the puzzle in my mind over what it is that sets North Korea apart from "similar" Communist regimes in Europe, or from tyrannical regimes in the West. When I speak with people from the former USSR about North Korea, I hear over and over again, "I know how that is; I lived under a regime like that." Unquestionably, there are parallels between European Communism and the Asian version, but there are perhaps more differences than similarities. The conservatism of North Korea sits well with the foundations of Korean culture and Korean history of the twentieth century. In general, those of us who grew up and were educated in the West naturally project principles that seem self-evident to us, upon people of other cultures; we are not always open and willing to internalize the cultural gaps and bridge them.

A word about the perception of the ruling class in the cultures of the East. The Eastern cultures have no word corresponding to "democracy;" certainly no such concept existed in that part of the world until after the end of the Second World War. Even today, only a minority of countries in Asia are democracies, and even these do not always reflect all the parameters of a democracy in the Western sense. The Western form of democratic governance is the result of processes that have taken place over the course of centuries in all areas of life: economics, religion, scientific development, and social theories. One has to keep in mind that in the cultures of Eastern Asia, the ideological basis underlying the regime is Confucian philosophy, which defines man's conduct within society on the basis of two main principles: social hierarchy and punctilious discipline. At the top of the pyramid we find the "heavens," which award the ruler – the embodiment of wisdom and heavenly benevolence – the mandate to rule for the benefit of all citizens. The citizens, for their part, have to maintain absolute obedience, since according to this approach, "Every person has to know his place in society." Once again, let us remember that the perception of reality held by the citizens of North Korea today is that their situation has never been better.

As to religion: Religions in the West are dogmatic and define all of a person's behaviors from the time he is born until he dies. In addition, Christianity – in most of its forms – is a central influence in public administration. While Communist ideology perceives the state as an entity whose purpose is to help the bourgeoisie to exploit the masses, religion is a full partner – according to this theory – in the exploitation, and must be fought. In Eastern cultures, religions are something else entirely. They would not be called "religions" in the Western sense at all, but rather philosophies that guide a person through the life cycle. For this reason, the religions of the East are not threatening, and Korea's opposition to religion is in fact an opposition to Western religion – i.e., Christianity.

The Communist revolution also claims that it can be realized only through destruction of the existing social organizational structure and its reorganization. Of course, the state, as an organ for the exploitation of the proletariat by the bourgeoisie, is meant to disappear, and the new reality will be one in which "Workers of the world, unite!" In North Korea, the "revolution" overlaps with the national liberation movement, such that the ideology of "Workers of the world, unite!" has no relevance. The ideology of creating anarchy for the purposes of rebuilding is likewise superfluous in the Korean reality, since the Japanese left chaos behind them and everything had to be rebuilt anyway. The rebuilding of North Korea relied on legends and traditions of the past, such as the legend of Mount Paektu, Chollima – the flying horse, and the stubborn fight to have Kaesong, the former capital, remain under North Korean sovereignty. The status of the ruler is maintained, in keeping with Confucian teachings, as the holder of the divine mandate to lead the people with benevolence.

Thus, in North Korea, Communist ideology is limited to the issue of social justice and the exploitation of the lower classes by the bourgeoisie. It is therefore not surprising that the principle of Songun awards preference to the army – in other words, patriotism – over the revolution.

Our journey continues, and so does the discussion. We ask Kim to tell us about military service in North Korea. Her response is surprising: "There is no obligation to serve, but we are patriotic, and so everyone aspires to serve in the army and to defend the homeland." I think to myself that in a country where everyone receives a salary from the state, it doesn't make too much difference who exactly is paying the salary; moreover, we have seen for ourselves that the army is involved in everything: construction, infrastructure works, helping farmers... Kim continues, explaining that there are two parts to the army. The first is something like national service; the other is the fighting force, which is a professional army, with the length of service determined accordingly. In Western sources, the information in this regard is less clear-cut. The CIA website, offering data on every country, shows that military service in North Korea is mandatory for men and women from the age of seventeen (ten years for men and six for women). According to this and other sources, the standing army comprises about a million and a quarter soldiers, with about a million more in the reserves. From my conversations with guides, and from my observations, the picture looks somewhat different. Studying, teaching, and countless other forms of service which are not exactly military service are included in the official definition. When we question Kim about mandatory service, she responds with an extraordinary and touching patriotic speech. Starting off in an informative tone, she reiterates that there is no obligation to serve in the army, but the aspiration to serve the country finds expression in every part of society. "We are a small country," she continues, "and we have been conquered over and over by neighboring and more distant powers." As she talks, her tone becomes increasingly passionate. "We were conquered by the

Khitans,[33] the Chinese, the Mongols, the Manchurians[34], the Japanese, and finally by the Americans, who still control half of our homeland. Over and over. We were conquered because we were weak. The lesson to be learned from our nation's history over the first half of the twentieth century is that we have to be strong to defend ourselves, and to rely only on ourselves because no one will do the work for us." Kim goes on, talking to herself more than to us: "We've never attacked any other nation.[35] In the First World War we fell victim to Japanese cruelty, and we were punished by having our country divided. When we tried to bring about reunification, a foreign force representing fourteen countries, led by the US, fought against us. It was only thanks to our heroes and our Leaders that we managed to maintain our independence – at least over half of the country. Why are we being punished, first with division and now with such harsh sanctions?" Again Kim asks, without expecting a response, "Who did we attack, and when?" There is silence in the bus. I cannot find the words for even a polite, non-committal answer. The silence is more powerful than any words. Kim's cry comes from the depths of her faith and her perception of

---

33 A nation that originated in central Asia, north-east of China. In the fourth century, the Khitans controlled the territories of Manchuria, Mongolia, and parts of Korea. The Khitan kingdom reached its peak in the tenth century, following the fall of the Chinese Tang dynasty, when it ruled over north-eastern China, Manchuria, Mongolia, and Korea. The kingdom came to an end at the beginning of the thirteenth century, the Khitan language disappeared, and the nation assimilated among the Chinese.

34 A nation that originated around the Manchuria region of today. The Ching dynasty of Manchuria, the last imperial dynasty, ruled over China from the mid-seventeenth century until the Japanese conquest. The Manchurians were completely assimilated among the Chinese, and their language was almost forgotten.

35 This is true if we regard the Korean War as a civil war.

Korean history. As I returned again and again to North Korea and spoke with the locals, I became increasingly convinced that this is the perception of the vast majority in the country.

After a few minutes of quiet chatting among the group, Kim starts asking me questions about life in Israel. I offer an overview of the history of the Jewish People, the Zionist movement, the story of the establishment of the State of Israel, and the "ingathering of the exiles" that is the Israeli reality. Once again, I discover that the Korean guides are surprisingly knowledgeable about our country, and are also aware of the Holocaust during the Second World War. Afterwards, our conversation drifts to Jewish faith and religion. I explain the special status of the Sabbath in Jewish tradition, and its gift of the day of rest to all peoples of the world. Kim is surprised and pays close attention. I describe the Sabbath Eve ceremony that is part of our culture, and muster the courage to ask whether it would be possible, on our next trip, to hold such a ceremony. Her answer is immediate and decisive: "No problem at all. On the contrary, you are our guests, and we'll be glad to facilitate your custom."[36]

*

We arrive in Myohyang in time to enjoy dinner and a relaxing evening in the beautiful hotel. In the morning, as on my previous trip, almost everyone in the group is awake and walking around outside, enjoying the tranquil scenery and the cool, clear morning air. After visiting the sites in the area – the nature reserve and

---

36 Full disclosure: I am not religiously observant at all, but during my trips overseas, I usually pay homage to the tradition of my people on the eve of the Sabbath and Jewish holidays by reciting the traditional "Kiddush" (literally, "Sanctification") – a declaration of the holiness of the day, followed by the traditional blessing over a cup of wine.

the Buddhist temple – we arrive at the region's top tourist spot, the International Friendship Exhibition. This time, at my request, we visit the collection of gifts given to Marshal Kim Jong-Il. It is no less impressive than the collection belonging to President Kim Il-Sung. There are gifts from all over the world, especially the Communist Bloc and the Non-Aligned countries, but also from Western leftist bodies. Ignoring for a moment the political aspect, it is a marvelous collection of treasures: handcrafted items made from rare raw materials; artistic pieces representing the folklore and culture of many nations, and more. The greatest surprise awaits us in the hall for honoring and bowing to the statues of the Leaders: in addition to the statues of President Kim Il-Sung and his son, Chairman Kim Jong-Il, a statue of Kim Jong-Suk, wife of the President and mother of the Chairman, stands in its own beautiful room (see box). With Mount Paektu in the background, dressed in combat gear and with a pistol at her waist, Kim Jong-Suk embodies the ultimate heroine. This was the only site where we saw a statue of her. We bow before her statue too, of course, and are then permitted to walk around the exhibition.

For this day of the tour, we have been joined by Andrea, who is the director of Uri Tours – the company via which we contracted the North Korean Koryo company. Naturally enough, our conversation concerns mainly the tour and its content. However, I cannot help asking about the custom of giving cigarettes to the officer at the border. I ask her, "Can this not be regarded as bribery?" Andrea answers with a smile, "In North Korea, people like to receive gifts! So long as they are within the bounds of reason and good taste, they are accepted without undue moralizing, with a smile and with sincere thanks." I note this for myself and decide to try it out on my next trip. Andrea also tells me, "When you speak with Koreans about their country, you should leave out the word 'North.' From their point of view, there is one Korea. Only if you are mentioning South Korea should you talk about 'North Korea.'" I decide to follow her advice.

Kim Jong Suk, 1917-1949

Kim Jong-Suk, wife of Kim Il-Sung and mother of Kim Jong-Il, was born in northern Korea under the Japanese occupation. Her father went to Manchuria and joined the underground forces fighting against the Japanese. Around the age of thirteen, Kim Jong-Suk crossed the border into Manchuria, together with her mother, who was looking for her husband, since contact with him had been severed. What they discovered was that he was no longer alive. About three years later, Kim Jong-Suk also lost her mother. The orphaned girl survived the difficult conditions of occupied Manchuria, including arrest and a period of imprisonment by the Japanese. At the age of about eighteen, she joined the underground in fighting the Japanese, where she met Kim Il-Sung, and they married in the Soviet Union, which was a base for anti-Japanese guerilla warfare. In 1941 she bore her eldest son, Kim Jong-Il. Kim Jong-Suk passed away in 1949. According to the Korean narrative, she died of complications from an injury sustained in the war. According to Western sources, she died after a stillbirth. A different version claims that she died of tuberculosis; there are even some who believe that she was shot.

In 1994, when her son, Kim Jong-Il became ruler of North Korea, he transformed the legacy of his mother from the model wife and helpmate of Kim Il-Sung into the immortal fighter and exemplary model of feminine heroism in the battle against the Japanese. Among other heroic deeds attributed to her, Kim Jong-Suk is said to have saved Kim Il-Sung from death when they found themselves caught in a Japanese ambush. She protected him and shot the attackers with her pistol (indeed, there seems to be some truth to this story).

In North Korea – in fact, in any human society – a legend requires no proof. This is part of its power. In the North Korean consciousness, Kim Jong-Suk is the wife of the President, mother of the Chairman, and a fearless fighter for the homeland.

*

Having finished our visits and after lunch, we are on our way back to Pyongyang. After about an hour of driving, there is a military roadblock, preventing us from continuing. One of the guides gets off the bus to see what is going on. He gets back on the bus, the three guides huddle together for a moment, and then Miss Kim telephones Mr. Cha in Pyongyang. There is no response. She turns to me and explains: "The heavy rains last week weakened one of the bridges, and it has collapsed. It's a bridge on the main road; a bridge that we drove over yesterday, on our way to Myohingsan." In response to my question of what this means for our tour, she tells me that she is waiting for instructions. A few minutes later, Kim summarizes her conversation with Mr. Cha, explaining the situation in a tone that sounds as though she is waiting for my confirmation or approval. She tells me that on the basis of the information at hand, the only practical possibility is to take a detour. When I ask what the impact will be on today's itinerary, she tells me that it will entail a delay of at least an hour. Since there is no choice, her waiting for my approval is nothing more than politeness. Of course, I "agree." The driver maneuvers the bus in the opposite direction, and about three kilometers further on, we turn onto a different road. In my mind this whole incident turns out to be a "fortunate accident." We miss our scheduled visit to the Children's Palace, but we end up driving on a road that has definitely never been traveled by any tourist before.

The road is narrow, winding, and full of bumps. The asphalt is patchy, and our speed is reduced accordingly. The road cuts through villages, and we drive among villagers walking about and between the houses. This is the unvarnished, undecorated, real Korea! Our guides, the photographer, and the driver are tense. It seems to me that it's the first time they've ever been on this road, too. For two hours, we are granted a unique anthropological experience. Every member of the group, myself included, is fascinated by the sights. Our guides ask that we take no photographs. I repeat their request in a tone less polite than the one they use. The group cooperates and refrains from photographing. The sights out of the window are entirely different from those that we see on the standard tour itinerary: there is poverty; not all the houses are connected to the electricity grid. The villagers, walking home from the fields, are dressed in "Maoist" style. Throughout the journey, we see no sign of any agricultural machinery. The farmers all perform their work manually. They are not an encouraging sight. But – and this is a big but – we see no signs of malnourishment, as we might perhaps have expected. While the scene is rather depressing, anyone who has traveled around certain areas of Asia, Latin America, and certainly Africa, has seen similar scenes, or worse. In short, our drive takes us through the essence of the North Korean reality.

On a lighter note, in response to the objections that I hear so often when describing life in North Korea – "You know that you're seeing only what they want to show you!" I have an answer: "That's not true. My group saw what they didn't want to show us."

In the fields

*

It is our last day in Pyongyang – a day meant for catching up and completing the itinerary. We start at the **Mansudae Art Gallery**, a huge complex housing workshop for sculpture, painting, woodcarving, an art exhibition, a souvenir store, and more. Clearly, this is politically sponsored art, leaving limited room for self-expression. The pride of the complex is the bronze foundry, where the giant bronze statues scattered all over the country are produced. The North Koreans have acquired great skill in creating these sculptures. Surprisingly enough, there is great demand around the world for monumental bronze statues, and this is one of the country's few exports. Following a short tour of the painting workshop, we continue to a rather impressive exhibition of pictures and sculptures – and, of course, the option of purchasing artworks, which some members of the group eagerly do.

From the Mansudae Art Gallery, we go on to visit the subway. As on my first visit, and as documented in countless articles and photographs, the tour of the subway includes just two stations. We board the subway train at the first station of the Red Line, Puhung ("Prosperity") Station, and disembark at the next stop, Yonggwang ("Glory") Station. There is a girl standing on the platform selling maps of the subway to tourists. I buy one and study it as we ride. I see two lines: the Red Line, with eight stops, and the Green Line, which also has eight stops. The booklet offers beautiful photographs of the different stations. I recall the well-known "fact" that everything is a show for tourists; thus, the map must be fictitious. I turn to Kim and ask, in a complaining tone, why we are only seeing two stations. Kim answers, "Because we're hurrying to dinner." I look at my watch; indeed, there isn't much time. I ask her, "On our next tour, could we see some more stations?" Kim looks at me, showing no agitation or discomfort, and says, "Yes, if time allows."

"Remember," I tell her, "I'm going to be back in two weeks."

"No problem," she responds. "I'll pass on your request to Mr. Cha."

"Let's see," I think to myself with skepticism.

*

Evening. A last dinner at which to sum up the tour. The Korean organizers make an effort to create a festive atmosphere. We walk a short distance from our hotel, the Koryo Hotel, cross a road, and we are at Pyongyang Number One Duck, reputed to be an outstanding tourist restaurant – and so it turns out to be. At the center of each table is a hemispheric cast iron grill, under which there are glowing coals. In addition to all the components of the standard tourist meal – rice, stir-fried vegetables, a sort of shakshuka, soup, and so on, there is a central platter on each table holding raw duck meat, and another platter with slices of squid, likewise for grilling. The waitresses help us to grill the pieces of meat and the calamari, and to wrap them in rice sheets with vegetables. Truly a culinary experience. The meal is accompanied by the waitresses singing karaoke, and when the atmosphere warms up a bit, they manage to draw us into a dance. Mr. Tang, president of Koryo, and Mr. Cha, the CEO, honor us with their presence. The meal concludes with some closing words by the president, as well as any members of the group who wish to speak, and myself, of course. The concluding meal can be summed up as an enjoyable and memorable evening – an appropriate ending to a unique, unforgettable, different, and very successful tour.

Among other things that I said, I praised the guides and the driver for their work. In conclusion I quoted the immortal line from *Casablanca*: "This is the beginning of a beautiful friendship." (For a second, I was surprised that my hosts did not respond; a second later, I realized that there was no chance that they would ever have seen the film.) Since I already had two more tours lined up, I asked that this team accompany me on the future trips, too. With a nod, my request was granted.

*

The final day of the first tour I have led in North Korea is over. What an amazing feeling! I have accumulated a wealth of experiences the likes of which I have never encountered on other tours. The tour was conducted with no problems or hitches, and all the participants – without exception – sum it up as one of the most profound experiences of their lives. And these are not tourists who have just taken their first trip and have been exposed for the first time to a different culture. They are all educated, intellectual members of the upper middle class, with extensive life experience, who have taken plenty of tours in the past. I do not allow myself to get carried away in euphoria; the time for that will come. For now, "it's not over until it's over," and I recall that ahead of us is the departure and the "return to planet Earth."

At first, I think about organizing tomorrow, trying to anticipate possible problems. But since it will all be routine activities, my mind wanders and I recall Kim's cry, "Why are such heavy sanctions applied to us? Did we ever attack anyone?"

On the subject of sanctions, I wonder about their purpose and the degree to which they help to achieve it. The Western narrative maintains that the Leaders of North Korea aren't interested in the Korean people, and their top priority is nuclear development, even if this causes the people to suffer. The purpose of sanctions is to pressure the Leaders to desist from the nuclear development program. But if the Leaders don't care about the people, how can sanctions help?

In May 2016, a delegation of three Nobel Prize winners visited North Korea, among them Professor Aaron Ciechanover, who won his award for Chemistry in 2004. The delegation made their trip conditional on it being an apolitical visit, and for this reason, as reported in the media, they did not meet with senior members of government, nor did they visit Mansudae Hill. Upon Ciechanover's return to Israel, some of his comments were publicized. The following are three quotes from the Israeli press:

"You can't use an embargo to play with people's lives. Let them impose an embargo on dangerous substances, but not on antibiotics, bandages, and medications for cancer."

"You can't turn penicillin into a nuclear bomb."

"It seems that the North Koreans long for peace."

Ciechanover's words are thought-provoking and should give us pause. It is interesting, though, to read the responses to his comments, the great majority of which are angry attacks. What they express is not a challenging of his positions, but rather a collection of the lowest form of ad hominem insults, and the insinuation that there is no connection between receiving a Nobel Prize and intelligence. I assume that many of these responders are highly intelligent people – presumably more intelligent than Professor Ciechanover, and hence, although they have never actually been to North Korea, their views on life and reality there can leave no room for questioning.

The encounter with the North Korean reality is a catalyst for thoughts on human nature. A visit to the country exposes one to a way of life in which everything that an ordinary citizen knows is directed and overseen by "Big Brother." The regime wages a fierce, ongoing battle against any possibility of undesirable information finding its way to the populace, and the results of the systematic brainwashing are therefore not surprising. But visiting there, one realizes that we, too, living in a world where there is unlimited access to endless information, undergo a process of consciousness-engineering. We form our views, our opinions, our positions, all based on the flood of information from the media, without stopping to ask ourselves how much of what we know comes from objective sources; to what extent we have turned assumptions into facts, in the absence of information and – most of all – how much of what we know has its source in biased disinformation. It is worth remembering that at least on one issue, all sides in the Korean conflict are in agreement. Everyone has an interest in showing that the leadership of North Korea is "crazy." News items about executions of an official by an anti-aircraft gun, and bizarre punishments, such as execution for falling asleep during a speech by the country's leader, are advantageous for all, regardless of what the facts might be.

The message of the North Korean regime is, "Look: we are crazy, and we have nuclear weapons, so watch out!" The US, Japan, and South Korea, on the other hand, say, "Look at who we're dealing with! Their behavior justifies whatever steps we might take; it certainly justifies our sanctions."

Do sanctions serve to promote change or to obstruct it? This is a real question. Seemingly, the answer is clear: sanctions cause economic distress, causing the population to rise up against the leadership, leading to regime change. Unquestionably, there are countries where this strategy has proved itself, but not in Eastern Asia. The Asian countries most similar to North Korea in terms of the processes that they have undergone since the Second World War are China and Vietnam. Both of these were subjected to isolation and sanctions by the West, especially the US. In both instances, it was internal economic processes that ignited a process that gained momentum as the countries opened up to international commerce and tourism. North Korea wants tourism. It instituted a series of economic reforms and changes recalling similar measures in China in the 1980s and in Vietnam in the late 1990s. Since the three countries share a similar cultural background, it is not unreasonable to posit that similar processes could produce similar results. Do the leaders supporting sanctions really understand the Korean people? To the Koreans, it is clear that everything that is good has come from the country's Leaders, while everything bad is a result of sanctions. Is the North Korean sense that their country has been repeatedly conquered, and that only a powerful military force can prevent this from happening again, completely baseless? Is there no room to even consider entering into commerce with North Korea with the aim of leading it to open up? Perhaps this sort of process would do more to restrain North Korea's nuclear program than could be achieved by pushing it into unbearable economic distress. Perhaps coming to an agreement on non-proliferation of nuclear weapons and technology would be preferable to having North Korea sell its nuclear secrets for the sake of obtaining desperately needed funds. Is it possible that sanctions are obstructing the desired change, rather than advancing it?

*

Our last morning in Korea. After breakfast, we head for the airport. The drive takes a little over twenty minutes, and we use this time to say our goodbyes to the staff, expressing our gratitude with generous gifts (extremely generous in relation to the average Korean income). At the airport, we find Mr. Cha waiting for us. He and the guides accompany us through the brief, efficient check-in. An emotional goodbye at the passport control counter, and we proceed to the departures hall. We stop at the small duty-free store and the cafeteria, and after a few minutes of free time, we board the plane. Take-off is at precisely the scheduled time (unsurprisingly, since this is the only flight taking off this morning). An hour and a half later, we are approaching Beijing.

*

It is exceedingly difficult to describe the feeling that envelops the group, myself included, as we land. We are in Beijing, the experience of a lifetime is behind us; all the fears and concerns have dissipated. The feeling becomes even more intense as we go out to the bus where the Chinese guide awaits us. We are back in the world of billboards, banks, stores, busy roads, wi-fi, instant communications, and multi-channel TV. Once again, I find myself thinking, "But this is China." The same country that we viewed just three decades ago as a reality that didn't make sense, a threat to the world we lived in. Now, as we return from North Korea, it seems like the pinnacle of sanity, representing the comfortable life that we are all used to.

The flight back to Israel is after midnight, and it is now noon. We have twelve hours to spend in Beijing. It seems that I didn't anticipate the level of strain and tension that I would experience. With the successful conclusion of this incredible tour to North Korea, I feel like I have completely run out of energy, and I barely function for these twelve hours. My mind oscillates between the satisfaction of completing this mission, and the missions still ahead of me: while the rest of the group will be returning to Israel, I will be staying on in China, waiting for the next group to arrive. The seven-day interval will be spent visiting Manchuria to weigh up the option of integrating it in the future as an add-on to the tour to North Korea.

CHAPTER 10

Second Tour, Fall 2016
(A Second Fortunate Accident)

B eijing. The group has returned to Israel; I have remained in the hotel. I'm happy to be alone. I feel more exhausted than I can ever remember feeling. All the tension has dissolved, and I am completely drained of energy. I regard my sub-standard functioning in Beijing with a forgiving eye; after all, the mission was North Korea. Guiding the first Israeli group ever in that alternative reality was a huge success! Tomorrow, I am meant to be flying to Manchuria, to look at three possible cities for future visits: Harbin and its Jewish heritage; Changchun, the capital and the largest city of Jilin province (between 1932 and 1945, it was the capital of the Japanese puppet state of Manchukuo); and Shenyang, the center of China's aircraft industry. Strangely enough, Manchuria and my visit there aren't in my thoughts at all. In contrast, when I imagine my next trip to North Korea, I feel a rush of adrenalin and am all at once focused and tensed for the next mission: guiding a second group. Since this group is meant to include some close friends, as well as my friend and colleague Eli Krispin, who will take charge of the group as far as Beijing, I ask them to bring some items that it didn't occur to me to bring on the first trip, which turns out to have been a great pity.

My request of Eli is that he bring some whiskey for the top brass of the Koryo Company, cigarettes for the border officer and the male guides, and cosmetic products for our head guide and for the local guides at the various tourist sites. I ask my wife to pack and send with Eli a jacket and tie, for the day of our outing to Kumsusan, and a kit for Sabbath Eve: kosher wine, skullcaps, candles, the text of the "Kiddush" blessing over the wine, and a booklet of traditional Sabbath songs.

The next five days are spent on a study tour of the three cities in Manchuria. During this time, I manage to detach myself completely from North Korea, and conclude that Manchuria is unquestionably well-suited as an area for a follow-up tour. I cut my planned six-day itinerary short. The fifth day is devoted to Changchun. Following a panoramic tour of the city and a visit to the palace of the last Chinese Emperor, I feel that the upcoming tour to North Korea is overtaking my consciousness, and once again, I am tensed and ready. I return to Beijing for a day of rest and organization.

The new group, led by Eli, arrives during the night. I meet them at breakfast for a day of touring in Beijing. In the evening, back at the hotel, we arrange a time to meet for a walking tour of a nearby pedestrian mall. Finding myself short of time, I hurry out so I won't be late. In my haste, I stumble over a step and crash down, falling on my knee. I ignore the pain, and continue with the program for the evening. Only when I return to my room after the tour do I realize that the injury needs attention. My knee has ballooned to a size that will make it difficult to pull on pants, and it's not looking good. I quickly weigh up the possibilities. Medical care in China might delay our departure for North Korea. Medical care in North Korea is an idea that I rule out categorically. There is no available substitute guide. Left with no choice, I decide to ignore the pain and the swelling, and hope for an improvement. Unsurprisingly, there is no miracle; the injury worsens and accompanies me throughout the trip, but I continue doing what I need to do. (Only upon returning to Israel am I admitted to hospital, and a few days later, I undergo surgery.) During the evening, as I am making my way back to the hotel from the pedestrian mall, I receive a call from Israel. Apparently, Rimon Tours has received an urgent appeal from the Koreans, via Uri Tours, requesting that I bring with me torches, batteries, and whatever else I am able to arrange, since floods in North Korea have caused significant damage, leaving large areas of the country without electricity. I quickly buy as much as I can, with my aching knee urging me to get back to the hotel as soon as possible.

*

In the morning, we head for Beijing Airport. Mrs. Yuan arrives with the visas, and for the third time, I board a plane headed for Pyongyang. A surprise awaits us on board: a group of about twenty Koreans, all of whom have some or other physical handicap. After takeoff, I approach one of the air hostesses and ask her about the group. It turns out that they are the North Korean Paralympic delegation, on their way home from the games in Rio de Janeiro. I turn to some of the Koreans who are sitting nearby me and ask, "Olympics, Rio de Janeiro?" The question is clear, and the answer is a nod; no translation necessary. I ask, "Medals? Gold?" and gesture with my hand, "Who?" In response, they point to one of the passengers. I walk over to him and repeat my question: "Medal? Gold?" my hands drawing a "V" shape down my chest, to suggest a medal. His face beaming, the man nods. I perform a slight bow and show a victory sign, adding "Hedad!" ("congratulations" in Hebrew).[37]

Our excitement at arriving in North Korea is set aside for a moment, making way for simple human emotion and commu-

---

37 North Korea won a total of seven medals at the Paralympics in Rio: two gold, three silver, and two bronze.

nication with the Koreans. Our enthusiasm spreads to include the surrounding passengers, too.

*

We land in Pyongyang. As usual, I am the last of the group to disembark, wearing a shirt that I bought on my previous trip with a picture of the Chollima monument and the inscription, "See you in Pyongyang," so that the policemen can see that it's not my first visit. The group goes through the entry procedures with no problems or delays. I requested that Miss Kim be assigned as our guide, and I am waiting impatiently to meet her. I look around the arrivals hall and see... Miss Li Mi-Soon, the guide from my first trip. Apparently, I fail to hide my surprise, and Miss Li asks, just as Miss Kim did last time, whether I am disappointed. After a fraction of a second, I manage to answer, "No, I'm not disappointed, but I am a little surprised." I add, "On the contrary – I would like to learn about North Korea from as many different guides as possible." This is the truth: at every destination I like to work with a variety of guides; this exposes me to the nuances of each of them. Still, I think to myself, Kim is more easy-going and less stern than Miss Li, but I soon reconcile myself to the situation.

We set off. Miss Li starts off with a concise geographical and demographic overview of Korea, as well as a brief summary of its history. Following this, she requests that we all respect the North Korean rules of etiquette. As agreed between us when we boarded the bus, she now passes me the microphone so I can give the group the Hebrew version – the rules that the previous group had received in written form, and which this group had heard from me when we met in Israel and then again in Beijing on the way to the airport.

We are in Pyongyang. Our first stop is the Arch of Triumph. The end of September is approaching, and the days are growing shorter. It is already after sunset when we arrive at Mansudae Hill, and our visit there finishes when it is already dark. The protocol, as we recall, includes laying wreaths of flowers at the feet of the statues of the Leaders, and respecting our hosts by offering the ceremonial bow, followed by an explanation about the site and various other monuments in the city. The sight of the statues, and the view of the city from the top of the hill, are enchanting, despite all my natural aversion to this personality cult and worship. Since this is already the second time that I have brought a group here, I am able to devote more attention to the participants and the effect that the visit is having on them. I observe them, and all I can see is amazement and exhilaration. Third time at the site, and so far, everyone has responded in the same way.

Our touring for the day over, we return to the now-familiar Koryo Hotel. We settle in our rooms and then meet for dinner at the revolving restaurant on the forty-fifth floor. As on our previous visit, Mr. Tang and Mr. Cha of Koryo Tours join us. Before the meal, I hand our hosts the gifts that we have prepared for them: for Mr. Tang, a bottle of good whiskey; for Mr. Cha, two cartons of American cigarettes; for the guides, some more cigarettes and a set of Dead Sea cosmetics, which I present to them noting with modest pride that the Dead Sea – the lowest point on earth – is in Israel. I enjoy seeing how they respond to the gifts with joy, thanks, and a proper degree of appreciation. There is no ingratiation, no greed, and no fear.[38] They simply smile happily and thank us. Andrea was right. I still have more gifts waiting to be distributed: more cigarettes, quality chocolate, body lotion, key chains with traditional Jewish designs, and more.

---

38 I had encountered reactions of this sort on my visits to Ceauşescu's Romania, where officials and functionaries expected or demanded their "due," and would then hide their gifts with lightning speed.

*

After the meal, we look over the tour itinerary: Mr. Cha, Miss Li, Eli Krispin as an observer, and myself. But before we can start discussing the subject at hand, Mr. Cha turns to me and asks what I have brought with me to help the flood victims. I explain the timing and the circumstances in which I received the request, and promise that in the morning I will give him the little that I have brought (as indeed I do). The attention now moves to the itinerary, and the discussion is conducted mainly between Mr. Cha and myself, with Miss Li listening and, from time to time, nodding in agreement. With two tours behind me already, it is very easy to understand what is important for the local personnel to show to tourists, and what they prefer to conceal. It is clear that that which they do not wish (or are not allowed) to show, you will not get to see. When you consider the tourist's "obligations" in North Korea, you realize that for the most part, what you want correlates with what they want. If you know where you've come to, then it's clear what you've come to see. You've come to see something different, special, the propaganda industry, the personality cult, and the brainwashing – with maybe just a peep at "real life." Thus, the game is going on all the time. The tour guide's aim, then, is to limit as far as possible the visits to sites where you see nothing of any importance, such as a train station in the port city of Wonsan, or an agricultural cooperative. The only thing we could be exposed to there is a page of messages that has been memorized and is recited in Korean by the local guide, translated into boring English by one of the tour guides, and then translated by myself into Hebrew, while the staff tries to follow and make sure that I don't leave out a single detail. What we want is to get to sites with maximum exposure to the life of regular Koreans. Mr. Cha reads out the itinerary, which has undergone some adaptations in response to our requests. Then comes my turn to comment and to make requests. The conversation is conducted in a polite, relaxed, and friendly tone – and, more importantly, with a positive approach. At no point do I begin with requests for changes; rather, I emphasize what cannot, under any circumstances, be omitted. It sounds something like the following: "The itinerary is excellent, but it may possibly be too full. Of course we cannot forgo the Museum of Victory, Mansudae Hill, or the DMZ (here I list the sites that are clearly important to our Korean hosts), but we'd like to see more subway stations, a school, local stores, and so on." Mr. Cha listens, internalizes the message, and with surprising mental agility, proposes adaptations that relegate the sites we are least interested in seeing to the lowest priority and, as usual, promises to check the possibilities that we have requested.

Morning. Mr. Cha informs Miss Li and I of the changes. All of my requests have more or less been fulfilled. Once again – none of the changes I requested was unreasonable. This morning we will be touring around Pyongyang, and after lunch, we will depart the city, heading eastward, and will spend the night at the ski resort near Wonsan. When we leave the hotel, we pass the nearby train plaza and see some cheerleaders. My friend Eli is thrilled and calls to me to stop so he can take photographs. "Eli," I tell him, "It doesn't work like that here. You have to ask permission from Miss Li at the proper time." Eli begs; I reassure him and promise that later on, I will ask permission. Eli is not happy, but reconciles himself to the situation.

Our tour of Pyongyang this morning is fairly standard: Kim Il-Sung Square, the Grand People's Study House, Juche Tower, a tour of the subway, and back to the hotel for lunch and to collect our baggage. During lunch, I approach Miss Li and present our request to stop at the "Cheerleaders' Square." Miss Li answers that this isn't a simple matter, and she will have to forward our request for a photograph stop to the company's CEO, Mr. Cha.

Then we visit the Mansudae production studio and the Mansudae Art Studio, followed by a drive to where we will be spending the night, outside of Pyongyang. The morning tour goes on longer than expected, and we find ourselves pressed for time. Miss Li decides that the visit to the subway will wait until after lunch. Upon reaching the hotel, we start loading up all our baggage. Suddenly Mr. Cha appears. I approach him and present our request to go to the Cheerleaders' Square, whether by bus or by foot. Mr. Cha's expression grows serious and focused. He thinks long and hard before offering a response: "That's a problem; I'll see how we can solve it. I'll let you know later on."

Cheerleaders at the ready

I update Eli: the ball is now in the Koreans' court.

My hope that the subway tour will include more than two stations is unrealistic in view of the time constraints. Even with just the two stations we don't have much time. We are supposed to start at Puhung Station and to finish at Yonggwang, which is close to the hotel. To save time, I suggest to Miss Kim that we reverse the order: if we were to start at Yonggwang, close to the hotel, the bus could drive in that time to Puhung and wait for us there, cutting some of the travel time for the continuation of our tour. Miss Li's answer is brief and unequivocal: "Impossible."

"But why?" I ask. "It wouldn't involve any deviation from our route."

Miss Li simply repeats, "Impossible."

I find this hard to accept. "I don't understand why. It's exactly the same two stops; the only difference is the direction of travel."

This time her response astounds me: "You ask 'why' too much."

I am dumbstruck for a moment, but quickly recover (outwardly, at least) and respond, "Okay, I understand; we'll do it according to the program." And so we do.

The expansive **Mansudae Production Studios** are the brainchild of the previous leader of North Korea, Kim Jong-Il, dating back to the time when he was still the "son of" and heir apparent. Kim Jong-Il was known for his love of films. He is said to have owned an enormous library of films, including many produced in the West. He reportedly showed them to North Korean filmmakers so they could learn and improve their work. The episode of the kidnapping of South Korean actress Choi Eun-Hee in 1978, while she was in Hong Kong, is well known. Shortly thereafter, her former husband, director and producer Shin Sang-Ok, was kidnapped when he rushed to Hong Kong to investigate what had happened to Choi. The North Korean regime maintained that the pair had come to the country of their own free will. They were afforded relatively comfortable conditions and artistic freedom of sorts. At the "recommendation" of Kim Jong-Il they remarried, and for six years, between 1980 and 1986, they made six films that were produced by the Korean leader. He needed this professional team not for propaganda films – there was no shortage of skilled professionals who could turn out countless works in this genre – but rather for quality cinema. The couple gained the trust of the regime, and in 1986 were permitted to participate in a film festival in Vienna, where they seized the opportunity to seek refuge in the US embassy. Kim Jong-Il's love for cinema spurred the development of production studios that are much larger than what one might expect.

The tour of the studios starts with a bow to the statues of the Leaders, located at the entrance to the administrative area. The bowing ceremony is brief and uneventful – or so it seems. Miss Li speaks with our hosts, and then with a troubled expression, she comes over to me and tells me that our hosts overheard one of the participants in the group mutter "Amen" at the end of the bow. Before I can respond, she tells me, "Look, we in the tourist industry understand you tourists and the fact that our customs are foreign to you. But the public, which hardly comes into contact with tourists, has a harder time understanding it. We have great respect for our Leaders, and we're offended by behavior that is disrespectful towards them." Her tone is serious, as is her facial expression, but the conversation is conducted in a friendly, explanatory spirit, not as a rebuke. When Miss Li and I get back to the bus, I convey the essence of our conversation to the group, who are all wondering what the huddled consultation is about. I add my own insights, explaining that in countries whose regime is based, inter alia, on "popular supervision," our guides are under close scrutiny from two directions. Firstly, obviously, there are the authorities, who are intolerant of any behavior that could threaten the basis of their authority. But there are also the ordinary citizens, who are eager to prove their loyalty, and who are likely jealous of the tour guides, who are better paid than regular citizens – even citizens of higher social status. The incident reminds me once again of the need to keep my hand on the wheel at all times. I think of guiding a tour as being comparable to the experience of driving. Guiding some tours is like driving a train: one has to ensure that the train is on the right tracks, and then proceed, accelerating, slowing down, sounding warning bells, and being ready to respond at all times. Other tours are more like driving on a highway. Others still recall driving on a winding mountain road, or in town, where one has to maintain maximum alertness. Leading a tour in North Korea is like driving on a racetrack: one second of inattention, or a delayed or inappropriate response, can result in a crash. On the spot, I come to an agreement with the group that is an extension of the "bowing protocol": when it comes to certain circumstances and events, we will keep our sense of humor, sarcasm, and cynicism under wraps, returning to them only once the incident is over.

The visit to the studios is interesting, indeed, even fun. For about half an hour, we drive in between different "neighborhoods": Koreans, Japanese, Chinese, battlefields, and so on. The fun, at the end, involves hiring items of traditional Korean attire, at a cost of one euro, for souvenir photographs. The members of the group are completely swept up in the enjoyment of the experience – a complete antithesis of the severe atmosphere that preceded the visit to the studios.

*

From the studies we set off westward, heading to Wonsan and the Masikryong ski resort. What I have in mind for the group is to spend this time relaxing, looking out at the view, and listening to quiet, calming music. On our previous trip, Miss Kim allowed me to play whatever music I chose, but to avoid causing antagonism, I was careful to play only instrumental music, with no lyrics. With all of this in mind, I ask Miss Li if I may put on some music for the drive. She answers sharply, "No music." I apologize, showing no surprise. She really is sterner and stricter than Miss Kim, I think to myself. Perhaps it might be defined as "more religious," observing every detail of the rules with greater punctiliousness. The main lesson that I learn from the incident is that there are different interpretations of the North Korean code of behavior. I immediately look for an alternative, asking – and receiving – permission to present a brief history of the country. Miss Li listens while I speak, and I take care to mention the names in English, too, so that she can follow. As always, I take care to introduce each new topic, explaining what I am going to talk about, and then conclude it by summarizing what I have said. Over the course of my talk, which lasts around forty-five minutes, her expression slowly changes; there is less suspicion, and growing wonder. What I do not realize in real time, and discover only afterwards, is that this talk is the turning point in Miss Li's professional attitude towards me. Her sternness and suspicion start to give way to admiration – not only with regard to my familiarity with the material, but also (and more importantly) with regard to the unapologetic presentation.

As we continue driving, the members of the group start opening their bags and taking out snacks. Predictably enough, they share whatever they have, offering their snacks to the staff too. The Koreans are quite happy to try out and enjoy the different treats. The atmosphere in the bus warms up, and Miss Li declares, "Great group," and "Nice people." She sounds surprised, giving me the sense that she was not anticipating the Israeli social dynamic. It seems that the ice is starting to crack.

*

Further on in the journey, we make a restroom stop at a facility on the highway overlooking a small lake. Afterwards, back on the road, a conversation develops and we start asking our guides questions about Korea. Of course, we bypass potential "landmines" and focus on day-to-day life. No one in the group is naïve enough to think that the picture arising from the exchange of questions and answers reflects reality, but I believe it is fairly reliable in conveying the way in which the local people perceive it. If one pays attention, it is clear that the questions that our group is asking also reflect the reality in which we live. At a certain stage, after the group discussion subsides, Miss Li starts asking me about Israel and our way of life. The questions are simple; the answers are less so. On one hand, I want to describe things as they are; on the other hand, I have to avoid saying things in such a way that they might be understood as criticizing life in North Korea. One way or another, the conversation turns to the essence of the establishment and existence of the State of Israel. All of a sudden, in a tone of curiosity that is devoid of any belligerence, Miss Li asks me a question that I am not prepared for: "Why are you allies of the US?" Taken by surprise, I take a deep breath before answering. From our conversations to date, I know that Miss Li knows about the Holocaust. I use this as the introduction to my answer and my description of Israeli reality. As in my conversation with Miss Kim during the previous tour, I give a brief review of Jewish history, starting from the ancient kingdoms of Israel and Judah in the Land of Israel; exile, and the movement of return to the land, prior to and after the establishment of the State. As strange as this sounds, it is easy to explain to a citizen of North Korea the existential situation of the State of Israel in its early years, right after the Holocaust. Miss Li listens, fascinated. I explain that we, too, have an ideology that is somewhat like the North Korean principle of Juche: we have no one to rely on but ourselves. However, part of our might depends on being aided by allies for the sake of our survival. It doesn't stop with the US: I go on to describe the decisive role of the USSR in the UN vote of November 29th, 1947, and in the Czech arms deal, as well as being the first country to grant de jure recognition to the new state, on May 17th, 1948, just three days after Israel's declaration of independence.[39] I tell her about how France was the main supplier of arms to Israel before the bond with the US was strengthened. It seems that for the first time it is not I but rather Miss Li who is surprised. It seems to me that our discussion over this section of the journey has completely changed the relationship between the North Korean Miss Li Mi Soon and myself – a citizen of Israel, an ally of the US.

Toilets at the Children's Palace

---

39 The US was the first country to recognize Israel de facto, on May 14th, but de jure recognition came only later, on January 31st, 1949. Only in March 1949, after two rejections (with the USSR supporting Israel's bid for acceptance) did the Security Council recommend accepting Israel as a member state of the UN, with the support of the USSR, Ukraine, US, France, China, Argentina, Cuba, and Norway, and with Egypt and Britain abstaining.

*

Arriving in Wonsan, we take an abbreviated tour of the Agricultural University. We skip the visit to the railway station and spend just a few minutes at the fishermen's wharf, so that we can spend more time at the children's camp. On the previous tour, there was not a child to be seen, and our group had concluded that the place was simply a deception set up for tourists; clearly, it did not serve as an actual recreational camp. This time around, that conception is shattered the moment we step off the bus and hear the tumult of children playing. As we tour the dormitories, we see children cooking in the kitchen; tidy, clean tables are set and ready for dinner in the dining room, and the entire facility is alive and busy. We meet a group of children, and my friend Eli pulls a small harmonica out of his pocket and starts playing for them. The children stand mesmerized for a few minutes, until a counselor directs them to continue their planned activities. All at once the children leave us and follow the counselor to the yard. It is time for evening roll call. The yard fills with children who find their places with lightning speed and wait for the roll call to begin. We stand on the sidelines, watching; we are also permitted to photograph. I spent twenty-three years in the army and I've seen hundreds of roll calls, and dozens of Independence Day ceremonies with the raising of the flag, but I've never seen a more disciplined, orderly, perfectly executed ceremony. When I watch military parades in North Korea on TV, I remind myself that I saw with my own eyes how training starts at an early age. Only in North Korea!

*

The next morning we are at the Masikryong ski resort. Three cable cars make a slow ascent. The view may not be especially breathtaking, but any time spent in natural surroundings is a relaxing break from the unique reality of North Korea. On our way to Pyongyang, we visit the impressive Ulim Waterfall. Arriving there, Miss Li asks to take a joint photograph with the waterfall in the background. "Of course," I agree, and stand next to her, taking care not to get too close which could make her feel uncomfortable. Miss Li gives me a naughty look and says, "Why aren't you putting your arm around me? Are you afraid of your wife?" Once again, I am taken by surprise, but I have learned not to let it show. With a smile, I put my hand on her shoulder for a friendly photographic memento. A rather banal moment anywhere else, but here in North Korea one has to learn the rules of behavior attentively and quickly.

*

On our way back to Pyongyang, I discuss the remainder of the itinerary. Over and over again, I discover that the "knowledge" that in any case I will have no control over the program is not only inaccurate, but simply wrong. Miss Li tells me that Mr. Cha has notified her that the road to Myohyangsan Reserve is still closed as a result of the collapsed bridge. As compensation, we will visit the International Friendship Museum of gifts to the Leaders in Pyongyang, and Mr. Cha proposes that we spend the night at a spa hotel near Nampo, where we are scheduled to spend tomorrow. He is awaiting my confirmation. I ask Miss Li a few questions about the hotel and discover that she knows very little about it, but she makes another phone call to Mr. Cha and hears some more: most importantly, that every room has its own spa bath, fed by hot spring water. It is a tempting offer, and the decision is up to me. I decide to go along with the suggestion. We then continue discussing the rest of the tour in view of the new circumstances. We need to replan the order of the sites to visit on the remaining days, and I take the opportunity to repeat my request that on one of the remaining mornings, we stop at the train station near our hotel, so we can photograph the cheerleaders. Miss Li once again refers me to Mr. Li, since Mr. Cha will have to give his approval. However, this time she continues: "Tell me your ideas for the itinerary; I like the way you think and present things. I'll discuss it with Mr. Cha." This is only the second group I have led in North Korea, but I have already learned that the Koreans are surprisingly flexible. As time goes on, I will be surprised each time there is official acquiescence to a reasonable request that I have raised.

*

We set off for the **Children's Palace** – a visit that we missed last time, owing to the "fortunate accident." While the children's camp provides a framework for children of a specific age-group during the summer vacation (like youth group camps in Israel), the Children's Palace is also a venue for regular extra-curricular activities. In general, extra-curricular activities take place in the afternoon, within the school program. On my future trips I will visit two schools – one in Pyongyang; the other in a city further to the north – Pyongsong. The extracurricular activities at school include every conceivable realm, from enrichment in school subjects (English, computers, etc.), to sporting activities (soccer, volleyball), to the arts (painting, playing instruments, dance, etc.). However, each of the big cities boasts a central Children's Palace, which caters to especially talented youngsters. The palace of palaces is to be found, of course, in Pyongyang, and the carefully selected, most talented children are sent here. Thursday of each week is an "open day" for visitors – mainly organized groups of Koreans visiting the capital, and, of course, tourists.

The Palace, a grey marble structure of impressive size, is in the eastern part of the city. We are greeted upon arrival by the local guide, Alu – a charming girl of about thirteen. She will lead us for the next hour and a half, in Korean, and one of the guides with our group will translate into English. At the stairs leading to the entrance plaza, there is a huge bronze statue of a chariot carrying a group of children, led by two winged horses – Chollima horses – that are galloping forward. The message is clear: the children are our future, and we, the adults, invest in them so that they will draw the homeland rapidly towards a promising future. Our guide leads us to the entrance hall, whose marble floor is decorated with bright colors. As expected, the cleanliness of the hall, as of the other rooms, is beyond belief. We have just arrived after a long trip, and need to use the toilets. Our young guide leads us to them, and here too, the cleanliness is dazzling. We then start the tour: the mathematics classroom, the painting room, the art room; the children in each wearing spotless uniforms. Unquestionably, this is a show – but not only for tourists. It must be emphasized that throughout all my tours in North Korea, wherever we met children – and we met them often, at schools, camps, and the Children's Palace, the museum, the theater, an early childhood day center, in the street, in Pyongyang and in outlying towns – the children are clean, immaculate, and very disciplined, but still children, giggling and excited to see us. It is clear that at the Children's Palace they are ready for us. It is a show, but not one that is detached from reality. We move on to the wing for stage activities. The children continue their activity while stealing glances at us from time to time. We see a room for music practice, a dance room, and a gymnastics room, for boys and girls aged seven to sixteen. The children, slightly tense, enjoy the attention; the teachers seem concerned mainly with avoiding any mishap. The tour takes about half an hour, and as it goes on, our amazement grows. The climax is the ballet class: the mesmerizing sight of young girls practicing, dancing, being rebuked, correcting themselves, and continuing. The teacher has a good understanding of what the audience will appreciate, and one of the most gifted dancers makes her way to the center of the room and the focus of our attention. Her performance leaves no room for doubt: she is the best dancer in the group. For a second, my mind flashes the thought, "It's not real; we're watching an animated movie."

Now we move on to the impressive theater hall, with about a thousand seats, all occupied. Most of the audience is Korean, along with all two hundred or so tourists who are in Pyongyang at the time. The performance lasts exactly one hour. It is conducted and executed from beginning to end entirely by children, mostly young teens. A children's orchestra, led by a child conductor, accompanies the show. And what an extraordinary spectacle plays itself out over the next sixty minutes: a shower of stage talent, including instrumental performance, dance, song, acrobatics, and humorous interludes – all reflecting taste and quality way beyond the age of the participants – altogether, a special and inspiring evening. It was a show (with the vast majority of the audience made up of local people), but what a show! Only in North Korea!

Afterwards, we are back on the bus, heading west of Pyongyang, to the spa hotel. Mr. Cha joins us for the experience. As noted, intercity trips in North Korea are extremely uncomfortable, to put it mildly. The main roads are very wide, but in bad condition; the driver navigates in between the potholes, and the drive is one long obstacle course. As for the side roads, their condition causes you to look back fondly at the bumpy main roads. If there is any compensation for the tribulations of the trip, it is the sights that one sees on the way: not the beautiful scenery, but rather the "reality show" of life in North Korea. We are driving at night, on a side road, in a rural area. While even in Pyongyang it is clear that night lighting is not one of the city's strong points, outside of the city there is complete darkness. The journey turns into a type of torture. The driver notices obstacles in the road only at the last second, and jerks the steering wheel to avoid them – not always in time. Here and there, he almost runs over people riding bikes; how the villagers find their way in the dark is a mystery. The curious traveler, seeking an anthropological experience, is compensated with the rather disconcerting illustration of an alternative reality. One has the sense that the journey is taking hours and hours in the middle of the night, while in fact it is only one hour, in the evening, immediately after nightfall. I sit at the front of the bus, feeling as though I am watching a thriller where some new bone-chilling surprise awaits us at every turn. To keep calm, I keep reminding myself that a hot bath of mineral water awaits us at the end of this terrifying drive.

We reach the hotel, and the surrealistic movie isn't over yet. Out of the dark, some weak lights shine here and there. A somewhat more promising light emanates from the main building around which the place is built. The main building houses a reception desk, a lobby, a dining hall, and activity rooms; surrounding it are huts housing the guest rooms. The hotel looks nothing like what I imagined. It is "interesting," in the Chinese sense of the word.[40] At this stage, the hotel is a given; there is no choice but to deal with it. We distribute the room keys to the tourists and invite them to dinner, which will take place in the next few minutes. I do not head for my room, but rather remain behind for a chat with Mr. Cha and Miss Li. We have a look at the menu: unsurprisingly, it offers no culinary surprises. Mr. Cha turns to me and tells me that he has an important matter to discuss. His body language projects discomfort, even apology. I naively assume that he wants to explain his recommenda-

---

40 "May you have an interesting life" is a traditional Chinese curse. "Boring" is a blessing.

tion that we come to this hotel, but in North Korea, it turns out, there is no end to the surprises. The topic of conversation is the damage caused by the floods. With surprising openness, he tells me about the disaster that has befallen parts of the population, with food shortages and even hunger. For a moment, I am silent; when I find my voice, I ask him, "How can I help?" After all, this isn't an intimate heart-to-heart talk; it is meant to lead to some practical result. Mr. Cha goes on to "wonder" whether we might help with a contribution of some kind – say, a truckload of grain; he mentions that this would cost seven hundred and fifty euros. I am dumbstruck. Fortunately, I have learned to conceal my feelings in North Korea. Still, before responding, I think to myself: This can't be true! This isn't really happening! I'm traveling in a country that's a nuclear power! They're asking us for a contribution of seven hundred and fifty euros in order to save citizens from hunger?! Is this real, or a scene from some parody? I am truly at a loss; I find myself in a situation that I would never have imagined could be possible. I seize upon the technique that Mr. Cha uses in response to my requests, and tell him, "I'll see what can be done." After a pause of a few seconds, I add, "I'll consult with the directors of the company in Israel, and with the group; I believe we'll be able to help."

Dinner is waiting for the group, and as the first few participants drift in, I ask what they think of the rooms. In response, I receive indulgent smiles and mutterings along the lines of, "When you see, you'll understand." Indeed, when the rest of the group arrives, I understand better. "There's no choice," I tell them – and myself; "It's just one night. We'll get through it." I won't describe the dinner in too much detail; suffice it to say that it justifies our impression of the hotel. In short, what you see is what you get. Towards the end of the meal, after reviewing tomorrow's itinerary with the group, I apologize and explain that my agreement to the change was given with the understanding that this would be a unique experience, and that locals would regard a sleepover at this hotel as a "treat." With some trepidation, I now make my way to my room. Opening the door, I realize that the picture I had imagined in my mind was overly optimistic. The room is large, cold, and not clean. The bathroom is even less clean, and there is no shower, only a tap for filling the tub, leaving that as the only option for washing. I choose not to lie in bath water, but rather have the water splash onto me. I wash off the soap the same way. The warmth of the water is the only pleasurable part of this experience. Before getting into bed I call Chaim and tell him about my conversation with Mr. Cha.

"So what do you suggest?" he asks me.

I tell him, "We'll make a donation, but on condition that we receive official, written confirmation that Israelis helped the citizens of North Korea in their time of need."

"We'll donate five hundred euros," Chaim declares.

"Great," I tell him, mentally committing that I'll make up the balance by contributing myself, along with whoever of the group is interested.

My mind is filled with the startling events of the day: the Children's Palace; the requested donation; the hotel. It's a reality of such contrasts: a nuclear power in need of a truckload of grain! This is the ideology of Songun in action: preference for the army over the revolution (or, to put it differently, the welfare of the citizens). Only in North Korea. An alternative reality.

I sleep restlessly. In the morning, I arrive at breakfast prepared and ready to face an angry group. A sizeable number of participants are my personal friends, and they have in the meantime forged connections with the other members, who I did not know before, forming a unified, lively group with a positive dynamic. They see my long face and ask what is wrong. When I express my disappointment with the hotel conditions, the general response is one of surprise and laughter. "What's the big deal? It was just one night, and it gave us a glimpse of a different Korea."

If we're already on the subject of a "different Korea," we are about to receive a generous helping of it. As the bus starts off in the direction of Nampo, we find ourselves driving on winding roads between fields, villages, and villagers. The sights are similar to those I described during the "fortunate accident." Farmers in faded work clothes are cultivating their fields using manual tools, and the houses and roads are derelict. This is unquestionably a Third World country. For me, this is a second "fortunate accident," but for the group it is a first and sole experience of a Korea that I'm not sure that we are supposed to see. (With other groups in the future I request a drive on one of these roads, and the response is invariably, "We'll see; we'll check." Eventually I understand that it's not going to happen.) After we rejoin the main road to Nampo, I address the group and tell them about my conversation last night with Mr. Cha. I connect his request with the hotel and the fascinating reality that we are discovering day by day. I tell them about the company's donation, and add fifty euro of my own, committing to make up whatever sum is still needed after the group's participation. Eli volunteers to collect the contributions. Within less than five minutes, the entire sum has been raised. Israeli tourists, together with Tarbutu/Rimon Tours, are contributing a truckload of maize to North Korea!

Nampo

Nampo is a port city located 55km south-east of Pyongyang. With some 750,000 inhabitants, it is the third most populous city in North Korea. Nampo is a major industrial center in diverse areas including cars, ships, sea salt, fish preserves, and more. Statues of the two former leaders are stationed at the entrance to the city. The architecture is in unimaginative Communist style, and the general atmosphere is rather depressing. Since there are no tourist attractions, we pass by without stopping. One eye-catching feature of the city is the solar panels installed outside the windows of the houses, producing enough electricity to provide lighting at night.

We continue towards the **Western Sea Barrier**, located 15 kilometers south-west of Nampo, on the delta of the Taedong River. It is a most impressive engineering feat; the pride of North Korean civil engineering. Pictures of the barrier are sometimes used as the background for TV news broadcasts. Built by the army over five years, from 1981 to 1986, it stops the seepage of salty sea water into the Taedong River, and creates a giant lake that serves as a source of water for agriculture and for more than a quarter of the country's population, including the city of Pyongyang. The barrier, eight kilometers long, comprises thirty-six sluices and three lock chambers, allowing for the passage of ships of up to 50,000 tons into the port. According to estimates, the construction project cost a total of some four billion dollars.

We pass by Nampo, driving along the road that crosses the barrier, and arrive at the visitors' center at the top of the hill which, prior to the construction of the dam, was an island. Our visit starts in the lecture room, which features a model of the barrier. A ten-minute film presents the impressive feat, emphasizing the devotion of the workers who completed the project before the deadline, in true Chollima spirit, to please the beloved leader, Chairman Kim Jong-Il. Then we go up to the roof of the visitors center, which looks out on the photogenic scene of the dam and the lock gates which allow passage for ships. While we stand there, taking photographs, Miss Li asks me what I think of the place. I express my genuine admiration. Then she asks whether Israel has similar feats to boast of. I tell her that half of Israel is desert. Moreover, I tell her, the Israeli ethos has elements that are similar to Juche. I go on to describe the National Water Carrier project which is similar to the Western Sea Barrier insofar as it represents a harnessing of mighty natural phenomena to serve existential needs. I fail to notice that the moment I mention "Juche," I lose Miss Li. She stops listening to what I am saying, convinced that I am still waxing enthusiastic about North Korea. She calls out proudly to the local guide (who is wearing a traditional Korean dress, causing tourists to photograph themselves with her) and says, "Do you hear what he's saying about us and about Juche philosophy?!" and then asks me to repeat what I said. Having no choice, and out of politeness, I repeat what I was saying, this time placing more emphasis on the North Korean aspect and less on the Israeli story. Thus I gain the status of a Friend of the People. Truly, only in North Korea.

From the Western Sea Barrier, we make our way back to Pyongyang. On the way, and as a continuation of the demonstration of technological prowess, we are taken to a factory that bottles mineral water. Of course, we are treated to explanations and praises of the Leader who thought up the idea of the factory. The only truly fascinating aspect of the visit is the thought that a Western tourist would be impressed. But again, it is the small things that illuminate the gap between the North Korean reality and the world we live in. On future tours, this attraction will not be included on the itinerary.

We arrive back in Pyongyang slightly earlier than scheduled. At the request of the group, we pay a return visit to the statues on Mansudae Hill. We had stopped there on the first day of the tour, in the evening. The power of that first impression, in the dark, had left the group wanting to go back, and the extra time available opens a window of opportunity. We conduct the visit in accordance with all the rules, and when we return to the bus, members of the group draw my attention to the fact that Miss Li is having what looks – even from a distance – like a rather heated exchange with the local guide. I walk over to them to try to find out what is going on, and Miss Li tells me that one of the group participants has violated the rules of the holy site. I ask her for more details, and am told that someone stepped off the path and trod on the lawn, seeking to pick a flower. I express shock and anger, and in a tone that even someone who does not speak the language can understand, I offer Miss Li a heartfelt apology for offending the sensibilities of the North Korean people, and promise that this incident will not be repeated. The site guide is appeased and softens her stance slightly, and we head for the bus. As we climb aboard, I discover that the guilty party is none other than my good friend Nissan, a farmer who lives on a moshav near Ashkelon. Since we know each other well, I ask him for an explanation, and he tells me: "When we got off the bus, I saw a flower alongside the path that is evidently suffering the effects of some sort of pest. I was curious to know what pest it was, and perhaps advise the site personnel as to how to deal with the problem. I did indeed take one step off the path; I bent down to have a better look at the flower – of course it never entered my mind to pick it – and then suddenly the site guide reacted to my 'crime.'" Fortunately, Mr. Li had been standing nearby Nissan when all this happened, and confirmed every detail of the story. I turn to Miss Li, whose face shows the tension she is feeling, and relay the story along with the explanation, backed up by Mr. Li. She doesn't answer, but now she looks angry. Without saying a word, she gets off the bus and walks back to the site guide. Their exchange is brief: this time it is Miss Li who talks loudly and then, without waiting for a response, turns her back and returns to the bus. After a brief pause, she tells me, "You know, most citizens of North Korea don't come into contact with tourists, and so they don't always understand them. They evaluate the behavior of tourists in relation to their own norms, and suspect and accuse us guides for every deviation from the rules of etiquette. They don't understand that tourists are used to different rules." In effect, Miss Li has apologized, without actually saying so. She looks angry and frustrated. I ask her whether the incident is going to cause her problems. From her response – "No, I'm not worried at all" – along with other indications, I understand that her status is more secure than that of the local guide. She also mutters something like, "That idiot; she always has something to complain about; it's not the first time." To ease some of the tension I respond with a smile and an expression I learned from my parents, originally in Yiddish, to the effect that "If you're an idiot, it's that way for a long time." She glances at me, unable to hide a smile.

Once again, I am reminded that leading a tour in North Korea is like driving a racing car: one has to be alert at all times, with both hands on the wheel, otherwise you might find yourself crashing.

We are now back on track with the planned itinerary, and our next stop is an opera or musical performance meant for a local audience. All cultural events take place in the early evening. The performance starts at five, followed by dinner, and at that point, nightlife comes to an end. By around nine everyone is back at home, and tourists – back at their hotels, where at least they can still order a drink at the bar.

The theater hall is nice, but not at all impressive. We are shown to our seats, somewhere around the tenth row, in the middle section. The theater, with seating for about a thousand people, fills up quickly and quietly. I watch as people come in – all locals, except for the thirty of us Israeli tourists. The show starts exactly on time. It is a musical, with the plot centering around the construction of a hydroelectric power plant. The laborers work long hours, their living conditions are minimal, and the weather is brutal, but they accede to the call of the Chairman (the previous leader of North Korea) and work tirelessly all day. At night they dance, rejoicing over their contribution to the homeland. There are choral bits in Red Army style, solo songs, dances, and movement. The singing and dancing are of Broadway quality. The props are conservative: pictures of the construction project in its stages of construction are projected onto a cinema screen. The plot reaches its climax when the workers receive the terrible news that Chairman Kim Jong-Il has passed away. The entire audience reacts, along with the actors, with expressions of pain and sorrow, but the plot continues. The workers, recovering from the shock, decide to accelerate the pace of their work and thereby fulfill the will of the late Leader. Their efforts pay off, and the project is indeed completed before the scheduled date. Here the drama reaches a new climax that none of us Israelis could have expected: the inauguration of the plant. The event is attended by the present leader, Marshal Kim Jong-Un, son of Chairman Kim Jong-Il (see box). A giant photograph of him is projected on the screen in the background, and the response is spine-chilling: the entire audience rises to its feet, and with cheers and enthusiastic, lengthy applause, accompanied with chants of support, they welcome the Leader whose likeness is now showing on the screen. We are sitting in the middle of the audience, surrounded on all sides by Koreans who are standing and applauding. Without any rational control over our actions, we too rise to our feet and join the applause. Of course, this is the grand finale of the show. Eventually the audience – including ourselves – starts making its way out. We all look at them, and then at each other. We are all in shock, gazing in confusion and bewilderment, as if to say, "What was that? Never seen anything like it!" I have no doubt that like myself, the others too are filled with wonderment, along with some embarrassment in light of the ease with which one gets caught up in the personality cult.

Only in North Korea!

Opera in Pyongyang. A leader on a different scale...

Supreme Leader Marshal Kim Jong-Un
(From the official North Korean tourist guidebook,
Panorama of Korea, 2017)

The cause of Juche, pioneered and led by President Kim Il Sung and General Kim Jong Il, are being carried forward by Supreme Leader Kim Jong Un.

Kim Jong Un is possessed of unbounded loyalty to the revolutionary cause of Juche, outstanding leadership ability, matchless courage and pluck, and popular traits. Thanks to his ennobling loyalty and moral obligation, a new phase was opened up in implementing the cause of immortalizing the Leader. Accordingly, the beaming image of General Kim Jong Il has been implanted in the minds of the people and the sacred history of his revolutionary activities continues without let-up. Through his energetic ideological and theoretical activities, Kim Jong Un formulated the great Leaders' revolutionary ideology as Kimilsungism-Kimjongilism, and he is leading the Korean people to march straight ahead along the road of independence, the road of Songun, and the road of socialism. A perfect statesman of the present era, he accompanied General Kim Jong II on the road of the Sengun-based leadership, working with devotion for the development of the Party, the country, and the army. Upon being appointed as Supreme Commander of the Korean People's Army, he has inspected one army unit after another, which is giving a powerful impetus to the enhancement of the country's defense capability and the victorious advance of the cause of socialism. In March 2013, when the situation on the Korean peninsula was growing acute owing to the uninterrupted war moves by the US, a plenary meeting of the Central Committee of the Workers' Party of Korea was held. At this meeting, he advanced a new strategic line of simultaneously conducting economic construction and building up the nuclear forces. In accordance with this line, he led the cause of building the country's nuclear forces to victory, thus increasing the strength of socialist Korea to the highest level and developing the country into the Juche-oriented nuclear power. By adhering to the principle of self-reliance and self-development, the Korean people have built monumental edifices for their well-being and raised fierce flames of the industrial revolution in the new century, pushing back the frontiers of science and technology. They have achieved one eye-opening success after another in the fields of science, education, literature and the arts, and sports, bringing about an epochal turn in building a knowledge-based economy and a civilized socialist power. Cherishing the lifelong motto of the great Leaders who believed in people as in heaven, Kim Jong Un administers politics of prioritizing the interests of the people and respecting and loving them in order to translate their beautiful dreams and ideals into reality. He shows paternal affection for and trust in the people to rally the service personnel and other people firmly around the Party. The traditional singlehearted unity of the country has been consolidated on the basis of his ennobling view of comrades and comrades-in-arms. All the people share the same destiny with their leader, advancing the revolution arm in arm and shoulder to shoulder with him. Thanks to his unshakeable determination to reunify the country, the national reunification movement is making rapid progress.

He has thwarted the imperialists' war moves and rendered an outstanding contribution to ensuring global peace and stability and promoting the cause of independence for mankind, thereby winning international recognition as the great guardian of justice. In reflection of the people's unanimous will and desire, he was elected Chairman of the Workers' Party of Korea and Chairman of the State Affairs Commission of the DPRK, and he was awarded the title of Marshal of the DPRK.

Kim Jong-Un
(As per Western sources)

Kim Jong-Un was born on January 8th, 1984, evidently the youngest child of Kim Jong-Il, with his fourth and last wife.

He studied at an elite private school in Switzerland, and continued his academic education with military studies at the Kim Il-Sung University in Pyongyang.

Kim Jong-Un was named Supreme Leader of North Korea on December 19th, 2011, two days after the death of his father. Upon his appointment he declared that he would not take the title "Chairman," since it belonged to his father, Kim Jong-Il, for all eternity.

Kim Jong-Un has accelerated the country's nuclear and missile programs to the point of war capability. He has held meetings with the President of South Korea (Panmunjom Declaration) and also held historical meetings with former US President Donald Trump.

Leadership

He is regarded by the people as a worthy successor of a glorious dynasty and as an energetic young leader who is leading the country at record speed towards progress.

He continues to accelerate the nuclear armament program.

Under his rule, the level of sanctions against North Korea have reached an all-time high.

He is spearheading economic reforms.

He is advancing unprecedented construction in Pyongyang and at potential tourist sites.

He is the first leader of the country to present his wife to the public.

Still blown away by the weird and foreign cult worship exposed in all its intensity, we make our way to dinner. It is Friday, the Sabbath Eve. During our drive this afternoon I told Miss Li about the status of the Sabbath (Shabbat) in Jewish culture, and requested her approval to hold a "Kabbalat Shabbat" ("welcoming the Sabbath") ceremony. Her response, like that of Miss Kim on the previous trip, is immediate, brief, and simple: "We respect your customs; we'll be glad to facilitate the observance of the ceremony."

I have brought along my "Kiddush kit," which includes a bottle of kosher wine, candles, the text of the Kiddush recital, a booklet of songs traditionally sung at the Shabbat meal, and skullcaps for the men. Most of the tour participants have completely forgotten that today is Friday, and never imagined that here, in North Korea, they would find themselves participating in a Kabbalat Shabbat ceremony with a Kiddush. I ask Miss Li to delay the waitresses' entrance to serve the meal. Once everyone is seated, my friend Nissan makes the necessary preparations and as agreed between us, starts reciting the Kiddush. We are not alone in the restaurant; a large number of Koreans are in the middle of their meal. Some pay no attention to the foreign ceremony going on, but many others fall silent and watch with curiosity. A ripple of emotion passes through the group – certainly through me – although most of us do not regard ourselves as religious Jews. The staff follow each stage with fascination. When we reach the Shabbat songs, their astonishment grows. Later on, they bombard me with questions, and I happily respond and explain. I believe that this was a unique event – the first time that a Kiddush was ever recited in North Korea. An extraordinary and emotional night to remember.

*

Saturday morning. Mr. Cha is waiting for us at the hotel with some news. I approach him and somewhat cheekily announce, "I have some news, too." I hand over the donation of seven hundred and fifty euros, reminding him that he promised to issue Rimon Tours with a certificate of acknowledgment. His face lights up. With no connection to the donation, his news concerns our request to make a stop at the railway square to photograph the cheerleaders. Since coming to the square with cameras is likely to offend the cheerleaders, and since the bus is not permitted to stop at the square, he proposes a simple solution: we will pass by the square on the bus, very slowly, and photograph them through the windows. Indeed, a pragmatic solution – only in North Korea. And that is in fact what we do. Afterwards we head southward, towards the DMZ. This is our fourth drive out of Pyongyang. A positive, cheerful atmosphere develops on the bus. Our tourists share the snacks they have brought with the staff. Had anyone told me a month ago that this is what a group traveling on a bus in North Korea would look like, I would have waved in dismissal and ended the conversation. Along with an overview of the processes leading to the division of Korea and to the Korean War, there is time for discussions between members of the staff and the tourists. The relaxed atmosphere concerns me slightly, in light of the incident with the flower and the "amen" after the bow, and so, while encouraging the positive dynamic, I take pains to remind myself and the group that after all, this is still North Korea.

We are visiting the DMZ, and once again I meet Captain Wang Ryong-Chu. We shake hands and exchange smiles. As we walk towards the observation post looking out over South Korea, I am in conversation with some members of the group, and I compare the border that we are now visiting to the border between India and Pakistan, close to the city of Amritsar. Every evening a flag-folding ceremony is held there on both sides of the border – a rather peculiar demonstration of patriotism involving the soldiers of two nuclear powers. There are similarities between the two borders, both of which cut nations in half: both are the products of insensitive Western intervention, with the local populations suffering the consequences. Miss Li is listening to the conversation. Picking up the name "Pakistan," she turns to Captain Wang, asking what Pakistan has to do with North Korea. I listen to their conversation and manage to catch the words "India," "Pakistan," and "colonialism," which tells me that Wang understands the parallel that I have drawn. At this point I intervene and clarify what my subject was. I speak with them in English, and Wang, who seems not to speak English, just listens and nods slightly. I turn to him and say, "You understand English." Caught defenseless, with an embarrassed smile, he answers (in English), "Just a little." When we return to the bus, I give him a carton of American cigarettes. Once again, as on the previous occasions when I distributed gifts, he accepts it in a most dignified manner.

After the visit to the DMZ, we pay a visit to Kaesong, including a stop at the Museum of the Koryo Dynasty, located in the

Confucian temple. As we arrive, we encounter a bride and groom and their families, who have come to take photographs in honor of the occasion. We watch as they pose, and when we ask, with hand gestures and with the help of our guides, to join in, we are welcomed with enthusiasm. The situation quickly turns into a mutual photography session. A few moments later, we come across another two bridal couples, and the scene repeats itself. It turns out that it is actually possible to forge a connection with the locals. While language and other practical difficulties preclude conversation, the Koreans don't avoid making eye contact with foreigners. It seems that Saturday is a popular day for weddings in North Korea, since Sunday is a day off work and allows some time for rest and recuperation.

*

There are two days left before our tour comes to an end, and we spend the time visiting different sites in Pyongyang, since up until this point, we have spent only a little more than two half-days in the capital. Sunday morning is devoted to the "holy of holies," the Kumsusan Palace of the Sun, the mausoleum housing the remains of the previous leaders of North Korea. Of course, we all dress up for the occasion. Miss Li is wearing a beautiful floral dress; I am wearing a jacket and a tie. This is one of those moments where the saying, "Clothes make the man" takes on real significance. I am not dressed in designer clothing, but what I am wearing is a sharp contrast to regular tourist garb. The tourists in the group perhaps find it amusing, but the reaction of the guides and local staff is completely different: their eyes express esteem and appreciation. Seeing their looks of admiration, I tell them, "We are, after all, visiting a place that is considered holy, and I thought it would be appropriate to dress the same way you do." If I were a businessman, such high returns on such a small investment would no doubt make me very wealthy... The visit goes off without a hitch, and once again leaves the group of tourists thrilled and elated.

Children at the Sci-Tech interactive science museum

Sci-Tech Museum

The atom-shaped museum is located on Ssuk Island which is located in the Taedong River. It was opened in 2015 and serves as an interactive science museum for children. The museum is open for activities in the afternoons, and children learn about science mostly through games, but not only. As usual, at the entrance, we are welcomed by a guide who seats us at the center of the building under a huge glass dome. In the background is a life-size model of a missile. Two of the seats are marked with special plaques; these are not to be sat upon. These seats will be used by the Leader, Marshal Kim Jong-Un, when he comes to visit the museum. The guide starts off, of course, with praise for the Leader who is leading the homeland to a dazzling future, with a focus on science and the younger generation. The complex is unquestionably impressive. The second floor houses a hall with computer terminals for children to learn and practice on, as well as study rooms and more. We are sitting on the entrance floor. This floor houses an amusement park for younger children, introducing them to laws of physics through play. The hall is full of children, and my friend Eli Krispin, who somehow attracts children wherever he finds himself, goes into action. With no shared language, he somehow creates contact with the children, and they happily respond to him. Our guides watch, smile, and allow the joyful interaction to continue. Needless to say, the entire place – including the children themselves – is spotless and completely tidy.

Our concluding dinner, as for our previous trip, is held at the Pyulmori restaurant. We enjoy a festive grill accompanied by singing, with the participation of Mr. Tang and Mr. Cha. Mr. Tang gives his farewell address, during which he hands me an official certificate of the Koryo North Korean Tourist Company. The certificate thanks the Rimon Israeli tourist company and its tourists for contributing a truckload of maize, worth seven hundred and fifty euros, as aid to the Koreans affected by the floods. Truly – only in North Korea!

The mood is amazing; there is a feeling of a unique life experience – not in the entertainment sense, but rather in the sense of experiencing something that is different. Different from anything we have encountered anywhere else up until now; a completely different reality from what we imagined, and even more different from what we were told. In short: an encounter with the most fascinating reality anywhere on earth.

*

Our last morning. A drive to the airport, goodbye to the staff, a short flight, and we are in Beijing. We have returned to familiar reality, and like the previous times, once again, despite the mind-blowing experience, we experience a letdown and a sense of emptiness. From my point of view, there are two significant differences between now and the same stage after my previous tours: firstly, this time I am mentally ready for the anticlimax, the feeling of "the end," and secondly, there is my injured knee, which has turned the color of an eggplant and has swollen to the size of a large grapefruit. The pain, which had been suppressed and ignored as I focused on the tasks at hand, makes itself apparent now that the tension has dissipated. A day's touring in Beijing goes by without any special incidents. One more flight and we are home. I have survived North Korea for the third time.

Letter of Confirmation

Pyongyang Koryo International Travel Company confirms that the Israel Rimon Tours and its tourists who travel in DPRK from 20th to 27th of September, 2016, donated 4 tons of maize (750 Euros) and 14 electric torches to give assistance to reconstruct the flood-hit northern areas of North Hamgyong Province, DPRK.

Pyongyang Koryo International Travel Company, Pyongyang, Democratic People's Republic of Korea September 25th, 2016

Certificate confirming donation of 4 tons of grain and ...
14 electric torches.

CHAPTER 11

October 2016 – Third Group

I am finally home, after two tours to North Korea, from September 4th to 28th, with a week in the middle spent alone in Manchuria. I am home, bursting with experiences, impressions, insights, and – above all – a sense of satisfaction that prevails over the tribulations of the flight and the condition of my knee. I show my knee to my wife: "Beautiful, isn't it?"

She looks worried and announces, "We're going right now to the ER."

With idiotic heroism I tell her, "It's waited ten days; it can wait another day. I've just landed from a long and tiring flight; I'm going to rest."

My objections are to no avail; I find myself at Ichilov Hospital (or, by its official name – the Tel Aviv Sourasky Medical Center). The initial treatment that I receive merely postpones the inevitable. On Monday, October 3rd, I undergo surgery on my knee. My next tour is scheduled for October 16th. It doesn't seem that I'm going to be fit to lead a tour by that date.

Since there is no choice, a substitute guide is recruited. Of course, he has never been to North Korea. We are all unhappy with the situation. While the local guides in North Korea know their job, and the plan is that I will provide close instruction to the substitute guide, we're still talking about a unique destination, where any misstep can entail serious problems for the future. I spend Rosh Hashana, the Jewish New Year, in hospital,

271

but my thoughts are in Korea. The more I think about all the points that I need to cover with the substitute guide, the more my dissatisfaction grows. One of the phone conversations that I have with Chaim, director of Tarbutu Tours, takes place in my wife's presence. She listens, and afterwards says to me, "You feel that you have to lead this tour, right?"

I contemplate her question in silence, remembering a conversation I had with one of the participants in the second tour. She had asked me who was going to be leading the next tour. "I will," I told her.

"I'm glad," she said. "I'm glad for the participants."

I told her, "Our company has a number of excellent guides who could lead the group."

"I'm sure that's true," she answered; "I'm not talking about the actual tour guiding. I see how you conduct yourself with the Koreans. It's a delicate and fragile relationship that still needs to be built up and consolidated before someone else can continue the job."

Recalling this, I tell my wife, "I feel like I'm teaching a toddler to walk, and suddenly, before he's able to stand firmly on his own two legs, I'm abandoning him." After all, at this stage, there is no other Israeli guide who has led a tour in North Korea, and no tour anywhere else can compare with the challenge. I've had the good fortune to be able to learn and gain experience; I've already made my mistakes and learned from them. "Yes," I finally agree, "I think I need to lead the upcoming tour, too."

After some consultation, the surgeon agrees for me to lead the tour, subject to some reasonable conditions. One is that I will need a checkup by October 25th at the latest. What this means is that I have to be back in Israel the day before the end of the tour. Over the phone with Chaim, it is agreed that I will lead the tour. Ami, the substitute guide, will join the tour as an apprentice. On the last day, he will fill in for me.

As usual, before every tour, I have to review the service supplier's itinerary and compare it with the program that was advertised to the group. A quick check turns up no special problems, except for one interesting point: during the last tour, I asked if we could visit Myohyang. There were two reasons for my request: firstly, the area comprises a group of sites that are both enjoyable and important to visit, especially the Friendship Museum, with its display of gifts accumulated by the Leaders. The other, less obvious reason is that I want to repeat our drive on the road that is not meant for tourists, cutting through the heart of the country. The visit appears on the itinerary, but I am left with the question of whether the bridge has been repaired, or whether the officials have decided to permit a drive through the villages.

*

We set off. Beijing-Pyongyang, passport control – all routine already for me. Miss Kim is our guide, for a second time. Alongside her, as usual, are the two apprentice guides. Mr. Cha is in charge of the local staff. I receive a welcome that is warm and appreciative, especially in view of the fact that despite my knee injury – of which the local staff are well aware – I am back with a third group. Eighty tourists within a month and a half is rather unusual in North Korea, and the attitude of the local personnel reflects this. It is October 18th, it's colder, and the days are significantly shorter. Near the bus the usual photographer and driver are waiting for us. When we emerge from the airport, the sun is already starting to set. Our guide, Miss Kim, starts off by introducing the staff members and goes on to a very concise overview of the geography and demography of Korea. I ask her to present at least the rules of etiquette, but Miss Kim thinks otherwise: "You know the rules well already, and you've already told them

273

everything." I repeat my request, telling her gently, "That may be, but I would like them to hear the rules from you." Kim gives a forgiving smile and of course accedes to my request, reviewing the code of behavior that is expected of us, the tourists.

The program for the day of arrival is in no way influenced by the short winter days. We visit the Arch of Triumph. Then Mansudae. No surprises. Mansu Hill and the worship there, as on our previous visits, is astonishing. No one is left untouched; every one of the participants is moved by the experience, which is so extraordinary for someone who has grown up in the West.

The festive opening dinner is held on the forty-fifth floor of the hotel, and the staff and I spend this time having a work meeting and looking over the itinerary. The main question that interests me is the route for the drive to the Myohyang mountains: has the bridge been repaired, such that we will drive on the main road, or will we be taking the rural route? I am told that the bridge has not been repaired, and therefore (to my great joy) the only possible route is the winding road among the villages. Later on, I will discover that I rejoiced too soon.

*

In general, the tour routes in Pyongyang have already become routine to me. The exception is our visit this time to the subway station. As usual, we are meant to start at Puhung Station and travel to the next station – Yonggwang. On the way to Puhung, I remind Miss Kim of her promise that if time allows, we will be able to visit more than just the two famous stations. Miss Kim glances at her watch and says, "No problem. How many stations would you like to see?" I am holding a map of the subway, which I purchased on my previous visit; a tourist map with pictures of the stations. I examine today's itinerary and after some discussion, we decide that in order to avoid wasting time, we will travel through a total of six stations, stopping at three of them: the usual two, obviously, and then at the sixth station, Kaeson (Victory), we will emerge for a visit to the Arch of Triumph. "Fine," says Miss Kim. This becomes the fixed program for all the future tours. On this trip, at each station, I hop off the train (alone, without the group, since we have agreed that we will not visit the intermediate stations as a group) to have a quick glance around. The stations are nice, and clean, but indeed not worthy of a visit. The first, second, and last stations certainly do justify a stop, owing to their decorative appearance and the message that they convey to the masses of passengers. The comparison of the embellishments of the subway stations to churches, as pointed out to me by the local guide who showed me around Moscow, is valid here, too.

Pyongyang subway, Victory Station. Seventeen stations;
one can visit all of them!

As we finish our tour of Victory Station and emerge towards the Arch of Triumph, I am filled with a sense of deep satisfaction and joy: I have discovered and managed to prove – at least to myself – that the story of North Korea in the free, multi-channel Western media, is a mixture of information, misinformation, and disinformation (sometimes biased), creating a confused and confusing picture. It is a "known fact" among travelers to North Korea that tourists can visit only two stations of the Pyongyang subway (I recall how, on my first trip, Mike muttered, "Two stations, of course"). This fact is so "well-known" that journalists have even written about how Koreans claim that the subway system includes seventeen stations, but no tourist has ever traveled between more than the same two. (Indeed, even the Wikipedia entry – as accessed in January 2024 – for "Pyongyang subway" notes that "Since 2010, tourists have been allowed to ride the metro at six stations, and in 2014, all of the metro stations were opened to foreigners... The previously limited tourist access gave rise to a conspiracy theory that the metro was purely for show. It was claimed that it only consisted of two stops and that the passengers were actors.")

The idea that the regime would set up the entire system as a show especially for tourists, including operating the subway and having hundreds of actors appearing on it, with this show on display at almost any given time (at least twice during my tours, the decision as to when to visit the subway stations was made in accordance with immediate time constraints) is at least a little bizarre. Nevertheless, it is reiterated in many accounts of personal experiences of tourists in Pyongyang – despite the fact that the *Lonely Planet* tourist guidebook states explicitly that one can travel the entire length of the Red Line. It turns out that myth can be stronger than any fact or logic.

On the second day of our tour, a problem that I have feared all along, surfaces. A few minutes after we leave the hotel, one of the participants notifies me that she's not feeling well, and asks to go back to her room. We both approach Miss Kim and notify her that the participant wants to remain in her room, since she isn't feeling well. She isn't looking for any sort of medical help, she simply wants to rest, and will take some medication that she has with her. This ostensibly simple, mundane matter that would be routine anywhere else in the world, is a very serious problem in North Korea, or at least so it seems. A tourist cannot remain alone at the hotel. Miss Kim calls Mr. Cha, who arrives quickly, listens to the woman and to me, and then takes her back to the hotel (or so I think) while we continue with our program for the day: a drive southward to Panmunjom in the DMZ. On the way, I tell the group the story of the Korean War. One can't make sense of the Korean War without addressing the historical processes that preceded it: the Japanese occupation (1905-1959), the division of Korea, up until the outbreak of the war (1945-1950), and the war itself (1950-1953) (see Appendix: Korea – History). Miss Kim is already used to my speeches, but nevertheless follows my words – and, even more so, the faces of my listeners – with interest. During the visit to the DMZ, of course, we will hear the official account of the events. I briefly review the Western version in contrast with the North Korean version, taking care to note that "Western sources maintain...." For the third time, I meet my friend Wang Ryong Cho, who now bears the rank of major. I congratulate him on the promotion, and at the end of the visit, I present him with a gift – cigarettes for the soldiers. As we part, I promise to be back in April 2017.

*

After the visit to the DMZ, where there is no phone reception even for Koreans, we continue to Kaesong, and I ask Miss Kim to check with Mr. Cha how the participant who was unwell this morning is doing. Miss Kim calls and notifies me that now, following treatment, she is doing well; she is resting in her room and one of the Koryo guides is with her. My face must register

277

some concern, since Miss Kim reassures me with a smile, "Don't worry, everything is fine." Considering that my options for action are exceedingly limited, I have to accept the reassurance for now and wait patiently until we return to Pyongyang. In the evening, as we arrive for dinner, I heave a sigh of relief. Mr. Cha and the participant are waiting for us at the restaurant. The woman receives us with a big smile; she is certainly looking much better than she did this morning. She tells us that Mr. Cha did not take her back to the hotel, but rather directly to a clinic. She describes the clinic as altogether acceptable: she underwent a thorough battery of tests, was given liquids via IV, and was returned to her hotel room for a rest. Now that she is feeling better, she is ready to rejoin the group. I had entertained grave doubts about the North Korean health system. When people in Israel asked me about it, I had answered – partly in jest, but also seriously – "It's better to be healthy." This first experience of medical treatment for a group participant has succeeded in lowering my level of anxiety, at least where the problem is a mild one. (On my future tours, four more participants would require medical care. In one instance, the circumstances facilitate the realization of my strong desire to join the patient and visit the clinic. The incident and my impressions appear later on here.)

*

I visit the Children's Camp in Wonsan for the third time. The first time, there were no children to be seen. The second time, we saw many children and a great deal of activity. This time, the camp seems to be full beyond capacity. I am astonished at the number of children we see in the yard. Kim and the local guide explain that the camp is full of children whose homes were damaged by the floods. Kim tells the local guide, on her own initiative, about the truckload of grain that our group donated to the victims of the flood. The guide, in turn, gathers the children and tells them about our contribution. The children surround us, somewhat shy but full of gratitude. They thank us warmly and gracefully for the aid. It is a simple, heartwarming gesture.

Beyond the excitement, I am once again filled with thoughts. A nuclear power desperately seeking 750 euros in aid, and torches? Seven hundred and fifty euros to buy grain? From whom? Here I receive confirmation that this is an accepted fact. If the guides are telling the children, it can't be a secret. Again and again, we see and hear that the regime tries to show off the country at its best, but that doesn't sit well with a request for aid. It also doesn't jibe with the narrative that they show only what they want to show, and that they don't want Westerners to see Koreans in distress. Perhaps the aim is to show the world how unjustified and cruel the sanctions are. That being the case, the story accords with the Korean "guide to life," which attributes everything good that happens in the country to the Leader, while every problem or deficiency has its source in the sanctions that are imposed by the West. Roads are potholed because of sanctions; agriculture flourishes thanks to the Leader. The unfinished Ryongyong Hotel – sanctions. An apartment for every citizen – the Leader. Nevertheless, the more I think about the story of the donation of a truckload of grain, the less I understand.

*

After lunch, we head back in the direction of Pyongyang, with the intention of continuing to the Myohyang mountains. As noted, the days are short, the journey continues into the darkness, and as described previously, driving on North Korean roads at night is an adventure best avoided. The bus maneuvers around the potholes, the bus's stereo system is faulty, and there is no bathroom anywhere on the way. Ahead of us is at least another hour of driving in the darkness until we arrive in Pyongyang for dinner, and then we're going to be driving through the villages at night – a journey that will become a nightmare. I approach Miss Kim and ask whether she could check with Mr. Cha the option of having us sleep over in Pyong-yang, and then continue the journey tomorrow. The response is that it's possible for us to sleep in Pyongyang, and then to set off for the Myohyang mountains tomorrow afternoon. "But then we'll be driving in the dark again," I conclude, and pro-pose a different plan. Miss Kim tries to help me in my efforts to bring about a situation whereby the drive through the villages will take place during the daytime hours, but all my ideas are politely turned down, and with some or other "interesting" reasoning. I beg her to try a different idea. Miss Kim knows ex-actly what I'm seeking. Moreover, she knows that this time I'm not going to get what I want. I don't give up. With a smile I tell her, "You, the Koreans, have a saying: 'Even a monkey can sometimes fall off a tree.' Please try again." Miss Kim likes my use of the local saying (which I learned from Miss Li Mi Soon) and once again calls Mr. Cha. Of course, my latest creative idea is also rejected. I understand that this time, Mr. Cha is going to stick to his position no matter what; the more I try, the more forcefully he will resist. It's clear to me that Mr. Cha under-stands very well that all my ideas have been directed to having our passage through the villages happen in daylight, and they are therefore doomed to failure, because the authorities aren't interested in exposing us to the sights we saw during the "for-tunate accident." Since I have already learned my lesson – "You use the word 'why' too often" – I yield. I forgo the visit to Myo-hyang, but ask that the time be filled with other visits with in-teresting tourist value. My request is fulfilled.

We sleep over at the hotel in Pyongyang. The question of whether there are available rooms isn't even discussed. Not only are there rooms available, but once again, they are the same rooms that we used before leaving for Wonsan. Since the climax of the visit to Myohyang is the two International Friendship Museum buildings, and we will not be seeing these, we are offered an alternative: the Korean Gifts Museum in Pyongyang, housing gifts to the Leaders of North Korea from Korean expats throughout the world. The museum is situated on a hill to the north of Pyongyang, and it too, like the museum in Myohyang, has a balcony with a panoramic view. This museum, too, holds an extensive, dazzling collection of gifts: wood carvings, ivory, jade, and every other type of precious stone, as well as crystal porcelain, paintings, sculptures, and more. We conclude this most impressive tour with coffee on the balcony. At least as far as content is concerned, this is an altogether satisfactory substitute for the visit to the International Friendship Museum.

*

On our way to the western port city of Nampo, we make a stop that was not originally on the itinerary, but was added to the program in response to my request for more content to substitute for the visit to Myohyang. Since the site does not appear on the program that I reviewed, I try to lower the group's expectations (as well as my own). I tell myself that there is nothing to lose: we'll go, and we'll see; in any case, it's a one-time visit. The site is the **Three Tombs of the Koguryo Dynasty** in Kangso. The Koguryo (Goguryo) Kingdom existed from the 1st century B.C.E. to the sixth century C.E., a period known in Korean history as the Period of the Three Kingdoms. Two kingdoms – Kakja and

Silla – lay in the southern part of Korea, while the Koguryo Kingdom occupied most of the territory of Korea, including extensive swathes of the south-eastern part of Manchuria. The kingdom had a series of capitals, the last of which centered around the Jangan Castle at the center of what is now Pyongyang, up until the kingdom's collapse in 668 C.E. Hundreds of tombs from the Koguryo Kingdom have been identified throughout the northern part of Korea and in China. Nearly a hundred of them are decorated with frescoes, about seventy of them in North Korea. The frescoes include portraits as well as divine and decorative motifs. Most of the tombs were looted long ago and were never subjected to scientific study. Ironically, it was under Japanese occupation that they received some scientific attention. In 2005, UNESCO included the tombs in Kangso on its World Heritage Sites list. Among other reasons for their inclusion, the organization listed the artistic value of the frescoes, the engineering skill demonstrated in the construction, and their influence on East Asian cultures, including Japan. Three of the tortoise-shaped tombs are located in Kangso. The largest of them is fifty meters long and nearly 9 meters high. The frescoes show human figures and scenes from aristocratic life, such as dancing, wrestling, and hunting. The tombs and paintings are of a surprising and impressive quality, certainly in view of their era, paralleling the early Middle Ages in Europe.

In addition to the visit to the tombs themselves, there is another big bonus for the group. The site is located in an agricultural region, a few kilometers north-west of the main Pyongyang-Nampo highway. The drive there, partly on dirt roads, passes through villages, between fields in which farmers are toiling away, working their fields without any mechanization; everything is done manually. The group, including myself, sits and observes with fascination what is unquestionably "real" North Korea. To my surprise, the guides make no effort to stop us from photographing the scenes. Clearly this is not a "show for tourists," but in the toss-up between concealing the North Korean reality and showing Korea's historical heritage, the latter wins.

We kept our expectations small, and the surprise is dramatic. The visit to the Kangso Tombs is added to the list of sites for future tours.

*

In response to the disappointment that I expressed to the Korean organizers of our previous tour over the visit to the agricultural cooperative and the mineral water factory, they take us for a visit to a "sample village." Of course, this is my first visit to the village, located in the suburbs of Pyongyang. When the houses of the village become visible from afar, the difference between this village and the type we have unexpectedly been exposed to, is immediately apparent. The houses here are painted in a gleaming white, and their roofs are green. The bus comes to a halt in the parking area of the village square. It is a very large square in relation to the size of the village. At one of its corners, there is a main building in which administrative and cultural activities take place. On one side of the square are some apartment buildings, and on the other side are some houses. The main building, the apartment buildings and the houses are all in good condition: newly painted in white, with roof tiles. The initial impression turns out to have been accurate.

First, we visit the main building – the "community center." There is a spanking new theater hall with seating for an audience of about eight hundred people; activity rooms; and administrative offices. We are invited to enter one of the houses. It stands about fifty meters from the community center (in the future, whenever I visit the village, it will be the same house).

All the houses are surrounded by gardens – not flower beds and lawns, but vegetable patches. The house is not fancy, but quite respectable, with all the basic comforts: a kitchen with all the necessary equipment, bedrooms, a living room with a television – all in all, a home at what would certainly pass in the West as a reasonable standard.

We return to the bus and after a short drive, we arrive at the hothouses. Once again, everything looks nice. The greenhouses are spacious, vegetables are growing, and there is drip irrigation – modern agriculture. We are given a thorough explanation about modern agriculture, all of course thanks to the initiative and resourcefulness of the Leader (the farmers among the group echo the local guide's praise for the greenhouse agriculture).

We return to the community center building and are invited to see the kindergarten – unquestionably the climax of the visit. Young children always manage to evoke smiles. Of course, the building is spotlessly clean, as are the children themselves, who appear well cared for and happy. We walk through a few classrooms, rooms for rest, a dining hall, and playrooms. In short – much like a "children's house" on a kibbutz in Israel, but there is something that is different: in the hallways and on the stairways, footprints have been painted to show the children how to walk in the public areas – just as at the Agricultural University in Wonsan: keeping to the right. Unquestionably, this is a show for tourists. And a successful one, too. The question is, is it just a show, or is it perhaps the archetype of a sample village? And if so, is this intended as a model for similar projects in the future?

*At a kindergarten: from the time the toddlers learn to walk,
it's this way and no other...*

*

It's the last evening of the tour, for me. Tomorrow morning, I'll
be heading back to Israel. The group will stay on for one more
day, led by Ami, the guide who is still learning this destination.
For the first six days of the tour I have shared all my ideas, conversations, deliberations, and decisions with him.

For some time, I have wanted to see another local pub, after
the one we saw on the last trip and that has been included on our
itinerary. The organizers have decided to accede to this request
as a gesture to me. And so before dinner, we find ourselves at a
pub which is actually a karaoke club. There are various rooms of
different sizes, and we are directed to one that is suitable for the
size of our group. Waitresses bring us beer from the bar, and we

have a private evening. Nice, perhaps, as a farewell party – for me as well as a couple who will be flying back with me for family reasons – but definitely not what was meant when we asked for a pub. The aim had been to mingle with the locals. We can order beer at the hotel – in fact, beer is served with lunch and dinner every day. Following this experiment, on future trips we stick to the other pub.

*

Morning. The couple and I take our leave of Mr. Tang and Mr. Cha, and of course the guides, and head for the airport. We have a quick flight to Beijing, a wait, and then back to Israel. I am back from North Korea for the fourth time. Routine.

CHAPTER 12

"Nuclear War" (?)

In view of the unexpected success of the autumn of 2016 – three groups, each with more than twenty-five participants – the company starts preparing for the spring of 2017. The nuclear test conducted by North Korea on September 9th has no effect on our preparations or on the demand for the spring tours, and we have about eighty registrations – three full groups. At the same time, other tour operators are starting to offer tours to North Korea. It seems we were the groundbreakers. The mysterious hermit kingdom is about to become the next tourist hit.

*

But slowly the sunny skies start to darken. The nuclear test of September 9th turns out to have been just the beginning of another fascinating chapter in the relations between North Korea and the US, South Korea, Japan, and the rest of the world.

In November 2016, Donald Trump was elected President of the United States. Although he had declared during his election campaign that he was willing to meet with Kim Jong-Un, no one entertained any doubt that his policy would be more belligerent and less accommodating than that of his predecessor, President Obama.

Trump was supposed to enter office on January 20th, 2017. Kim Jong-Un's "congratulatory" gift to him upon his entry into the White House took the form of an announcement that his country was in the final stages of developing an inter-continental ballistic missile that could reach the US. Trump's response was, "It's not going to happen."

North Korea did indeed conduct tests, which failed, but in February 2017, a missile landed near Japan. Trump: "We're going to respond very forcefully."

In March 2017, North Korea launched four missiles. Three of them landed in Japan's territorial waters. Trump officially canceled President Obama's strategy of patience and shifted "from words to actions." On April 6th, he met with Xi Jinping, President of China. The two leaders reached agreements concerning the political measures for dealing with "the problem of North Korea."

The rhetoric was ramped up in anticipation of April 15th, 2017, the 106th anniversary of the President (the eternal President, even after his death). Remember that April 15th is one of the two most important dates on the North Korean calendar. In 2017 this date marked the 106th New Year on the North Korean calendar.

The world has become accustomed to the Leaders of North Korea exploiting holidays for "national celebrations" and demonstrations of might and power. We recall that on September 9th, 2016, the country had conducted its fifth nuclear test. Now, in 2017, there is anxiety and concern as to what lies ahead.

Indeed, Marshal Kim Jong-Un does not disappoint; he announces that a major event will soon be taking place, adding fuel to the fire by inviting two hundred foreign journalists to watch the event and report on it.

On April 14th, a day before the threatening date and the military parade, which is traditionally a show of power, President Trump declares that he is adopting a policy of maximum pressure and intervention.

The Leader of North Korea, Marshal Kim Jong-Un, responds:

"In the event that we are attacked, North Korea will respond with total war that will cause grave harm to its enemies."

The entire world waits with bated breath for April 15th: the military parade and the "great event." "Unilateral rhetoric has been exhausted," the Leader comments. It seems that the frightening scenario of an all-out nuclear war is now a real possibility. (Or is it?)

*

The world prepares for war, while we, at Tarbutu-Rimon, prepare to take three groups to North Korea. As the departure date draws closer and the drums of war beat louder, participants start having doubts and begin rethinking the adventure. Unsurprisingly, some want to cancel their participation. Who would want to step into the eye of an approaching storm? The initial cancellations are followed by many more.

In early April, the Israeli Foreign Ministry publishes a "sort of" travel warning. The slew of cancellations has dealt a serious blow to two of the three groups. Family members, friends, and acquaintances are worried, and urge me to cancel my trip. "Those in the know" share their insights with me, concluding decisively that of course I have to cancel my participation, so that the tour will be canceled. Outwardly I display confidence and determination to go ahead, but inside, a battle rages. On one hand, the atmosphere is scary; on the other hand, I remember very clearly the speech by the "handsome" Mr. Li in September 2016: "We are strong. We will not start a war..."

For some reason, I believe that the regime in North Korea is not as insane as its portrayal around the world (and its portrayal of itself, perhaps, as a deterrent). I also believe that the balance of fear that has kept the world from nuclear war for seventy-two years will continue to have its effect. The combination of these two assumptions decides the issue in favor of the trip – specifically at this interesting and challenging time – to North Korea.

About two weeks before our departure, I meet with the group. I ask them, only half in jest, "Are you sure that you want to travel right now, in the midst of this tension, to North Korea? Aren't you afraid?" The response is decisive and unanimous – "We're going." Still three groups, but two of them, each of which started off with over twenty participants, have shrunk. The first group will be led by Eli Krispin. The number of participants is down to twelve. The second group, which is down to five, will be led by Yaki. Only my group, for some reason, still numbers thirty participants, with no cancellations. My tour will be the first to offer a continuation tour to Manchuria, as well as a train ride from Pyongyang to the city of Dandong, on the Chinese border. Perhaps these attractions explain why there are no cancellations.

*

On April 15th, the military parade is held as promised, displaying the might of the North Korean army. The event is given wide coverage in the international media, but there is no report of any sort of "big event" such as a nuclear test or the appearance of a sophisticated new missile. The West continues to wait tensely for the event.

On April 17th, two days after the parade, I land in Pyongyang for the fifth time. I am given the sort of reception reserved for national heroes: a group of thirty people, at a time when many tourists are canceling their trips, is no small matter, especially considering our own cancellations. Our hosts regard me as personally responsible for the arrival of this relatively large group, and the more I try to explain that I don't think they have all come because of me, the more firmly they become convinced that it's all thanks to me. After all, it's my face that they see returning time after time.

As I understand it, I happened to be in the right place at the right time to become the focus of their appreciation, but the credit goes to two objective facts that are not connected to me:

1. With the advertisement of this new destination, we received enough registrations for three groups, each of them larger than what the North Koreans are used to (i.e., over 25 participants).

2. Israeli tour directors generally approach their work as though they were tour guides; indeed, the Israeli public refers to us as "overseas tour guides." While tour directors around the world – and certainly in North Korea – confine themselves to management, Israeli directors lead the tour on the ground, ensuring that the participants experience everything on the itinerary and more. In North Korea, the local guides are used to having exclusive control and being able to follow a program that doesn't necessarily accord with the itinerary. When they encounter (for the first time, it seems!) a guide who talks, lectures, and explains, they are impressed. Moreover, when the guide reviews the operative program and concludes that it is technically unrealistic, offers a heads-up in good time, proposes changes, and turns out to have been correct, it is no wonder that Kim On-Hee says, "Why do you say that our idea of changing the program was a good one? It was all your idea," and Li Mi Soon says, "I like the way you think."

There is also, I believe, a subjective factor that contributes: the fact that in my contact with them, I take care to show respect, and an understanding of their truth, their worldview, and the reality of their lives as they see it.

Following the usual entry procedure, I meet the mostly familiar local team: Mr. Cha, the CEO; Miss Li Mi Soon, who is the lead guide for the third time; two new apprentice guides; and the usual photographer, Mr. Kim.

We board the bus. Miss Li, as usual, introduces the team and then goes on to present an overview of Korea. I am glad to hear her list the rules of etiquette in a serious and authoritative tone before she hands the microphone over to me.

The program for the first day has become routine, as has the first dinner, where we review the itinerary. The skeleton program has already become consolidated, but every tour requires adaptations arising from the different days of the week of the arrival, holidays, and other events going on in the country, and so on. During this tour, as always on April 15th, there are celebrations of the birthday of President Kim Il-Sung – in other words, the New Year marking the 107th year of the Korean calendar. As described previously, the celebrations include the Flower Exhibition with the Kimilsunia and Kimjongalia, a mass picnic on Moran Hill (to be discussed below), and more. We have introduced a major change this time: at the end of our tour of North Korea, we will proceed to China by train, traveling from Pyongyang to the border city of Sinuiju, on the banks of the Yalu River, facing Dandong.

After dinner come the gifts, which have also become routine, with some polite conversation. After we have finished reviewing the updating the tour itinerary, Mr. Cha asks me, "What happened to the other two groups? Why are they so small?" Seemingly a simple question, but my answer has to be honest without causing offense: it is almost certain that the local guides are not aware of the "facts" that are known to us; and even if they are, the different manner of presentation of those "facts" changes the picture entirely. In response to his question, I describe carefully the hostile atmosphere in the international media surrounding North Korea and the fear of war. "War?" Mr. Tang asks with surprise, and goes on to repeat the same mantra: "They won't dare declare war on us, and we certainly won't declare war, so there's no danger!" After a brief pause, I divert the conversation: "Representatives of the international press were invited by Chairman Kim Jong-Il to participate in an important event. Which event did he mean – the parade of April 15th?" Mr. Cha isn't sure what I mean. While he and Mr. Tang, both with weak English, puzzle over the question, Miss Li jumps in and says, "The opening of Ryongmong Road." The three of them burst out laughing together, and Miss Li tells me, "They inaugurated a new road – Ryongmong Road – "the Dawn." The road was built at the instruction of our Leader, within a period of ten months."

I hide my surprise (is the opening of a new road an event worthy of wide coverage in the world press?) and ask Mr. Cha, "Is it possible to visit there?"

He hesitates for a moment and then answers, "As soon as they are finished populating the road, it will be possible to visit."

In a pleading tone, I tell him, "We would very much like to see it."

Mr. Cha thinks some more and then, as usual, tells me, "We'll see what can be done. I'll try."

At night, in my room, I am lost in thought. What a great abyss separates the image of North Korea from what actually goes on in the country. From Israel, it looks as though we'll be flying into a war zone, but when we arrive, I feel as though we've landed in a quiet, tranquil pasture. Why is the inauguration of a road an event worthy of worldwide interest? And if it is indeed so special, why isn't it possible to visit there? I don't understand. Only in North Korea. An alternative reality.

*

On the second day, we visit the holy of holies – the Kumsusan, the Sun Palace – as usual, dressed in our finest. The guides are tense, and the group is eagerly anticipating the dramatic visit. Miss Li and I have become much closer; our conversations are more open and less formal. As we stand in the entrance hall to the mausoleum, I notice that she is having what looks from afar like an unpleasant conversation with the apprentice guides. Afterwards, I try to reassure her: "Smile, the visit is going to proceed without any problems; the group will respect the importance of the site and behave accordingly." In a slightly calmer voice, but still sounding angry, Miss Li answers, as she points to the apprentices: "They are children; they don't understand anything. I bear all the responsibility." Her words and her manner indicate the degree to which the guides are constantly subject to very close scrutiny. The visit goes smoothly, and what remains with me from the visit is my conversation with Miss Li.

*

We set off. As we leave the hotel, we pass the Cheerleaders' Square. In the past, we "visited" in accordance with Mr. Cha's guidelines (approaching the square by bus, driving by slowly, photographing as we go) but I am not satisfied. I ask Miss Li, "Is there any possibility that I could come to the square with one of you, one of the guides? Without the group?" I understand the claim that having the whole group arrive and photograph the cheerleaders would embarrass them (it is certainly possible that this is true). Miss Li agrees without hesitation. "On one of the mornings, before the day's program begins, we'll do it." This is duly noted.

April 15th is behind us, but the celebrations continue. The festive atmosphere can be felt everywhere. Women are going about in their colorful dresses; we see groups of people who are clearly dressed in their finest clothes, and we guess that they are from other towns and villages and have come to Pyongyang as organized groups. There are five sites where the celebrations are especially conspicuous: Kumsusan, Mansudae Hill, the house in which President Kim Il-Sung was born in Mangyungda, the Flower Exhibition, and Moran Hill. The biggest surprise is the military presence in the city. Open trucks full of soldiers are driving on every street. The soldiers are the same ones who participated in the parade, and it is clear that they are excited and enjoying themselves. The pedestrians welcome them with cheers, and the soldiers smile back and wave. There are dozens of trucks; a never-ending convoy. Bearing in mind that in general, it is forbidden to photograph soldiers, we ask permission to take some photographs, and the guides happily agree. The entire group, including myself, is thrilled by the scenes. Once again, as someone far removed from being an enthusiastic proponent of militarism – especially that of a totalitarian regime – I find myself embarrassed at my excitement, but decide to go with what I am feeling. After all, for the soldiers and for the masses, this is a celebration.

A fun day in Pyongyang – a "treat" for soldiers of the North Korean army following the May Day parade.

We arrive at the Flower Exhibition, and the atmosphere is festive. The entrance is full of celebrants, women in their holiday dresses and exuberant children. I remind Miss Li that in April of 2016, on our first tour (as tourists), the visit to the exhibition was led by the guide, and was tedious. We were a group of only nine people, but even this small number was difficult to lead collectively. "What do you suggest?" asks Miss Li. I suggest that we make a time to meet back at the bus. The local guide will give an overview of the exhibition for a few minutes at the entrance, and then we will allow the tourists to walk around freely. "Fine," Miss Li agrees. "How long do you propose giving them?"

I think quickly and ask, "What do you think – about an hour?"

It's a deal. It's only the second day of the trip, everyone is impatient, they want to get off the bus, and join the happy bustle. I'm not sure that the group has internalized the code of behavior, and so I ask for their attention and explain that what we are about to do will deviate from the known "facts" concerning going about freely in North Korea. I tell them the exact place and the exact time for meeting, and the rules concerning photography. Many of them ask whether they can photograph the women in their festive dresses. "You can, if you ask permission," I tell them. "Let's practice." We get off the bus, and as we approach the stairs to enter, two women are waiting to go inside. I approach them and ask, with hand gestures, pointing to the camera, whether we can photograph them and be photographed with them. Their response is a happy, smiley, positive one. We photograph ourselves with them. The tourists grasp the idea, and repeat the procedure themselves. The local guide reviews the wonders of the exhibition. We are told about the flowers at the exhibition – the Kimilsungia and the Kimjongilia – that together create pictures, symbols, and geometric shapes for decoration, all around the Leaders, their personalities, and the country's achievements under their rule. We are left with about forty-five minutes in which we are free to walk about, take in the sights, and enjoy. I am glad to walk about alone and watch the celebrants. The real party is at the exit: hundreds of children and their parents sit facing a stage while artists appear and keep the children occupied. I stand for a few long moments, watching the people. I receive many curious glances as well as smiles in response to my own. I have become very quickly accustomed to this surrealistic situation in which I, as an Israeli, stand in the midst of hundreds of celebrating Koreans. Of course, when I describe all this to my friends and acquaintances upon my return, their reaction, predictably enough, will be, "You know that it's all a show for the tourists."

"Of course," I'll answer. "Thirty Israelis arrived, and the North Korean propaganda machine mobilized thousands of extras, including children, for a huge show, the biggest show in the world..."

At the entrance to the Flower Exhibition

A girl at the Flower Exhibition

*

The visit to Nampo and the Western Sea Barrier was described at length in the previous chapter. It starts off, once again, with a presentation of the engineering feat, a ten-minute film, and a talk including a model of the project. Seemingly there is nothing more to add – but on this visit there is a surprise. When we enter the lecture room, our guide, Miss Li, and the local guide have a whispered consultation and then Miss Li comes over to me and says, "You know everything about the barrier, so instead of a lecture with a translation, you can give the lecture directly, while we prepare coffee or tea for whoever is interested. A euro for a cup." She goes on without waiting for my response, "I'll take orders, and you can begin." I don't manage to say anything, so she addresses the group in English, asking that whoever would like a cup of tea or coffee for one euro should lift their hands, and then she counts the number of cups of each drink to prepare. I take their confidence in me as a great compliment, but the real story here is the tea and coffee on sale. It turns out that the guides aren't doing anything that they aren't allowed to do – clearly, the income is to their benefit, too, and hence their ambition to make the service more efficient. Here we have another illustration of the economic revolution taking place in North Korea. It's a very small step, but as the saying goes in neighboring China, "Even a journey of a thousand miles starts with one step." Incidentally, in every place in North Korea where one can buy anything, the service unquestionably demonstrates that the service provider receives personal remuneration in proportion to the volume of sales. I also understand very quickly at which places our guides want us to buy and at which places they prefer us not to.

*

Yaki arrives with his group on Friday, and when we meet at the hotel in the evening, I propose that he joins me the next morning for the visit to the Cheerleaders' Square. Yaki readily agrees, and Saturday starts off with great excitement for both of us. Before breakfast, accompanied by one of the guides, we go off to the square, where we take some photos, including of ourselves, and simply watch with wonder. Dozens of women who look to be around sixty, in uniform, perform movements that are somewhere between a dance and military drill exercises, accompanied by military music that they are playing, to encourage the passers-by to hurry to work. They perform their cheerleading with complete seriousness, so focused on what they are doing that they do not even notice us, the foreigners with the cameras.

My description fails to capture the story. One has to be there, to see and to feel the alternative reality in order to understand. Only in North Korea.

*

Moran Hill is located at the center of the city's central park, with the Arch of Triumph to the west, the Chollima Monument to the south, the Taedong River to the east, and the Kim Il-Sung Stadium inside the park itself. The Kaison amusement park is also part of this "green lung," intended as a venue for a range of recreational activities. On holidays, Pyongyang residents and local tourists from outside the capital come to the hill for picnic lunches, as in parks all over the world – but North Korea isn't anywhere else in the world. Here, the most elementary things – a hardware store, a pub, or a school – are tourist attractions. Every unmediated encounter with locals is an achievement, especially when you see crowds of people enjoying "normal" recreational activity – certainly if you manage to make eye contact and conduct some sort of communication with them. You feel a sense of satisfaction from the discovery that "they're people, too," and that not everything that's been written about life in this insular country is true and accurate.

At lunch, Miss Li informs me that this evening we can go for a walk on Ryongmong Road, now that it has finished being populated. I am delighted. I'm curious to know the meaning of the term "new road," and what it means to be "populated." I understand every word she says, but I can't manage to imagine what it is about a new road that would justify turning it into a central event of the New Year celebrations and inviting journalists from all of over the world to see and report on it – certainly not after we've become accustomed to associate major events reserved for holidays with the prospect of nuclear war. Just before we leave to see the new road, Miss Li tells me that Mr. Cha has asked if I have any objection to having Yaki's group join mine for the tour. "Not at all," I tell her, "I'd be more than happy, and I'm sure that all the participants will be happy with that too." Ryongmong Road is home to Kim Il-Sung University, the most important university in the country, and it leads to the Kumsusan, the mausoleum. Ryongmong – "The Dawn" – signals the new era that began for North Korea with the appearance of President Kim Il-Sung. In March 2016, Marshal Kim Jong-Un proposed rebuilding the road. In August of that year, the plans were completed and approved. In April 2017, the new road was opened. The renovation had included the construction of forty new apartment buildings, the tallest of them two hundred and seventy meters high, with eighty-two floors. In addition, thirty-three existing apartment buildings were renovated along with another thirty-four public buildings, including six schools, three kindergartens, and three early childhood centers. The project will ultimately include another seven buildings for the nearby Kim Il-Sung University as well as fifteen commercial buildings.

Thirty-seven Israelis set off for a walk along the road whose opening was the event that led the world to believe that North Korea, with its provocative behavior, was leading inevitably to hostilities that could turn into a nuclear war. Thirty-seven Israelis and a few dozen other tourists, on a road crammed with thousands of Koreans who have come to marvel at this wondrous sight. The road is excessively wide, considering the volume of traffic. Its sidewalks are no less generous, and there are strips of lawn and play areas for children. The first floors of the buildings look as though they are reserved for shops, restaurants, and other services for residents. The exteriors of the buildings are painted in soft shades of green, pale blue, and lemon. The place reflects twenty-first century living conditions.

The crowds in the street create the atmosphere of a special occasion. We agree to walk about freely, but together. Miss Li and I will lead; Yaki and his local guide will bring up the rear, and the other guides will be dispersed amongst the group. Since the road can be crossed only via underground crossings, we agree to proceed at a comfortable pace until we reach the first crossing (about three hundred meters away), and then we will cross the road and return to the bus. Upon reaching the crossing, I stop and suggest to Miss Li that we check that everyone is with us before descending. "Don't worry," she says, "The boys [i.e., the male guides] are making sure that everyone is together."

"Still," I propose, "let's make sure." Our conversation is conducted quietly, in a friendly tone. When "everyone" is assembled, it turns out that two participants are missing. The "boys" quickly advance a few dozen meters; they find the tourists and turn back towards us. It's not a big story, but when I read articles and hear stories, over and over, by people who once visited North Korea and who warn against the dangers of being alone for even a second, I wonder how this situation comes to its simple conclusion on my tour.

Now we understand why the opening of a new road is an event worthy of inviting Western media, and we also understand what "populating it" means. All apartments in North Korea belong to the state. This project includes several hundred apartments; once they are ready, they are handed over to their new owners, who all move in within a couple of days, and then it is time to celebrate. The festive inauguration of a new road — only in North Korea!

All of us are swept up in the carnival atmosphere: Mr. Cha, both teams of guides, and especially us, the Israeli tourists. The good mood is maintained during our visit to the pub. I am already familiar with the place; for Yaki, and of course for the groups, it is a first encounter. The pub is not big. Some locals are sitting around the tables, and when we walk in – all thirty-seven of us Israelis; five guides; Mr. Kim, the photographer; and Mr. Cha – they are unable to hide their astonishment. They try to appear focused on their affairs, but the attempt is doomed. We order drinks for all the tourists and the guides, the atmosphere warms up, and there is some level of interaction with the locals, expressed mainly in the exchange of smiles and glasses raised in toasts. We spend about an hour in the pub – thirty-seven Israelis and about the same number of Koreans, sitting, drinking, and chatting. As the minutes go by, we all become more accustomed to the scene, and the unusual sight of an encounter between Israelis and Koreans starts to feel natural and to make sense.

Mr. Cha decides to maintain the social momentum and decides that the two groups will eat dinner together at the grill restaurant that is usually reserved for the concluding dinner at the end of the tour. Mr. Tang, president of Koryo Tours, joins us for the festive meal, which is accompanied by beer and sake (rice wine). Looking back, it seems to me that that lunch represented a sort of release: the atmosphere in the days leading up to our departure had been filled with a lot of tension, albeit unspoken, and when you participate in what you thought was a frightening event that would threaten the world, and discover it to be anything but threatening, there is a sense of relief.

In the evening, at the hotel, I call Chaim as usual and update him as to the day's events. Chaim informs me that a well-known journalist wants to interview me. "Gladly," I tell him. "We'll call her," referring to Yaki and myself. Once again, it's important to note that communications between North Korea and Israel are easily and conveniently conducted via a regular landline telephone. Calling North Korea, on the other hand, while possible, is slightly problematic. When my wife hears about the planned interview, she expresses reservations, not wanting trouble: she is afraid that I will be accused in North Korea of being a journalist. Yaki, on the other hand, is quite willing to be interviewed. We call the number that Chaim gave us, and the journalist asks us some questions about what is going on in North Korea. In response to a specific question about the dramatic event to which Western journalists were invited, Yaki tells her about our afternoon, the celebration, and the carnival atmosphere. Then comes the immortal response: "You know that it's all a show for the tourists." Yaki is unable to contain his irritation and answers, "Tell me, does it make sense to you that the Koreans would organize thousands of actors just because thirty-seven tourists have arrived from Israel?! Are you listening to what you're saying?!"

Ryongmong Road

*

It's our last morning in Pyongyang. After breakfast, we will be heading for China: our trip to North Korea will end off with a tour of the Manchuria region. This time, our return journey won't be via the quick, familiar flight to Beijing, but rather a train ride from Pyongyang to the border city of Sinuiju, some 170 kilometers away. I had assumed that we would be accompanied during the train trip by one of the local guides as far as the border, but when I question them as to the details of our train ride, I suddenly understand that the team in Pyongyang has no knowledge or experience of either train rides or border crossings. I am even more astonished to discover that from the moment we board the train until our arrival in China, no one is with me to help during the journey and – more importantly – with the border crossing. With some hesitation, with no escorts and no choice, we set off.

We travel by bus from the hotel and within a minute, we are at the train station. The cheerleaders encourage and urge the passers-by on their way to work, as they do every morning, but this time, their gestures look to me as though they are waving goodbye. Mr. Cha and all the guides accompany us to the train, and each of us receives a lunch tray. After an emotional farewell, we are on the train, on the way to Sinuiju.

The journey takes about three and a half hours. The train drives slowly, and for me, as an inquisitive tourist, that's a good thing. The tracks pass through the agrarian heartland of the country. Assuming that the Koreans – despite their zealous protection of their image – have not planted Potemkin villages (see box) along the route, there is much to see. Much that the authorities would perhaps prefer for tourists not to see, but there's no way of hiding it. It's April, and spring is coming late to Korea. The fields are just starting to awaken from their winter hibernation and are turning green. We already know that we will see very few, if any, tractors or other mechanical equipment. Almost all labor is carried out manually. I have already driven through farming areas, and the sights are not surprising. Most of the roads are unpaved. People go about on foot, or on bicycles. One of our tourists, formerly the sales manager for a fertilizer manufacturer, looks at the fields and comments, "The fields need fertilizer. A bit of fertilizer and everything would look different." He turns to me in consternation: "Why don't they fertilize the fields?"

"Sanctions!" I tell him. The sanctions are indeed causing great distress to the population; the intention behind them is that the population will rise up against its leaders. Is this strategy going to succeed?

It would be an understatement to say that the villages do not enjoy outstanding standards of housing, roads, and electricity – but as already noted, anyone who has traveled around the world outside of Europe and North America isn't surprised by what they see here.

At around 13:00, the train enters Sinuiju station, and comes to a stop. The instructions that I received were simple: do as you are told. Outside the train, uniformed personnel energetically move about; inside the train absolutely nothing happens. Near us are some Chinese passengers, seemingly businessmen. Yes, despite the sanctions. I communicate with them via hand gestures, asking, "What is going on?"

They gesture in return: "Patience; wait." I don't feel very patient, but there isn't much choice. After what seems like a long time, two uniformed men climb aboard, survey the passengers, and distribute customs and immigration forms. The forms are in two languages – Korean and ... Chinese. I run after the border policemen, who are already walking to the next carriage. When I catch up with them, I wave the forms and say, "English, English!" They give me a look that says, "Your problem, what do you want from us?" shrug their shoulders, and walk on. I am now quite worried. The border station, far away from anyone I know in North Korea, looks cold and hostile. There are no English-speakers – and that is disconcerting. Somewhat at a loss, and slightly cynical, I return to the group with the decision that we will wait patiently and see what happens. As usual in such situations, within a group that is consolidated and at ease with each other, the sarcastic humor and pieces of advice help to relax the atmosphere. Within this mess a simple idea suddenly comes to one of the participants: when we entered North Korea, we filled in similar forms. I always hand out sample completed questionnaires, so that it will be easier for the participants in the group to follow the same idea. He asks me, "Do you still have samples of the forms for entering North Korea?"

"Of course," I tell him, delving into my bag and taking them out. Working together, locating the different questions on the form, we manage to fill in the answers, and then pass the form around for everyone to fill in their forms accordingly. We are still busy writing when two officers, one male, the other female, wearing different uniforms from the ones we saw previously, approach us. The female officer addresses us in reasonable English, requesting our passports. She takes them, counts them, thanks us, and takes them away with her.

A few minutes later, two officers with yet another set of uniforms appear. They start an inspection, and at first it is rather alarming. Their faces impassive, they ask us to open our suitcases and bags. They look over the pictures in our cameras and on our cellphones, asking here and there that some of them be erased; they look at the newspapers we are carrying, books, and pamphlets. As the inspection continues, the atmosphere becomes slightly more relaxed, and the officers seem to be working less thoroughly. Conversations develop between us and them as they review our photos and the newspapers. While all this is going on, one member of the group offers them some small halva snacks. One of the officers takes one and examines it, looking doubtful. The tourist who offered it to him takes another one himself and eats it. The Korean watches, and then agrees to taste his. His serious expression slowly morphs into one of satisfaction. He finishes the snack and makes it clear that he would be glad to receive another. Each of the officers receives another two snacks. Towards the end of the inspection, one of the officers climbs onto the seat to look at the shelf above us. He finds a few North Korean banknotes. I shudder: we are in North Korea; a tourist was sentenced to fifteen years' imprisonment for removing a wall poster. What will happen to someone who transgresses the prohibition against taking local currency out of the country? My fear grows as the officer looks at me and asks, "Whose money is this?" Fearfully but decisively I answer, "Not ours." The officer doesn't bat an eyelid; with an apathetic expression he stuffs the banknotes into his pocket, and continues the inspection. The whole process takes about half an hour, and is concluded without any further incident. The two officers bid us a friendly goodbye, and move on.

I am relieved, but still not relaxed. The border passage procedure is completely different from what happens in Pyongyang. In fact, the procedure at the Pyongyang airport is the fastest and most efficient I have encountered in any international airport; while here the minutes go by, the uniformed officers walk back and forth, and nothing seems to be getting done. All of a sudden, the female officer reappears with our passports, looking displeased. She calls out loudly, "Abraham, Abraham!"

I answer, "Is there is a problem?"

"Yes," she tells me, pointing to my passport, which shows my birthdate as 00.00. 1948. (Starting from my second tour, I have made a point of entering North Korea with my Israeli passport.) "How can this be?"

308

I relax; I'm already used to the reactions of immigration personnel to the strange date. I explain that this is already my fifth visit to North Korea, and at the airport at Pyongyang no one raised any questions. "Really?" she asks. She thinks for a while, comes to a decision, and starts handing back the passports, identifying each passenger. She doesn't give me my passport, but says, "A moment," gesturing that I wait, and steps off the train. The mood amongst the group is improving, and of course there are now jokes about the group parting ways with me, leaving me here and continuing to China without me. This time the wait is just a few minutes. The officer returns, hands me my passport, apologizing for the delay. (I will travel by train to China another three times; each time I encounter the same officer, and she will always remember me and remind me about my "birthday.")

Our stop at the train station – the Sinuiju border station – lasts about two hours. A nerve-wracking two hours, but also quite entertaining, and – most importantly – offering yet another perspective on this alternative reality. The train starts moving slowly towards the Yalu River. On the other side of the river is the Chinese city of Dandong. It takes about three minutes to reach the river; I am glued to the window, filming our crossing. I am filled with illogical tension as the train, with theatrical slowness, crosses the kilometer-wide river. In the middle of the river, on a bridge, the flags of North Korea and China mark the border. Just as we pass that point, my cell phone comes to life with a 'ping' indicating that I have received some messages. Immediately, while still on the train and in the middle of the river crossing, I send my very worried wife a message: "We're in China." Back to civilization! There are billboards, banks, McDonalds, and coffee shops, and one can walk around independently without an accompanying guide, like anywhere in the "free world." We're in China! At the Dandong station, we are greeted by Mao Zedong – or at least a statue of him. It was Mao who led the catastrophic Cultural Revolution, and who was once viewed as the greatest threat to Western civilization. Ironically enough, his statue represents China – and China, for us, symbolizes the return to the freedom that we are accustomed to.

This is the fifth time that I have left North Korea. I will do so another three times in the future. The excitement and intellectual stimulation that I have experienced on each of my visits have caused me to return again and again. Each time I depart feeling relief and joy at having returned from "the most remote place from earth on the planet." This time, however, my sense of relief exceeds anything I have felt in the past. When I recall the intensity of the thrill and analyze the reasons for it, I attribute it to two factors. Firstly, the visit to North Korea has taken place at a time when the world was expecting an escalation of hostilities, to the point of nuclear war. Secondly, the border crossing. When one flies into the country, getting through the entry procedures is quick, easy, and familiar. The slow train journey, dealing with unfamiliar procedures all on my own, the length of the process, the frightening and even threatening atmosphere – all of these elements collectively created a tremendous level of tension, and the relief when it is all over is similarly enormous. On the next trips, I would be ready. I would already know how to prepare and how to instruct the tourists – and hence the following trips would look completely different.

Potemkin towns

In 1783, under the rule of Empress Catherine the Great, Russia realized a long-held dream. Five years after the Crimean Peninsula achieved independence from the Ottomans, it was conquered and annexed to Russia. This allowed Russia direct access to a "warm" sea – the Black Sea, through which they could sail to the Mediterranean. In 1787, the Empress decided to take a tour of the conquered territory, to see this outlying area of the Russian Empire with her own eyes. The plan was for her to sail southward on the Dnieper River – the main commercial and transportation artery of the southern part of the Empire. Since the Empress was known for her close attention to details, the upcoming tour presented a headache for her advisers, since in describing the area to her they had exaggerated its assets in order to glorify their achievements. At the time, General Grigory Potemkin was the Empress's closest confidant. Legend has it that he thought up a solution to the problem: he instructed that facades of houses and public buildings be quickly constructed to resemble the towns that the Empress expected to see. These facades were then assembled at a spot where the barge carrying the Empress would pass by, and at night they were disassembled and reassembled, with some adjustments to make them look different, further down the river, ready to be sighted the next day.

There is considerable doubt as to the historical accuracy of the tale. It seems more likely that Potemkin instructed that the facades of the village houses facing the river be repainted and decorated – but as often happens, the myth "beats" the facts. The term "Potemkin village" has become a synonym for an external façade intended to make the situation look better than it is.

CHAPTER 13

September 17 – "We're Going to War!"

Since the weather in North Korea during the hot summer months is not conducive to touring, our next tours are scheduled for September, and of course we start preparing for them. In the meantime, North Korea remains a fixture on the international agenda and in the news; and between April and September 2017 there are some dramatic developments. The president of the USA is Donald Trump, and the combination of the unique nature of the North Korean regime and the volatile personality of the US President makes for a political roller-coaster.

Current events are certainly doing nothing to encourage registration for tours to North Korea, but there is growing demand in the media for "experts" who can be interviewed on this topic. Whenever I am contacted by investigative reporters – radio, TV, written or online news – I ask to be introduced as someone who has visited North Korea a few times, rather than as an expert. To my mind, the title "expert" suggests someone who devotes himself or herself professionally to studying the country. The way in which the title is bandied about makes me nervous. I recall my period of studying Political Science in the '70s, including courses in Sovietology. Although the lecturers were presumably experts on the subject, none of them ever speculated aloud that the Communist Bloc was going to collapse within the next decade. Endless articles were written and speeches delivered explaining what was going on in the USSR on the basis of the standing or seating arrangements of its leaders during the Victory Day parade in Red Square. In hindsight they turned out to be irrelevant and in no way helpful for an understanding of what was happening behind the Iron Curtain. No one guessed that the visit by the American table tennis team to China, in March 1971, at the height of the Cultural Revolution, would signal the beginning of a process that would change the political face of the world. The defeat of South Vietnam by the North didn't end up causing a domino effect sweeping the entire Third World into the arms of Communism, as experts had warned. On the contrary: if anything, it was a catalyst that drove the Third World towards openness and an open market economy. All of this taught me a simple lesson: even expertise has its limits. Certainly when it comes to North Korea. A great distance separates the insights I have arrived at, following my visits to the country, and the title "expert," but I am glad to share my subjective observations and experiences as a curious traveler who observes, listens, and thinks, with anyone interested in hearing them.

It is Yaki who gives the first interview, to a major Israeli online news site. The Israeli media has reported on our tours to North Korea, and as the tension surrounding the Korean conflict grows, Tarbutu is flooded with requests to talk with someone who has visited the country. These requests are naturally directed to me. Between May and September, I am interviewed some fifteen times by different media outlets, including the three main TV stations. Of course, each interview is different, but almost all of them echo the usual questions and clichés. Over and over again, instead of questions, I got lectures in which the interviewer explains either that what I saw was only what the authorities wanted me to see, or the other standard cliché – that everything was a show for tourists. Immediately after the death of Otto Warmbier, the story is covered by one of the TV studios and I am invited to participate in a secondary item about trips to North Korea in light of the incident. During the discussion of the Warmbier story, I am (quite rightly) excluded. I sit patiently, alone, in a small room in the studio in Tel Aviv, in front of a screen and a camera, ready to respond as required. When the discussion ends, the news presenter turns to me and asks how we could be traveling to North Korea. In my response I emphasize that my intention is not to explain, justify, or represent the North Korean regime; rather, I will talk about the trips to this secluded country, and that I will try to explain my own position, since I have been asked about tourism to North Korea. Before I can finish my first sentence, the interviewer flashes me a "yellow card." A reprimand. A few more words, and a "second yellow card" – in other words, "Stay away." The interview ends with a detailed and well-substantiated declaration by the interviewer: "We're against trips to North Korea." With that, he moves on to the next item. (This doesn't stop him from contacting me about a month later, to request my help in organizing a visa to North Korea. And here I was, innocently believing that he was opposed to traveling there.) Another interviewer lectures me about life in North Korea, on the basis of the film, *The Truman Show*. Once again, I experience firsthand the absolute advantage of image and cliché over a description of the complexity of the North Korean reality. And in many cases, I understand that my fear that I might be presented as an expert was groundless; my interviewers sound quite sure that they themselves are the experts.

On the other hand, I also discover how easy it is to keep the interviewer spellbound. Once you break through the shell of shallowness, you find curiosity and attentiveness. In all the studios where I waited for my interview, when the producer asked each guest which item he or she was invited for, and everyone in the room heard that I had been invited for the discussion on visiting North Korea, all other conversations ceased and I became the center of attention, peppered with questions from all sides, including some interviewees who were well-respected experts in their fields. In the wake of the first few interviews, I had already learned not to answer the question, but rather to state the truth as I saw it. Indeed, one of the interviews in which I felt that I had managed to convey the message that I wanted to share, ended with the conclusion: "Still, we don't recommend traveling to North Korea." Immediately thereafter, the interviewer added, "Not that I'm not dying to go myself!" Curiosity about what was going on in North Korea seemed to have spread to audiences that I would never have imagined would be interested, and I was interviewed twice by ultra-Orthodox journalists, as well as for an ultra-Orthodox newspaper and radio station. Notably, it was actually these forums where I was asked sensible questions, where close attention was paid to my answers, and where the interviewers were not ashamed to acknowledge their very limited familiarity with the subject.

As noted, media interest is fueled by the dramatic events on the Korean front between April and September of 2017. The collision between Trump's "interesting" style of leadership and the North Korean regime was clearly going to produce headlines that are anything but boring. The following is a concise summary of the events and declarations:

April 27 – Trump is interviewed and sounds conciliatory when asked whether Kim Jong-Un is insane. He answers that he is impressed by his success as a ruler: he was a young man when he rose to power, and his ability to deal with the tough figures surrounding him, who sought to remove him from power, gives the impression that Kim Jong-Un is smart. At the same time, Trump notes that if the talks fail, there is a significant chance of a major conflict.

May 2 – Surprisingly, Trump reports in an interview that it was an honor to meet Kim Jong-Un; he adds that he could meet him over a hamburger.

May 10 – A new president enters office in South Korea – Moon Jae-in. North Korea prepares a "friendly" welcome.

May 13 – There is a North Korean missile launch, in what the Pentagon defines as another stop on the path to long-range missiles.

June 13 – Otto Warmbier, the American student sentenced to fifteen years' imprisonment, is released from prison – but the supposed gesture aimed at lowering the intensity of the conflict quickly turns into fuel for the flames. Warmbier is released in a vegetative state, and six days later he dies. Trump denies that the US paid two million dollars for his release, and adds that the North Korean regime is cruel – but he knows how to deal with it.

July 4 (!) – North Korea launches a long-range missile capable of reaching Hawaii or Alaska. US Secretary of State Rex Tillerson defines this as an escalation of the threat to American national security. In a speech in Berlin, the President of South Korea presents a roadmap to peace by 2020, including the nuclear disarmament of North Korea.

July 29 – North Korea conducts a successful intercontinental ballistic missile launch. The US responds by announcing a joint military exercise with the South Korean army.

August 5 – The US initiates a resolution of the UN Security Council tightening the sanctions on North Korea, with China's support.

August 8 – "We will respond with fire and fury like the world has never seen," warns Trump following the angry North Korean response to the UN Security Council decision. North Korea then claims that Trump is "leading the situation towards war."

August 9 – North Korea releases – alive and unharmed – a Canadian priest of Korean origin who was given a life sentence in 2015 for missionary activity in the country. The item is played down in the international media (my guess is that none of the readers remember this event).

August 17 – The US and South Korea announce a joint military exercise.

September 2 – US President Donald Trump and South Korean President Moon Jae-In announce that the two countries' armies will hold a joint exercise.

September 3 – North Korea conducts a sixth nuclear test, the most powerful to date, and announces that it involved a hydrogen bomb. Despite the power of the explosion, sources in the West express doubt that a thermonuclear weapon was indeed involved.

September 4 – Ten brave tourists and myself meet at Ben Gurion Airport. We are flying to Beijing; our destination is Pyongyang, capital of North Korea. While the media in Israel and around the world is covering the process that is "inexorably" leading to "inevitable" war in the Korean peninsula, we at Tarbutu are preparing for the company's eighth tour there (my sixth). The group is small, but considering the atmosphere, the interest of even ten participants is surprising. Once again, my friends, relatives, close family, and especially my wife, are trying to persuade me to forgo the trip. It's easy to understand why. The trip in April helped me understand how the events look from the North Korean perspective, and how they see reality: "We were weak; we were victims. Today, we're strong. Every missile and every nuclear explosion reinforces our power in the eyes of our enemies, and that distances the danger of war." In the global arena, and in the conflict between India and Pakistan, that's called a "balance of fear." This knowledge helped me to consolidate my position on trips to North Korea in general, and this tour in particular. The media shows interest in the trip. A phone interview is scheduled with a major Israeli TV station for the day I arrive in Pyongyang. The agreement is that an item about the trip will be included on the nightly current events program on the eve of the Jewish New Year. They ask me to send footage (when I reach Manchuria); and then when we return to Israel (if we return...), they will meet with the whole group, at Ben Gurion airport, and interview us.

September 7 – We are in Pyongyang. About half of the seats on the flight are empty, unlike my previous visits, when the planes were always completely full. On the other hand, there is a conspicuous group of about twenty North Koreans who are on their way home, apparently from some sort of national mission (a hint of the future?). The flight and entry procedures proceed smoothly. The inspection is slightly quicker than usual.

When we emerge into the arrivals hall, Mr. Cha is waiting for us, with a guide who I am meeting for the first time; her name is Miss Ann Sang-Wu. Miss Ann is young – in her late twenties; nice-looking, tall (shattering the stereotype of short Koreans), and very pleasant to talk to. She is certainly less experienced than the guides I have worked with previously. I take the fact that she is assigned to our group as a compliment – especially since, as we walk to the bus discussing how we will operate, she does not hide the instructions she has received to follow the procedures that have been consolidated on our previous trips. The rest of the team is mostly familiar: along with Miss Ann, we have the two Messrs. Li as apprentice guides – one of them new to me, Mr. Kim, the photographer, and of course the CEO of Koryo Tours, Mr. Cha. After our enthusiastic reunion, while still walking towards the bus, Mr. Cha can no longer contain his surprise, and he asks, "What happened that you brought only ten people?" His question sounds almost like a complaint or rebuke. My response is simple and honest: "You know," I tell him, "the international situation surrounding North Korea is causing people not to come here right now."

"Situation?" he repeats wonderingly.

As usual, the first day of the tour is devoted to visiting the Arch of Triumph and Mansudae Hill. In the evening, at the hotel, I am waiting for the elevator when suddenly out steps a man with a Western appearance. I always talk to every tourist I see in North Korea and ask about his visit and his impressions. This time a surprise awaits me. "I'm not a tourist," he tells me. "I'm a British journalist, living in Hong Kong, and I am licensed by the authorities here to cover North Korea. I'm here quite often." I see that he is in a hurry, so I tell him, "I don't want to keep you, but I have to ask..."

"I know what you want to ask," he interrupts with a broad, reassuring smile. "Don't worry, there isn't going to be war. You can be sure of that, and you can reassure your group and your relatives at home." His smile widens as he turns to continue on his way.

At dinner, my traditional chat with Mr. Tang and Mr. Cha once again turns to the small group that I have brought, and the fear of war. In my innocence I had assumed that they were unaware of the international tension and the one-sided belligerence. But by the end of a delicate conversation in which I sidestep potential landmines, I understand that the local media has reported proudly on the "threats" by the US and the steadfast position of the Korean people, led by Marshal Kim Jong-Un, in the face of the cowardly enemy. The motto, "We are strong, no one will dare attack us, and we will never declare war," runs through every conversation I have with the local staff. To tell the truth, the words of the British journalist and my Korean hosts only reinforce my view that, as Shakespeare said so long ago, it was all "much ado about nothing."

In the evening, in my room, I call Israel, as usual, to calm everyone – first and foremost my wife, then Yaki and Chaim. After that, I have another call: as agreed, a telephone interview with a TV news channel. Since North Korea is five and a half hours ahead of Israel, our conversation is broadcast as part of the current events program at five in the afternoon. The interviewer is focused and interested; her questions are to the point, and not intended to display control or to challenge. As requested, I describe the relaxed atmosphere in Pyongyang, in contrast to the tumult throughout the world – or, at least, in the world media – and she asks to what extent we are free to move about as we wish. My answer was, and remains, "The reality of North Korea is an alternative reality that is different from anywhere else that I know of. As a tourist, you are restricted to the space between two parallel lines. In between the two lines, there is a surprising amount of room for maneuvering – so long as you are respectful towards your hosts, and keep your requests reasonable. You're not going to see nuclear facilities, and you're not going to visit internment camps." (By the way – where in the world would you be able to?)

At the end of our conversation, the interviewer adopts an empathetic tone and tells me, "Take care of yourself" – her words implying that she views the very fact that I am in North Korea as dangerous. My response was, and remains, "Since I value my life as much as any reasonable person, and I don't regard myself as either a hero or an idiot, the reason I visit here over and over again is because the more I see of the reality of North Korea, the simpler it is for the visitor. Respect your hosts, behave in accordance with the instructions, which are simple and logical, and if you make an innocent mistake, it will be understood and forgiven."

*

Our young guide, Miss Ann, proves from the start to have been a successful choice on the part of the tourism company. She is intelligent, open to listening and learning, and she quickly implements new insights. Like all tour guides, she is attentive to the needs of the group, and, above all, she has an easy, pleasant manner. Two incidents illustrate what I mean about her functioning as a guide, while at the same time shedding light on the way in which tours are run in North Korea – in contrast to the myths that have no basis in reality. The drive to the DMZ and Kaesong is devoid of any problems or delays. As we enter Pyongyang, Miss Ann and I discuss how to best make use of the time that has become available to us, since it is now about six in the evening and all we have on the program is dinner. I ask her, "Miss Ann, what do you say about us going to the pub now, instead of tomorrow?"

Miss Ann looks at her watch and answers, "Fine. But I don't know where the pub is."

"That's no problem," I tell her. "The pub is near the Juche tower. Let's drive to the tower and I'll show you the pub."

Miss Ann consults with the driver and decides to head to the pub. While on the way, I ask her, "You haven't been to the pub?"

She replies, "No. When I go out to drink with friends, it's in the area around the university."

We reach the building. "The pub is on the second floor," I tell her. She asks us to wait, and then goes up to the pub to check that it's the right place, and whether it's possible for us to come in. We wait for about two minutes. Miss Ann comes down, points to a room on the ground floor, and tells me, "Let's go in here." I have a look: we could go there for a drink, but it's not as nice as the pub that I'm familiar with. I ask her, "Why not upstairs?"

She tells me, "There are a lot of locals there."

"Great," I tell her, "The whole point of going to a pub is to meet locals!"

Miss Ann answers gently, "But you won't feel comfortable there."

"On the contrary," I assure her. "We prefer to be upstairs."

As we are talking, I think to myself – Hold on, this is North Korea. We're a group of tourists; we've arrived without coordinating in advance, and off the itinerary. Perhaps I'm creating complications for Miss Ann. I quickly come back to myself and suggest that we move away from the entrance. Then I ask her, "Miss Ann, is it a problem for you?"

"No, no," she replies. "I just want you to feel at ease."

I press further: "Miss Ann, look at me and tell me that you have no problem with this."

Miss Ann smiles and says decisively, with a smile, "No, no problem at all."

In view of her unequivocal answer, we go up to the pub. Indeed, a considerable number of local patrons are seated there. It has become something of a tradition: on behalf of Rimon/ Tarbutu, I invite the group, along with the guides and the photographer for a drink, and even the driver has a soft drink. We spend about an hour there, chatting, communicating with the locals via hand gestures, and in short, enjoying ourselves. "It's all a show for the tourists" and "You know that they take you only where they want you to go" are two mantras that I hear over and over. So, okay: the locals in the pub are actors planted there by the Party. They have been summoned at a quarter of an hour's notice, so as to put on the perfect show for a group of eleven Israelis.

Back on track with the itinerary, we are on Mira (Science) Road. As we are walking, we meet a bride and groom together with family members who have come to be photographed against the background of the buildings and gardens. Of course, the tourists want to take photos too. I turn to Miss Ann to ask her to request permission on our behalf from the celebrants. Her body language conveys embarrassment. "You're not comfortable asking?" I question her.

"That's right," she nods shyly.

"Can I ask?"

With a hand gesture inviting me to go ahead, Miss Ann allows me to address the family. I approach them with the camera, and with hand gestures and head movements I ask their permission. As in previous instances, the locals agree with a smile, and they also invite us to join them in their celebratory photos.

Further on, we reach the sports shop. I ask Miss Ann if we can go inside, and tell her that we once entered this shop but on a later visit, we were refused. Miss Ann asks us to wait; she goes inside, speaks with the salesladies, and returns with a positive response. We enter and walk about, perusing the merchandise and making purchases, for which we pay in euros. Seemingly, a rather mundane experience. Or so it would be anywhere else in the world. Only here in North Korea, it's a real story – especially in view of the fact that journalists and tourists who have once visited the country report that there is no possibility of even the slightest deviation from the itinerary and the route. They also recount what happens to Koreans who make eye contact with tourists... Again, it turns out that the so-called "facts" are not axioms, but rather theories that are there to be proven or disproven.

*

The festive atmosphere is everywhere. Tomorrow is North Korea's sixty-ninth Independence Day. It seems that celebrating the holiday is even more important than work, and the city is decorated accordingly. Everyone is going about in their finery, and groups of Koreans from out of town are enjoying the festivities in the capital. Our morning is devoted to a visit to the **Workers Party Foundation Monument**, which was inaugurated on October 10th, 1995, exactly fifty years after the foundation of the party. The monument, stretching over a plaza of around 27,000 square meters, was designed by the Mansudae Art Studio, and is made of granite and bronze. Of course, every detail and every element has symbolic value. One's eyes are drawn to three pillars of pale granite, fifty meters tall – alluding to the fifty years since the party's establishment. At the top of the three pillars are, respectively, a scythe, a hammer, and a paintbrush. The scythe and hammer are symbols familiar to us from the Communist world, and represent the farmer and the laborer. The paintbrush, a Korean addition, stands at the center, symbolizing the (traditional) writing instrument of the intellectual – indicating that the laborers and farmers need education to lead them towards their goal. The three pillars are bound together with a ring of the same pale-colored granite, representing the unity of forces in society. The outer circumference of the ring measures fifty meters (of course), and the inner ring measures forty-two meters; together they symbolize the year of Chairman Kim Jong-Il's birth (1942). The ring-shaped 'belt' is made up of sixteen blocks of granite, alluding again to the birthdate – February 16th. The monument stands exactly 2,016 meters away from the Mansudae monument – once again underlining the Chairman's birthday. The background of the monument is formed by staggered buildings of red granite that create an opening to the sky. The combination of colors – the white of the granite, the red of the buildings, and the blue of the sky – is the same as the flag of North Korea:

Blue – two thick stripes, at the top and at the bottom of the flag, signify the courage of the nation in its pursuit of peace;

White – two thinner stripes, symbolizing the unity of the Korean people (in terms of land, language, and culture)

Red: at the center, filling most of the flag and symbolizing patriotism, determination, and the blood of battle against the Japanese.

Red star – at the center of a white circle, against the red background – originally a symbol of the Communist Revolution. Despite the numerous changes to the country's constitution, including the replacement of references to Communism with the Juche ideal and later also Songun, the star has remained.

We visit the monument on September 8th, a day before the national holiday, and we are therefore fortunate enough to catch a view of the dancers in the plaza, practicing for the dancing in the streets tomorrow. For me, this is the first experience of its kind, since these are rehearsals and not the real thing; there are no "masks." The dances look less polished than they did on the previous occasions I watched them; there are no smiles, the faces are glum, and the dancing looks mechanical and devoid of spirit. Perhaps this bleak sight is a more genuine reflection of their reality, or maybe it's just the admonishments of the dance director...

*

On this tour, for the first time, we manage to visit a school. We had asked to visit a school or a "children's palace" meant for all children, not like the model one where all the tourists go. As usual, when one requests any sort of change, the answer is, "We'll see; we'll check; it's a problem...." But at lunch, Miss Ann comes over to me and says, "We have some time available in the afternoon. There is a high school that's like any other school. During the afternoon hours, there are extra-curricular activities, paralleling those at the Children's Palace. Would you like to visit?"

"Of course," I tell her.

Just before we leave for the school, Miss Ann adds: "There's a tourist couple from Holland that also wants to visit the school. Are you agreeable to having them join us?"

"Gladly, there are only ten of us; no problem to add another two."

And off we go to the school. The building is completely different from the splendid, sparkling Children's Palace. It's not especially attractive, but it's in fair shape in terms of maintenance, highly functional, and of course clean and tidy. In the yard, children are playing soccer; two teams are on the field, and another team is waiting. In another part of the yard, there is a volleyball court with a game in progress. A teacher, who is leading us around, asks what we would like to see. I answer, "Whatever you think is important for us to see." She thinks for a moment and then says, "The painting group, the gymnastics group, the music group, and the English group."

"That's fine," we agree. We pass from one classroom to the next – what an experience! The children are very excited, stealing shy glances at us and smiling. They happily agree to our request to photograph them. Slowly their behavior becomes more relaxed, and they are unable to hide their curiosity. Towards the end of the visit, we go into the English class. The students are aged about sixteen or seventeen. The teacher encourages them to recite sentences in English and to ask us questions. The interaction becomes more real when she turns to us and requests that we ask the students questions. The tourist from Holland – a powerfully-built woman who, it turns out, plays soccer on Holland's national women's team – addresses them: "I'm from Holland. Do you know where Holland is?" There is an embarrassed silence. She tries again: "Do you know what the capital of Holland is?" More silence; no one says a word.

I decide to try my luck. I say to the students, "I'm from Israel. Have you heard of Israel?"

"Yes!" a few students answer in chorus. "Israel is next to Egypt."

It seems that the children do know a little, and I assume that their familiarity arises from the fact that Israel is widely reported on in the news.

We may presume that the children at the school were prepared for the visit before our arrival, but later on in our tour, in an incident which could almost certainly not have been planned in advance, I encountered a surprising degree of knowledge about

Israel. Snags can be frustrating, but they can also lead to situations that could never have come about otherwise. Once again, one of the participants is not well. Unlike the previous case, this happens on a day when we are in Pyongyang, just before lunch. My professional obligation and personal curiosity coalesce into a decision to absent myself from the meal, and to escort the tourist to the hospital. The smallish medical center is located in the "Forbidden City" – the area that houses foreign embassies and consulates. It is quite evident that in general, the hospital is not meant for the local population. The place appears clean, tidy, and reasonably well equipped. The treatment provided to the tourist, as far as I – a complete layman – can judge, is professional, efficient, and polite. An IV is required, and it takes about two hours. I choose to remain at the hospital. While I am waiting, a conversation develops between the doctor and myself. His English is not very good, but certainly sufficient to hold a conversation. Firstly, he asks where we are from. When I tell him that we're from Israel, a conversation develops about our country. The doctor has some basic knowledge about Israel, and he expresses genuine curiosity. Once again, I discover that the Koreans are relatively knowledgeable about Israel. Afterwards, he asks me about my impressions, and those of the group, of North Korea. Surprisingly, we end up chatting for about two hours – the duration of the tourist's infusion. A conversation between two people, from two distant countries, representing two vastly different regimes, and two very different cultures. And still – a conversation between people.

*

September 11th. Our last day in North Korea; the day we will be taking the train to China. As on previous occasions, I am glued to the window for hours, watching the sights, smiling to myself as I think of all the times I have been told, "You know that...." I look out at the same sights that I have become accustomed to.

The train reaches the border station. This time I am better prepared – I know the procedure. I have brought English forms with me, and more importantly, ten tourists who are full of experiences in North Korea. When we return to Israel, a TV team will be waiting to interview and photograph the brave "lunatics" who have returned from the eye of the storm. We agreed that I would send them preliminary photographic material for the news item, which is scheduled to be broadcast on the magazine program on the eve of the festival of Sukkot (Tabernacles). I am therefore keeping a close eye on the road, photographing and filming sections of it that tell the story of North Korea outside of Pyongyang. When we reach the border city of Sinuiju, I already know what to expect, but it is still long, tiring, and stressful. After about two hours at the border station, it is time to move on. The train, with the same majestic slowness, makes its way towards the Yalu River, heading for the Chinese city of Dandong on the other side. Everyone is glued to the windows, photographing the Chinese shore as it draws closer. From the middle of the bridge there is cellular reception. Although I am not experiencing the return to civilization for the first time, the power of the experience is still tremendous.

Throughout the six days we spend in Manchuria, we are able to communicate freely with Israel. As agreed, I send the photos and the video clips. The news editor also asks me a series of questions, so he will be properly equipped and ready for the interview.

*

On Monday afternoon, September 18, 2017, we land at Ben Gurion Airport. The tour participants are aware of the "ambush" awaiting us, and although Rosh Hashana (the Jewish New Year) is only two days away and everyone is in a hurry to get home, they accede to the producer's request that we all emerge together. As soon as the group is ready, as per the producer's request, we enter the arrivals hall. I have returned to Israel hundreds of times, but it was clear that this time would be different, and I knew that. To tell the truth though, I wasn't ready for the barrage. I had already become accustomed to media interviews but at the end of the day, I'm a regular person, not a TV personality. It is a rather strange feeling for those who aren't used to it: the moment you enter the hall, you are pounced on by someone holding a microphone and others holding cameras. Naturally enough, there are also other people waiting in the hall, curious to know what is going on, and they, too, gather round. You find yourself in a situation that you never imagined you would be in. I was told in advance that first the group participants would be interviewed, so that they could go home, and so it was. They faced a storm of questions with responses along the lines of, "No, it wasn't scary or threatening at all. It was a fantastic experience; highly recommended. We enjoyed it; the reality we encountered was completely different from what we expected." But the participant who stole the show was the one who was asked, "What did you eat in North Korea?" and answered, "We ate noodles; meantime, you've been fed *lokshim*!" (In Yiddish, 'lokshen' refers to the egg noodles used in a variety of Ashkenazi dishes. In Hebrew slang, "feeding someone lokshim" means feeding them lies.) When the interview materials were edited, his answer was retained and it was broadcast as part of the item.

After a few minutes of questions and answers, the members of the group head home, and I am left with the technical team and Gil, the interviewer. We sit down in the arrivals hall, and he interviews me for about an hour. He asks all the usual questions about the atmosphere in North Korea, my opinion of the risk involved in traveling there, how one conducts oneself, the degree to which there is freedom of movement, and of course the claim that everything is a show for the tourists. I am surprised when Gil repeats a series of questions that I have already answered in our preliminary discussion and which I had assumed we had already covered.

"You always stay at the same hotel, right?"

"Correct," I answer.

"Did you visit the fifth floor of the hotel?"

"No."

"Why not?" he asks.

"Because my room was on the twenty-second floor," I answer with some impatience.

"You know that the offices of the North Korean Security Services are located on the fifth floor." It is somewhere between a question and a statement.

"No, I didn't know that," I answer. "I've lived in Israel for seventy years, and I still don't know where Israel's Security Services are located. You haven't ever visited North Korea, but you already know this?" I am by now quite angry. "And anyway, even if it's true, why does it matter?"

He answers, "They keep their security forces there so they can monitor the tourists and the Korean guides."

For a moment I am stunned. Then, instead of losing my temper, I say to him, "Gil, are you serious? The security services personnel of North Korea – a country with nuclear capabilities and ballistic missiles – need to stay with tourists in their hotel so as to track them? What about when we're out of the hotel? How do they track us then?"

Gil has a faint smile on his face, and it is only when I watch the broadcast and see this fragment that I realize that it was an intentional provocation.

Finally, he asks me to sum it all up. After a couple of seconds' thought, I say, "North Korea – the furthest place from planet Earth on planet Earth. The ultimate experience."

The program is broadcast on October 4th, 2017. In general, the editor has done a good job of conveying what the tourists and myself said. But sitting comfortably in the studio are some "experts" on North Korea, including a photojournalist who once visited the country as part of an Israeli group. He is given a broad platform to share his story, and of course I have no way of arguing with his subjective experience. But it strikes me as inappropriate how his personal experience becomes "fact," how hypothesis and reality become blurred, how supposed "facts" are regurgitated, and most of all, how a layman becomes, with dizzying speed, an expert – at least in his own eyes.

A screen shot from the TV item on Israelis visiting North Korea

CHAPTER 14

May 2018 – A New Dawn

As noted, in Chinese culture, "boring" is a blessing; "interesting" is a curse. The fast-moving events surrounding the Korean conflict leave no room for boredom.

September 3rd, 2017 – North Korea carries out a powerful nuclear test and announces that it is considering launching missiles towards the American territory of Guam.

September 19th, 2017 – In a speech delivered at the UN, President Trump refers to the ruler of North Korea as "Little Rocket Man." Lest there be any misunderstanding, he goes on to warn that the US is ready to "totally destroy" North Korea. Kim Jong-Un doesn't let this pass quietly. He calls Trump "the mentally deranged US dotard." The North Korean Foreign Minister joins the fray, comparing Trump's speech to "the sound of a dog barking." Trump tweets in response: "If he echoes thoughts of Little Rocket Man, they won't be around much longer!" The next day he asserts that Kim Jong-Un is a lunatic who doesn't care if his people die of starvation.

October 1st, 2017 – In an attempt to restore some order in the midst of this exchange of childish verbal blows, the US Secretary of State, Rex Tillerson, pays a visit to China. In his meetings with the Chinese leaders, he tries to advance a diplomatic breakthrough. The President offers some "moral support," declaring: "I told Rex Tillerson, our wonderful Secretary of State, that he is wasting his time trying to negotiate with Little Rocket Man." He tweets, "Save your energy, Rex, we'll do what has to be done!"

November 29th, 2017 – After a period of relative calm, North Korea tests a long-range missile which it claims is capable of striking "the whole mainland of the U.S." Immediately thereafter, in an official statement, Kim Jong-Un declares the country's missile program complete.

December 22nd, 2017 – Against the background of reports that the US is planning a military attack, the Security Council ratchets up and expands the sanctions against North Korea, with a focus on exports of energy-producing materials to the country. Just then, with events seemingly having led themselves to a dead end, on January 1st, 2018, Kim Jong-Un declares his willingness to dispatch a North Korean delegation to the Winter Olympics, to be held in Pyeongchang, South Korea, starting on February 9th. President of South Korea, Moon Jae-In jumps at the opportunity and proposes that North and South Korea participate jointly.

February 9th, 2018 – The opening ceremony of the Winter Olympics is held in Pyeongchang, in the presence of Kim Yo-Jong, sister of the North Korean leader. Her presence is intended to lower the level of tension between North Korea and the US and South Korea. For the first time, the Olympics witness a joint Korean team playing ice-hockey. Its sporting achievement is not newsworthy, but the North Korean cheerleading team steals the show.

March 8th, 2018 – An official spokesman of the South Korean government announces, on a visit to the US President, that the Leader of North Korea has announced that he will act for nuclear disarmament throughout the Korean peninsula, and that North Korea will hold no more nuclear and missile tests. Surprisingly, Trump announces that he is agreeable to meeting the Leader of North Korea.

March 26th, 2018 – Kim Jong-Un holds a meeting with Chinese leader Xi Jinping.

March 31st, 2018 – US Secretary of State Mike Pompeo pays a secret visit to Pyongyang. The purpose of the visit is to coordinate a meeting between Trump and Kim Jong-Un. Trump issues an official announcement that the meeting will take place within a few weeks.

April 21st, 2018 – North Korea officially announces that it will halt its nuclear and missile tests, and focus on the economy.

April 27th, 2018 – An historical meeting takes place between the President of South Korea, Moon Jae-In, and the North Korean leader, Kim Jong-Un. This is the third meeting between the leaders of the two countries. The first had taken place in 2000, at the Sunan airport in Pyongyang, between Kim Jong-Il and Kim Dae-Jung, President of South Korea. The second was in 2007, once again in Pyongyang, but this time the President of South Korea, Roh Moo-Hyun, made his way from Seoul to Pyongyang overland (195km) in order to meet Kim Jong-Il. The first meeting had concluded with an eight-point agreement, which expressed an encouraging level of conciliation between the two sides on the declarative level, but produced little in the way of practical results over time. The second meeting concluded with a recommitment to the eight-point agreement.

The Panmunjom meeting

The Panmunjom meeting was the third such encounter between the leaders of the two Koreas, but some aspects made it historically unique. First of all, the meeting succeeded in its intended aim of halting the dangerous deterioration in the rhetoric – and not just between the two sides.

Secondly, in Panmunjom in the DMZ, both leaders physically crossed the border from south to north and from north to south. This represented the first time that a leader of North Korea had set foot upon South Korean territory.

Thirdly, this meeting marked the beginning of a process that led to action, including two meetings – between the North Korean leader and the US President, and between the Korean leaders themselves, again, in Pyongyang in September 2018.

The central agreements reached included the establishment of direct telephone contact between the leaders; the establishment of a joint liaison office in Kaesong; the connection and renovation of land roads between Seoul and Pyongyang; and the transformation of the DMZ into an economic peace zone.

Along with the important political and practical resolutions, there were also some elements of the event with special symbolic value. These included a meeting (for the first time) of the wives of the leaders; a decision that North Korea would move its time zone a half hour forward, thereby eliminating the time difference between itself and South Korea; and a decision to bring forward the Winter Olympics of 2018 – in other words, the joint delegation to the Winter Olympics of 2018 would continue to represent Korea in future international sporting events, too. The two leaders planted a "peace tree "on the border, in mixed soil from the north and south. A cornerstone of peace was likewise laid at the border, signed by both leaders.

Time will tell whether this was indeed a turning point in Korean history, or yet another summit that will be remembered by few and regarded as just another anecdotal incident.

*

The world is preparing for the historical summit between US President Donald Trump and the Supreme Leader of North Korea Kim Jong-Un. As yet, there is no official confirmation that the meeting will take place, and no date or venue has yet been determined, but the rhetorical blows and exchange of insults have given way to more conciliatory and even complimentary discourse.

We at Tarbutu are preparing for our eighth tour (my sixth), which is meant to depart in early May. Interestingly, the prevailing atmosphere of reconciliation has little impact on tourism from Israel, and we received only twelve registrations. The media – throughout the world, including in Israel – is breathlessly awaiting the summit between the Korean leaders, and the meeting between the leaders of the US and North Korea. The media interest revives the demand for an interviewee who is an "expert" on what is happening in North Korea, and I am approached by two out of the three main TV networks. I came to an agreement with one of them that I would be interviewed by telephone when I reach Pyongyang; the other invited me to participate in an afternoon program before the trip. The interview is only a few minutes long, and after I briefly describe my impressions of the country and the way I ran the previous tours, I am asked two questions that should be addressed to an expert, not to me. I point out that I don't have the expertise to answer, but the interviewer, with a reassuring smile, asks me for my opinion, as someone who has visited North Korea and met with locals there. The first question concerns the anticipated summit. I have no idea if and when it will take place, but what I can say with certainty is that in North Korea, the meeting will be perceived as a great achievement by their outstanding Leader, and it will further aggrandize his stature in the eyes of his people. (After all, how many world leaders have an official meeting with the President of the United States?) The second question is whether I believe that the North Koreans will agree to give up their nuclear program. I am at a loss to answer, but once again, the interviewer provides gentle encouragement: "From what you know of the Koreans, what do you think they're thinking?"

I respond, "The Koreans, as far as I can read them, believe that the nuclear weapons in their possession are a deterrent factor that is preventing war: They have never attacked a foreign country, nor will they do so unless they have no alternative and are forced to. They don't understand why it's legitimate for other countries, such as India, Pakistan, Israel, and even France or Britain, to have nuclear weapons and why they have any less right than the US to maintain a nuclear arsenal. I don't think that they'll give up their nuclear capabilities in the foreseeable future. In the Koreans' historical perception, their country was conquered and trampled over and over again, because it was weak. Its independence is completely bound up with its power."

On May 3rd, 2018, we land in Pyongyang. As usual, Mr. Cha awaits us with a hearty welcome. He is accompanied by the friendly and by now familiar Miss Kim. Miss Kim starts the tour, as usual, by introducing the staff, presenting an overview of Korea, and then handing the microphone over to me. I insist, as before, that she presents the rules of etiquette.

The itinerary for the first day, as previously noted, has already become routine. In the evening, at the hotel, we enjoy the traditional dinner in the revolving restaurant on the forty-fifth floor. Mr. Tang joins us, and the gift-giving ceremony is also repeated. Seemingly, everything is as usual. We launch into our after-dinner chat, starting with the usual exchange of pleasantries. Before we move on to discussing the tour itinerary, my hosts ask what the world is saying about the expected meeting between the US President and their leader. I respond, and they question further, hungry for more details. An ordinary conversation for a meeting between representatives of two different cultures. The discussion proceeds naturally, and at first it doesn't occur to me that until now, they have never asked what is being said about their country in the international media. In the past, they have never raised the subject, even obliquely, and yet now the first question that I am asked is how the current developments concerning Korea are viewed around the world. Within a day, I realize that the change in the atmosphere and the discourse is ubiquitous. Each morning, the guides and their directors ask me whether I have spoken with home, and what is being said about them. Our rooms are furnished with televisions that offer Chinese and Hong Kong channels which our hosts have never mentioned, nor asked what is being broadcast on them. Now, they ask for an update each morning. It's not just a request to hear news from the world; but much more: the fact that the Western media is speaking about North Korea in positive terms makes them happy. The most important thing, for them, is that the leadership's policy of making the country's power a priority, is bearing fruit. The country's power is what has led to a positive meeting between the leaders of the two halves of Korea, and of course to the imminent meeting between the Leader of North Korea and the President of the United States – a summit meeting between equals. This is how they perceive the situation.

The feeling that I pick up from my conversations with the guides at every location – aside from the Koryo personnel, with whom I have already developed friendly ties – is one of victory, and, more importantly, the hope of an improvement in their situation, including the removal of what they regard as unjust sanctions and boycotts, and a longing to rejoin the family of nations.

On May 5th, we are at the International Friendship Museum at the Myohyang mountain reserve. On this day, there is an event of great symbolism and significance: North Korea shifts its time zone half an hour forwards, closing the time gap with South Korea. One of the guides at the museum, Ms. Min, who I have met on my previous visits, approaches Miss Kim, pointing to her watch and looking at me, and asks whether we are aware of the time change. I don't wait for Miss Kim's response; I nod my head, and she asks me if I know the reason for the change. Again I need no translation, even though I don't understand any Korean, since her body language conveys her meaning so eloquently. I nod again, with a smile of encouragement.

On our visit to the DMZ, as we reach the border, I ask my "friend," Maj. Wang Ryong-Chu, to show us the cornerstone of peace and the tree planted by the leaders of the two Koreas. Maj. Wang is delighted by the request, and promises to show us these important markers – which he does.

At the Museum of Victory, the meeting with my "friend" from my first visit, Cha On-Jung, who has now returned after her maternity leave and has been promoted to the rank of major, leads to a fascinating conversation. I had never dreamed that I would ever have such an open discussion – certainly not with an officer of the North Korean army. Our relaxed, friendly conversation concerns North Korea, the way in which it is viewed by the rest of the world, and the change that is currently taking place. It is Major Cha On-Jung who initiates the conversation. I do not have the sense of talking to a "page of messages." Not at all. (Incidentally, it is very easy to tell when the speaker is simply reciting a well-rehearsed text.) My impression is that she is expressing her thoughts, and what she says implies very clearly that she is aware of her country's image in the world. During our chat, she expresses the hope that now the world will understand her government's policy and the fact that the Koreans are peace-seeking people. [I emphasize once again that I am not expressing my own opinion as to the North Korean regime or its policy. What I am describing is my feelings and my opinion as to how the North Koreans perceive their own situation and their country's policy.]

On this trip, in all my encounters and conversations with anyone I happen to talk to, without exception, I sense a new, different feeling; a sense of optimism and (relative) openness.

*

On May 6th, as scheduled even before we left Israel, I am interviewed for the afternoon program of one of the main Israeli TV channels. After some technical clarifications (where I am located; how I have called Israel, and so on) we come to the real questions. The central question concerns the reaction of the people that I meet concerning the anticipated summit. This conceals another, secondary (and legitimate) question: is the Korean public even aware of the developments surrounding the summit? In my response, I describe the atmosphere that I have encountered in the country, emphasizing the fact that the Koreans view what is happening as a victory, and as such, it is clear that the Korean media is keeping the public informed and highlighting the achievement. One of the major newspapers in Israel reports the interview on its online news edition. The headline reads, "Israeli in North Korea: The North Koreans view the talks with Trump as a victory." It is fascinating to read the readers' reactions. I am treated to a range of "compliments" as to my idiocy, my blindness, and even the suggestion that since I am a tour leader by occupation, I have to give a favorable report. I feel a certain sense of satisfaction: I have joined the ranks of some very respectable "idiots," such as Yaki, for example (CEO of Rimon Tours), and – more importantly – Nobel Prize laureate for Chemistry, Professor Aaron Ciechanover. I reassure myself with the old adage, "Tell me who your friends are, and I'll tell you who you are..."

*

As usual, the itinerary includes a visit to the Western Sea Barrier, near Nampo. On the way there, for the first time, we drive on a new section of a highway, built to modern, Western standards! It is only about ten kilometers long, and one can see, after the paved section ends, the continuation of the roadworks. After our visit to the sample village near Pyongyang, I decide to pay attention whilst on the roads and to look for similar villages. And indeed, somewhere in the middle of the drive, I make out some buildings in the far distance whose white exterior and tiled roofs resemble those of the sample village. Is that actually a residential village, or perhaps some sort of government institution? Of course, I have no way of knowing. The visit to Nampo and to the Western Sea Barrier have been described as part of a previous visit. As always, we start with the ten-minute film presenting the engineering project and a lecture accompanied by a model. This time I am ready to fulfill my duty. When we enter the lecture room, Miss Kim and the local guide have a whispered exchange, which has also become routine. Miss Kim comes over to me and says "You can give the lecture; we'll prepare coffee and tea for whoever is interested. The price..." she continues without waiting for my response. "I'll take orders, and you can begin."

*

As on our previous visits, our itinerary includes a night tour. The aim, of course, is to see the monuments and tourist sites illuminated at night, but there are some differences this time in comparison with our previous visits. First of all, the night tour includes a boat ride on the Taedong River. Secondly, it will take place on our last night in North Korea, while the regular barbecue finale dinner is brought forward to the previous evening.

Towards sunset, we find ourselves on a wharf on the Taedong River. The riverboat awaiting us looks new and inviting. We had seen it on previous trips, but it had been stationary, not sailing on the water. It seems to have undergone renovation and some adaptations to allow for a panoramic sail down the river, including dinner and entertainment. The boat includes two tourist decks, both closed, with large windows. Each offers a large outdoor area allowing the passengers to enjoy the view. Each deck can hold about a hundred people. We are ushered to the top deck. The tables are set in a horseshoe shape, leaving space for dancing and a stage. When we enter the hall, a girls' orchestra and girls' choir start performing. The hall fills up. Aside from us, there are another two groups of tourists, as well as a group of about twelve members of the diplomatic corps from Poland. When one of the members of our group brings this to my attention, I approach them and introduce myself as an Israeli citizen who also carries a Polish passport. I explain that I often travel to North Korea, and I ask for their contact details in case I run into any problems. The Consul, with whom I am having the conversation, smiles, gives me his business card, and says, "From my experience, I don't think you'll have any problem that will require our intervention." I certainly hope not.

Most of the crowd on the boat is made up of locals who have come to enjoy themselves. At nightfall, the boat sets sail. Food is served when we are on the water. The meal is accompanied by beer and soft drinks. Our attention is divided between the food, the singing, the dancing, and the reflections of the city on the windows. Some of the passengers stand outside, photographing the monuments and other buildings that are lit up against the dimness of the streets in other parts of the city. The illuminated sites are unquestionably impressive, but this boat ride isn't about the city sights; it's about what is going on in the hall. Everyone seems to be in a highly convivial mood. This is certainly true of my group. When the girls invite the guests to dance, a number of participants in our group accept the invitation, and gesture to the locals and the other tourists that they should join, too. In the midst of all this enjoyment, the Koreans, as well as the other Western tourists, come to realize that we are from Israel. I stand on the sidelines, observing and wondering at the mingling on the dance floor. The party continues even after we anchor. In view of the fact that we still have a night tour ahead of us, our guides urge us to hurry and disembark. As they leave, they wave and sing to the Koreans, who wave in return and applaud. It's a show for the tourists, I think to myself. In September 2018, I will be back in Korea, and I will take another boat ride like this one and it will be nice, but the magical atmosphere won't be the same. So it seems that it's not a show for the tourists, but rather an evening of spontaneous joy, and the thought occurs to me that this is connected to the Koreans sensing a warming of international relations. They sense an approaching spring of openness, hope, and pride. Time will tell if the spring will be followed by a summer that will succeed in melting the deep freeze surrounding the sanctions and the international isolation in which North Korea finds itself.

As noted, the night tour is a regular fixture on the tour itinerary. The national monuments are well-lit, creating a breathtaking picture made even more prominent by the dimness of the lighting elsewhere in Pyongyang. Of course, our panoramic visit is conducted by bus, and the highlights include the Juche Tower, Kim Il-Sung Square and the Grand People's Study House, the Chollima Monument, Mira Road and Ryongmong Road, the Parliament Building, the Museum of the Revolution, and more. As usual, we get off the bus at two points to take a walk around the site: at the Victory Arch, and at Mansudae Hill. Alongside the Kim Ill-Sung Stadium is Kaeson (Victory) – the amusement park. At night, the roller coaster and other rides offer a nice picture as a memento. The most impressive stop is at Mansudae Hill. The sight of the illuminated statues on the hill, and the view of the monuments from the top of the hill, has already been described. The impression that the site made on the tourists on their first evening led them to request that we return, and indeed we do. Thus, arriving at the hill this time later at night and not immediately at nightfall, we find the dancing fountains in action. The fountains are on a par with any similar tourist site anywhere in the world. Located at the base of Mansudae Hill, specifically because of their beauty, they symbolize the surrealistic reality of North Korea. Once again, we see no locals enjoying the special sight. I wonder to myself: why is this? The more I think about it, the larger the question looms in my mind. The explanation that makes the most sense to me is that there is no street life at night in North Korea; no movement of people. The few places of entertainment that exist close at around nine or ten at the latest, and then the locals go home and the tourists head back to the hotels. Since private vehicles are all but non-existent, whatever activity there is, is limited to public transportation. At the Arch of Triumph there is a metro station, and thus it makes sense that the amusement park is open. But there is no train or bus line that comes to Mansudae Hill, and so the only visitors who benefit from the illuminated fountains – except for holidays and special occasions – are tourists, who come on tour buses.

The highlight of the night tour for me is the lookout point where one can view the illuminated Ryugyong Hotel. The monstrous building is a monument to failure and to pretentiousness detached from capabilities and costs. But a use was found for it – at least at night. Laser lighting and a range of pyrotechnic effects create a dazzling picture. In North Korea, once again, I cannot help but wonder: am I really here in Pyongyang, or in Las Vegas? And then, a few seconds later, the bus is again making its way through the darkness of the city.

*

I am already accustomed to the routine of the last day in Korea. Goodbyes to the staff. A three-minute drive to the train station. Three interesting hours of journeying through agricultural areas in rural North Korea. The drawn-out border inspection at Sinuiju has become less threatening. The bridge over the Yalu River takes us from the alternative reality to the "homely" comforts of the reality that we are accustomed to. But this time the feeling is different: there is a sense that perhaps North Korea has embarked on a long journey that will connect it back to Earth. Will it happen?

CHAPTER 15

Seventieth Anniversary Celebrations –
Celebrating "Victory"

September 2018. In terms of the weather, summer is making way for autumn, but in terms of politics, the Korean spring that began in April is continuing well into September. The relationships between all parties to the Korean conflict are less strained, and scary news headlines have been replaced by more encouraging signs. It is in this optimistic spirit that we at Tarbutu are planning our next tours for September.

On September 9th, 2018, North Korea will celebrate seventy years since its establishment. Clearly, there will be grandiose events marking the occasion, and we will want to be there with our groups. Like the rest of the world, we are closely following the developments surrounding the anticipated summit between the leaders of the US and North Korea. The situation calls to mind the prophet's question, "Will two walk together, except they have agreed?" (Amos 3:3). These two leaders don't seem to have intended this meeting – but they are both unpredictable.

As noted, on April 27th, a positive meeting between the leaders of South Korea and North Korea took place in the DMZ. The meeting produced the Panmunjom Declaration, heralding a significant shift in the direction of lessened tensions in intra-Korean relations, which had been fraught since the end of the Second World War.

On May 9th, following a meeting between the South Korean President and US Secretary of State Mike Pompeo, North Korea released three American prisoners. (One of them, of Korean descent, had been jailed for the crime of "anti-regime activity." Another had been found guilty of leaving behind a New Testament – which is forbidden to bring into the country, under the prohibition against missionary activity. The third, seeking political asylum, had torn up his entry visa into the country.) All three, according to US reports, were released in good physical condition.

It therefore came as no surprise when President Trump announced, on May 10th, that he would meet the North Korean leader on June 12th in Singapore. It seemed like a direct continuation of a process in which, ironically enough, what had previously seemed logically impossible was becoming most likely and self-evident.

However, the nature of roller coasters is that there are unexpected twists and turns. On May 15th, North Korea announced a freeze on talks with its southern neighbor, citing an imminent joint military exercise between South Korea and the US.

In response, as was to be expected, on May 24th, the US President announced the cancellation of his meeting with the Leader of North Korea. Then, two days later, following talks between North and South Korea, Trump announced that in light of the fact that he had received a positive message from North Korea, the Singapore meeting could still take place.

On June 1st, 2018, the US announced that the summit in Singapore would go ahead.

On June 6th, Singapore announced that it was preparing for the summit.

On June 9th, Trump announced that preparations in Singapore were going well, and that the summit would be a "one-time shot" for North Korea. He added that he hoped that the summit would conclude with an agreement on Korean nuclear disarmament.

On June 12th, the incredible happened: "Little Rocket Man" and the "dotard" (the complimentary titles that each of the leaders had used in reference to the other) held their historical summit in Singapore. In practical terms, the main significance of the meeting lay in the very fact that it took place at all. The rhetoric was positive, and included mutual compliments. A memorandum of understanding was also publicized, comprising four points:

- A mutual commitment to establish a new relationship between the two countries, expressing the need for peace and prosperity.
- Both countries would exert efforts to establish a stable and lasting peace in the Korean peninsula.
- North Korea reaffirmed the Panmunjom Declaration and committed to work towards nuclear disarmament of the Korean Peninsula.
- Both countries would work to bring home prisoners of war and MIAs.

The meeting and agreements were unquestionably cause for hope. A follow-up meeting between the two leaders took place in Hanoi, capital of Vietnam, in February 2019. It ended prematurely, and without any agreement. To date – 2024 – it seems that the meetings might be summed up, in the words of the ancient Book of Proverbs (25:14), "as vapors and wind without rain."

*

The public in Israel, as throughout the world, is fascinated by the summit and its results. Unfortunately, there is no correlation between the positive process underway and registration figures for our upcoming tours to North Korea. Ultimately, when a group of fourteen participants is finalized, it turns out that all the flights from Beijing to Pyongyang are already full. The positive atmosphere, along with the 70th anniversary celebrations planned for September, have increased the demand considerably, while the supply remains limited. All the trains from Dandong are fully booked, too. After our Chinese service supplier does some searching, we manage to secure places on a flight from Shen Yang in Manchuria. Since our tour includes Shen Yang and other areas of Manchuria in any case, we invert the order of our destinations. We will land in Beijing and take a connection flight to Harbin, where we will spend three days. Then we will travel by train to Shen Yang, and spend another two days there. From Shen Yang, we will fly to Pyongyang.

*

Our visas await us when we arrived at the airport in Shen Yang. The group includes my wife, Drora, who, up until now, has been firmly opposed to visiting North Korea. Now that the ice has thawed somewhat, she has joined me for this new experience. Two couples who are old friends have also joined us. Another participant is Dr. Itai Gilboa, a political scientist and a guide at Tarbutu, who has joined us out of interest and with a view to guiding future groups here.

September 2018. As expected, the plane is completely full. The flight from Shen Yang takes less than an hour, and we are in Pyongyang. As usual, I am wearing my "See you in Pyongyang" shirt, to indicate to the border guards and customs officials that I'm back again. The passport control and customs procedures are routine for me and no longer stressful. As usual, Mr. Cha is waiting for us. But from this point onwards, nothing is as usual. Alongside Mr. Cha stands a guide I haven't met before – Miss Yong Mi Si. "Call me Yongmi," she says. She is much older than

Miss Ann, and a little older than Miss Li and Miss Kim, but less experienced. Nevertheless, like all the previous guides, she will prove to be fully cooperative and do everything she can to ensure a successful tour. Later on, I will also come to understand why a less experienced guide was appointed for our tour,[41] but at this stage, I don't dwell on this. On the way to the bus, I start discussing the afternoon program for our first day with her. The arrival time for the flight from Shen Yang is earlier than the flight I am accustomed to, from Beijing, so I want to consult Miss Yongmi and Mr. Cha as to what we might add to the program today. Here I encounter another surprise – and not the last in the series of surprises awaiting me on this trip. "We won't be sleeping in Pyongyang tonight," they inform me. "Tonight, we'll sleep in Myohyang; tomorrow you'll visit the International Friendship Museum and the other sites at the reserve, and then you'll return to Pyongyang to sleep at the Koryo Hotel, or another hotel in Pyongsong." This information catches me somewhat off-guard. I have no problem with a change in the order of the itinerary, but now that the rooms that we use for the first night are customarily reserved for us when we leave the capital for a night or even two, it seems strange. "The seventieth anniversary celebrations have brought many visitors," notes Mr. Cha, but adds nothing further. What concerns me is the possibility that we'll be sleeping at a hotel in Pyongsong, which is about a forty-minute drive out of Pyongyang. It's not the distance that troubles me so much as the question mark over the hotel. The memory of the night spent at the hotel in Ryonggang, at the hot

---

41 The seventieth anniversary celebrations brought an unprecedented number of tourists to North Korea, and the tourist infrastructure was stretched to its limits. In order to meet the demand, creative solutions were found. In view of the Koreans' experience with our tours, they picked an inexperienced guide for our tour, to work in close cooperation with me.

springs, is still fresh in my mind, and it is clear to me that the change in plan represents a dramatic decline in the quality of the hotel and the group's enjoyment. That's North Korea, I think to myself; we're here at a very special time; perhaps this is the price we have to pay for having confirmed the tour late. At the same time, in view of the relationship that I have built up with the management of Koryo Tours, I do not hesitate to convey – gently and politely – my concern and dissatisfaction at this possibility. Mr. Cha, as always, listens, thinks, and offers his classic response: "It's a problem, but let me check." Having little choice, I thank him for his efforts.

We start with our usual visits in Pyongyang: the Arch of Triumph and Mansudae Hill, all as usual, but nevertheless different. In comparison with my previous trips, the city in general, and the tourist sites in particular, are full of tourists and not just local visitors. Since we are about to take a drive of two and a half hours with no restroom on the way (or so I think), the Korean guides and I make an effort to cover both sites in less time than usual.

We leave Pyongyang and head north in the late afternoon, but it's still early enough that more than half of the journey will be in daylight. After about an hour and a quarter, I approach our guide and ask that we find somewhere convenient for a "natural restroom" stop, as we have done on all previous trips. Miss Yong leans over to the driver, exchanges a few words, and turns back to me, nodding: "In a few minutes we'll stop at a highway restroom." I smile indulgently, thinking to myself, *Great – at least she has a sense of humor*. About ten minutes go by, and then a building comes into sight on the right side of the road. As we get closer, I see that it is new, and it does indeed look like a roadside restroom. We come to a stop. There is a counter with various snacks for sale, and one can order (instant) coffee or tea. Another part of the facility is furnished with counters and shelves that appear to be meant for shirts, souvenirs, and other tourist-oriented products. The toilets, at the back, have no running water at this stage. Instead, there are large water cisterns, and smaller containers to fill with water for rinsing the bowl. It's not at Western standards, but it is a small step in the right direction: a roadside restroom, in North Korea!

The hotel and sites in the Myohyang mountains haven't changed. Today is Friday and, as on previous tours, we welcome the Sabbath as per the ancient custom, with the Kiddush being recited by my friend Chaim.

*

Saturday morning. We finish our visit to the Myohyang reserve and set off on the way back. I'm tensely awaiting the moment when we arrive at the hotel in Pyongsong and I will have to inform the group of the change in the itinerary. We always prepare our groups for the possibility of changes that are decided upon by the Korean organizers and for which we don't understand the reason. The move from the nice hotel in Myohyang and from the luxurious hotel planned in the capital, to an unknown hotel in another city, which is certainly going to be of a lesser quality, is going to cause some surprise and disappointment, which may eventually turn into dissatisfaction. I address the group and give them the facts. I start by noting that we have arrived in North Korea at a special point in time; I ask that we all treat this as part of the alternative reality that we have come to experience, and I emphasize that we have no control over this anyway, adding, "I suspect that we may have more surprises." To my own surprise, the participants accept the change of hotel matter-of-factly and without complaint – after all, this is the sort of change that they had taken into consideration as a possibility. The only one who has a hard time accepting it is myself, perhaps because I am the only one who is familiar with the hotel in Pyongyang and understands what a great difference separates it from the hotel that we will be staying at.

*

We arrive in Pyongyang in the late afternoon. There is still time to visit the Workers' Party Monument and Kim Il-Sung Square before we go on to the hotel. Pyongyang is different from the city I've come to know: a festive feeling pervades everything, even though there's nothing one could put one's finger on. It is my eighth visit to the country and I have repeatedly experienced the main holidays (April 15 – birthday of the President and the Korean New Year; and September 9th – the anniversary of the country's independence), but this is different. It is even different from the historical day in May 2018, when the clocks in North Korea were changed to synchronize with South Korea, and one could sense the beginning of hope for change. This time, the hope for change comes combined with a sense of victory: North Korea is euphoric.

When our visit is over, we set off for the hotel. The bus is heading in the direction of the Koryo Hotel, which is just a five-minute drive from Kim Il-Sung Square. As we near the hotel, I ask Miss Yong Mi-Si, "Are we eating dinner here?"

She answers simply that in the end, we will also be sleeping over here, at the Koryo Hotel, but perhaps tomorrow we will sleep in Pyongsong. The group is happy – both at the news that we'll be at the Koryo Hotel, and because they have been surprised even earlier than expected. Everyone is exuberant, but I, as usual, am worried. A change from a good hotel to one that sounds as though it is of a lesser quality can be disappointing, but the experience of the move once one has actually experienced the better hotel is bound to be much more so. While the group participants go up to their rooms, I remain with the guides and Mr. Cha, who has come to meet us for some final arrangements before dinner, which is scheduled to take place on the forty-fifth floor. I cannot allow myself the luxury of dealing with future problems; I have to deal with matters requiring immediate attention. I pull myself together and apply the advice that I gave to the group, telling myself, *This is North Korea, don't try to change what can't be changed.* On my way to my room I look around: I have stayed at this hotel on all my visits and have come to know it well, but here again, like everywhere else we have been so far, the change is immediately apparent. The hotel is bustling with tourists – local and overseas visitors alike – in numbers I have never seen before. It is clear that the occupancy is high; a very different feeling from the half-empty state that I have encountered up to now. We eat dinner, and afterwards, the head guide, Miss Yongmi, Mr. Cha, and I discuss, finalize, and update the itinerary. My colleague, Itai Gilboa, joins us for this meeting. We discuss all the changes relating to the change of hotel, but the focus of the discussion is the events surrounding September 9th, 2018 – North Korea's 70th anniversary. In Eastern culture, seventy isn't just another number. It is the symbol of long life for humans, and now, in 2018, the country itself is celebrating seventy years of existence, while – according to the way the Koreans see reality – the summits with the President of South Korea and with the President of the United Sates are a huge achievement and proof that a just cause, determination, and prudent leadership bear fruit. A record number of tourists have come to celebrate with the Koreans at this historical moment, and joy and excitement pervade the country.

Two major highlights await us: one is a visit to the Kumsusan – the Sun Palace, the pantheon-mausoleum to which thousands of Koreans and hundreds of tourists will be making their pilgrimage. The other, in the evening, is the mass games at the Rungrado 1st of May Stadium. Mr. Cha and Mr. Tang, who also joins our meeting for a change, are visibly tense and stressed. In my innocence, I assume that this is because of our hotel problem, but I will discover the real reason only tomorrow night. We agree to adhere to the routine for the visit to the Kumsusan, which entails being dressed in our best clothes. Then we will return to the hotel for lunch, change our clothes, gather our baggage, and despite the inconvenience, take it all along with us for our afternoon tour. Towards evening, we will watch the mass games (the first in many years), then eat dinner, and then continue on to our hotel in the nearby town of Pyongsong.

*

September 9th, 2018. As usual, in anticipation of a visit to the holy of holies, I wear a jacket and tie, and elegant shoes rather than my usual hiking boots. My wife is dressed very elegantly too. We go down early for breakfast, and as we leave the elevator towards the dining room, we hear a commotion. I don't understand what is happening. At the entrance to the dining room I stop, not believing my eyes: the place is simply crammed with tourists. Waiters are hurrying about to fill empty buffet dishes. At the toast and coffee stands, where guests are being served rather than being able to help themselves, there are long lines, and the staff is struggling to keep up with the volume. I have eaten dozens of breakfasts in this dining room; the quiet and emptiness have always been the central feature that struck me, since the meal itself was reasonable but no more than that. Now the masses have arrived, and it is very noisy. Unquestionably, this is a new era.

While I meander in between the buffet tables, my eyes are drawn to an African man of about sixty, wearing a striking African robe. He has a dignified appearance, and his face radiates confidence and amiability. Wherever I go on my tours, I like to strike up conversations with other tourists – and particularly in North Korea, since it is clear that anyone who chooses to tour North Korea is out of the ordinary. Accordingly, I approach the venerable gentleman and half-say, half-ask: "You seem to be part of an official delegation." He looks at me and introduces himself with a smile: "Professor Obi Samuel of the University of Lagos, Nigeria, head of the Department of Kimilsungism." I introduce myself, emphasizing that I am from Israel. We converse for a while, and he expresses his surprise at discovering that there are Israeli tourists visiting North Korea. His surprise grows when I tell him that this is my eighth visit, and my seventh as a guide. I ask him in turn what "Kimilsungism" means. (It's a term that anyone who has visited the Juche Tower has encountered. At the entrance to the tower, on the wall next to the door, there are plaques expressing admiration for Juche philosophy, mostly from political parties and countries of the Third World. Among the plaques are some that mention "Kimilsungism.") Prof. Samuel is happy to set forth the main principles of this philosophy, which was developed here, in North Korea, by President Kim Il-Sung. It combines socialistic and patriotic principles, promoting national independence and development through the efforts of the popular masses themselves – Juche. I enjoy listening to him. In the coming days, we will meet again several times, like old friends, and in our discussions about North Korea, I will hear further elaboration on Kimilsungism and its relevance for the changes that need to take place in African countries, according to Prof. Samuel, in order for them to progress.

*

After breakfast, there is a "clothing inspection" in anticipation of the visit to the Kumsusan. As usual, the tourists cooperate with the instructions and the request that they dress respectably. This is the group's first morning in Pyongyang, and as we set off, the sight of the cheerleaders arouses great excitement and a request that we stop to take photographs. We are not surprised; the same request has been voiced by every previous group, too. This is my first tour with Miss Yong, but it seems that she has been instructed (and we also agreed in a conversation between us) to follow Mr. Cha's compromise. The bus slows almost to a halt. We open the windows and photograph as we are passing slowly by, and then continue on to the Kumsusan. The celebratory atmosphere is all around us; celebrants are walking about on the sidewalks. These are groups of Koreans who live outside Pyongyang, and who have come to the capital for the holiday. The women are in their colorful dresses, which look less bright than those of the Pyongyang locals, and the men are in their "Mao" suits – seemingly their most dignified attire, reserved for special occasions. For them, being in the capital for the seventieth anniversary celebrations is a once-in-a-lifetime event; a dream come true. Miss Yong and I use the last portion of the journey to review with the group the rules of etiquette at the holy of holies: to respect the local customs, to walk silently, and – especially – the three bows taken in rows of four, in front of the embalmed bodies of President Kim Il-Sung and Chairman Kim Jong-Il. Since there have been no problematic incidents to date involving our tourists, I am relaxed; nevertheless, I emphasize once again the obligation of bowing, and I compare it to the rules of etiquette for tourists at the Western Wall in Jerusalem: the separation of men and women, modest dress, and the obligation to cover one's head.

The parking area of the Kumsusan has never looked like this. Dozens of buses disgorge streams of foreign and local tourists. The foreigners are directed to the hall meant for preparation and waiting; the locals prepare in the open area adjacent to the parking lot. After about half an hour, we are called to enter. The Koreans use a different entrance, and when we reach the rooms with the embalmed bodies, groups of Koreans and groups of foreigners enter alternately. We progress in rows of four to the room in which the President lies in a glass coffin. The two lines – one for Koreans, the other for foreigners – have a short wait to enter the hall. We enter the room illuminated with pale reddish light. Soldiers are standing at attention, frozen in position, in all four corners. We stand in rows of four; each row in turn takes a step forward and then bows deeply in front of the casket.

One of the tourists does not bow. I whisper to him that he must bow, and he refuses. This is a most serious affront to the Koreans and the code of conduct in their country. Over and over, they reiterate that the honor they gave their leaders is a supreme value. They ask that we respect them, and they provide an option for those unwilling to follow the local custom in this regard: anyone refusing to bow is exempt from doing so, on condition that he refrain from entering the room in which the Leader's body lies embalmed. I sense that we have a serious problem on our hands. During our first days of touring, in Manchuria, it had become apparent from time to time that "Moshe" (a fictitious name) behaved "somewhat strangely." This worried me, and I had even considered not allowing him to continue with us to North Korea. I had a stern talk with him, and he had promised to put an end to his caprices. Indeed, during the last couple of days in Manchuria and on the first day in Korea, while his behavior had been not altogether normative, he was tolerable – or so I had thought. When we visited Mansudae Hill, he had participated along with everyone else in the wreath-laying ceremony and the bow before the statues of the Leaders, and so I was unprepared for his behavior at the Kumsusan. A tourist had been sentenced to fifteen years' imprisonment in North Korea for pulling a picture off a wall; what would be the sentence for such brazen insolence in the "holy of holies" of the Korean religion?

We file out of the hall, and I am agitated. I approach the apprentice guide, Mr. Chol, and ask him to remove Moshe from the building, so that he will not repeat his behavior in the room in which Chairman Kim Jong-Il lies.

Moshe asks innocently, "Why do you want them to take me out?"

I answer angrily, "In case you still haven't understood, you're in a country where a tourist was sentenced to fifteen years' imprisonment for offending the Leader's honor. So if you want to put yourself at risk, I have no problem with that. The problem is that you're endangering all of us, especially myself, since I come back here again and again." I ask him, "How would you feel if a tourist came to the Western Wall on Yom Kippur (the Jewish Day of Atonement), insisted on remaining together with his female partner, and ate in public?"

It seems that the significance of what I am saying dawns on him. With the facial expression of a child caught in the act, and with a contrite tone, he promises to behave in accordance with the rules. In the meantime, Mr. Chol returns and tells me that there is no possibility of cutting short Moshe's visit, and it will not be a problem if he doesn't bow in the room housing Chairman Kim Jong-Il. We continue our visit, and Moshe bows along with everyone else.

Once outside the building, I turn to our guide, Miss Yong, and apologize, explaining that Moshe suffers from certain problems. Miss Yong answers calmly, "We know." It turns out that while I had thought that Moshe's behavior during our first day in North Korea was more or less normal, the team of guides and the reception staff at the hotel had already noted his strangeness and decided to let it pass. Miss Yong reassures me – at least outwardly. Inside, I am troubled and angry. My greatest fear is that the trust that I have worked so hard to build up has been dented, and that there will be repercussions.

To my great relief and joy, the incident is behind us, and we move on with the itinerary. Our next stop is the Juche Tower. The elevator isn't large enough to hold our entire party. Itai goes up with most of the group, and I follow afterwards with two of the participants. When the elevator door opens at the top and we are about to step out, I see two African men, dressed in expensive suits, waiting for the elevator together with a guide. Of course, I don't miss this opportunity for a chat, and I address them with what has already become the standard opening line in many encounters on this trip:

"You seem to be part of a formal delegation."

The elder of the two men, more or less my age, extends his hand and says, "I am Ruhakana Rugunda, Prime Minister of Uganda."

Without missing a beat, I shake his hand and reply, "My name is Avraham. I am the tour leader of a group from Israel. It's my eighth time here in North Korea."

The Ugandan Prime Minister mumbles "Israel," and then launches into a sermon about the need for us Israelis to reach an agreement with the Palestinians. He also goes on to set forth the details of the agreement he has in mind. I listen to him attentively, and when he is finished, I express my admiration and my agreement with his ideas. Proud of my contribution to improved relations between Israel and Uganda, and to advancing peace with our neighbors, I step out of the elevator and return to the more mundane matter at hand: leading a group of Israeli tourists. Only in North Korea.

*

As planned, we return to the hotel for lunch. Afterwards there will be a site visit, the mass games, and then the drive to the hotel in Pyongsong. Arriving at the hotel, we are met by Mr. Cha, who informs us that we will not be moving to the other hotel after all. We will stay at the Koryo Hotel in Pyongyang. Hallelujah! Only in North Korea! Another update – we will be leaving immediately after lunch for the mass games. I wonder aloud, "But the production is only in the evening – what will we do for four hours until it starts?" Mr. Cha responds, "Those are the instructions." We are in North Korea; I have already learned that I use the word 'why' too much, and so I keep my response short: "Okay." After lunch we are given some time to rest before the long afternoon and evening awaiting us.

At the entrance to the hotel, a large number of buses are lined up. We climb aboard our bus and wait to set off. Everyone is excited: the Korean staff, including Mr. Tang and Mr. Cha, and of course us, the tourists. After all, this is a unique event – the central production in the celebrations of North Korea's seventieth anniversary. Mr. Tang and Mr. Cha are not their usual selves: tense, impatient, and unsmiling. To ease the tension, I ask them, "Where are we going now?" Mr. Cha answers, "They'll tell us." I ask him, "Will the Leader of North Korea, Marshal Kim Jong-Un, be in attendance at the production this evening?"

"We don't know," he answers.

"Okay," I tell him with a smile, "The Leader will be participating."

Mr. Cha offers no response to my declaration, and changes the subject, noting that ultimately, we didn't need to move to the other hotel. Of course I thank him all over again, and praise him for his efforts to ensure us maximum convenience. After a wait of about twenty minutes, all the buses waiting in line start driving. We don't know exactly where we're headed to. This is North Korea; even if one doesn't know, one doesn't ask too many questions. After a few minutes we reach an enormous square, in front of the Pyongyang City Museum. I remember the square as the place where the street dancing performances take place on holidays, but this evening it has become a parking lot for dozens of buses. In all my visits to the country, I have never seen such a large gathering of tourist buses. We are asked to disembark with our bags, and are directed towards the museum for a visit.

The museum includes several large halls, and an exhibition of pictures whose importance is not immediately apparent. It seems that the museum is not so much the end in itself, but rather a means. Like all the other tourists, we reconcile ourselves to visiting the museum, and go out onto the balcony that looks out over the square, where we are not permitted to go. We all wait patiently on the balcony that is raised eight steps above the square, and watch what is going on in the parking lot. Military vehicles start arriving and soldiers swarm the square, along with security and bomb detection teams, who start checking the buses. The search includes the underside of each bus and the interior. It takes about an hour, and then, as per the order in which the buses are lined up, the tourists are called to return to the vehicles. I watch this strange sight and wonder to myself: clearly, the security check is related to the Leader's participation in the event, but where in North Korea would a potential assassin come from? And if he were to come, the buses would obviously be at some distance from the Leader's car. I think and think, seeking some logical explanation for this behavior. Finding no answer, I decide to let it rest. In any case, even if I ask, I won't receive an answer. Just another small example of the reality that exists only in North Korea.

The performance is at seven in the evening. It's now a little after five, and all the buses, with their passengers, are waiting. Finally, it seems that the long-awaited go-ahead has been given: the convoy, accompanied by military personnel, makes its way to the 1st of May Stadium – the largest stadium in the world. As we approach, the buses are directed to an enormous parking lot where hundreds (!) of buses are already parked. Ultimately, the event will involve more than 160,000 people, including spectators, participants, ushers, and security personnel. We are asked not to take anything along with us, with the emphasis on cameras and cellphones. We receive promises that everything will be safely stored in the buses and we have nothing to worry about. To tell the truth, neither I nor any of the group participants is the slightest bit anxious. In North Korea, there are no pickpockets, no theft, no loss of property – at least, as far as tourists are concerned.

Disembarking, we find ourselves amidst an endless stream of people heading in all directions towards the dozens of entrances to the stadium. Mr. Cha, the team of guides, Itai Gilboa, my wife, and I all join forces to maintain our group cohesion. It's not an easy job, in view of the highly unusual (for North Korea) level of crowding. Eventually, we manage to gather and seat the group together. Mr. Cha counts repeatedly to make sure that everyone is in his or her place. I sit next to him, and once I have had a look around to take in the scene, I turn to him, and for the first time today, I see a hint of serenity. The stadium fills up. Although everyone knows, officially there is still no clear indication that the Supreme Leader, Marshal Kim Jong-Un, will be honoring us with his presence. There is still about half an hour to go before the event begins. Ten minutes before the start, we hear over the loudspeakers a list of all the guests of honor who are present, and then, after a pause for dramatic effect, comes the "surprise" that everyone has been waiting for: the long-awaited announcement of the great honor for all those present – the arrival of the Leader of North Korea at this evening's performance. The crowd's response, although altogether predictable, is unnerving. Some 150,000 people applaud in tense anticipation, and then, with the Leader's entrance, the applause is drowned in roars and cheers, which sweep up everyone in the stadium, including ourselves. After Marshal Kim Jong-Un waves a thank-you to the crowd, everything is ready; quiet descends, and the show begins.

Mass Games

As far as shows are concerned, I've been lucky. Thirty years of working as a tour guide have taken me to many of the greatest shows on earth. Musicals in London and New York; operas and ballets at the Bolshoi in Moscow and the Mariinsky Theater in St. Petersburg; the best clubs and shows in Paris and Las Vegas, carnivals in Rio de Janeiro, Venice, and more; mass games and the Circus in China, and even some productions in North Korea. But then, just when you think you've seen everything, you attend the mass games in Pyongyang and you say to yourself, "Well, no, I haven't seen everything, because what I'm seeing this evening is different from everything I've seen and experienced up until now." The very experience of sitting in a stadium that holds 150,000 people is extremely powerful, even for someone who has been in stadiums with tens of thousands of spectators in Barcelona, Rio, London, Italy, and elsewhere. The welcome shown to the Leader, regardless of your attitude towards the regime, is also spine-tingling. When the show begins, the entire western side of the stadium, with its 50,000-odd spectators, becomes a human background scene that is constantly changing; you sit and you are simply carried away by the show, which lasts for about two hours, with more than 10,000 participants displaying acrobatics, dance, and marches. All of this is accompanied by the finest pyrotechnic effects: lasers, drones, and fireworks, along with "regular" lighting and music. The greatly increased quantity and quality create a sense that what you are watching is a once-in-a-lifetime show. For five years, there had been no mass games; this year the country was marking its seventieth anniversary, and in view of this, combined with the sense of change and victory sweeping the country, the greatest show on earth was even more spectacular. No words can really describe the power of this incredible experience, suspending – at least temporarily – the unease and embarrassment at being so completely swept up by a show that glorifies a regime that is highly problematic (to say the least). Excerpts of the show can be viewed on YouTube (search for "North Korea Mass Games 2018") and on various websites. But again, it's just a sample, a taste, of the real experience.

*

Tuesday, September 10th, 2018. We head south, towards the border with South Korea. The visit to the DMZ jibes perfectly with the euphoric atmosphere pervading North Korea. My "friend," the guide, Major Wang Ryong Cho, is far more relaxed and smiley than in the past. In his presentation, he uses far fewer "juicy" superlatives concerning the enemy – the US – and is happy to tell us about the summit meetings between the leaders of North and South Korea.

Lunch is, as usual, in Kaesong, but today is also the 1st day of Tishrei in the Jewish year 5779 – Rosh Hashana, the Jewish New Year. I had the Kiddush kit for Rosh Hashana with me last night, but in light of the circumstances, there was no possibility of holding the ceremony welcoming the New Year, and so we postponed it for lunch today. Now, here in Kaesong, the historical capital of the Kingdom of Korea, my friend Chaim Bar-Noam recites the special Kiddush for the New Year. Of course, the ceremony is conducted in traditional style, with kosher wine, even though the great majority of the group considers itself completely non-religious. The restaurant is filled to capacity; the diners are presumably all tourists. As the Kiddush is recited, they maintain a respectful silence. Some even rise to their feet as they see us standing for the ceremony. (Recalling the scene, I believe that this was one of the most moving experiences I have had in my life – a group of Israeli tourists welcoming the year 5779 with a Jewish ceremony, in Kaesong, the historical capital of North Korea.)

Later, we have dinner with music and dancing on a boat on the Taedong River. In my mind, the memory of the boat trip from the previous trip is still clear: the exultant mood, the interaction with the Koreans, the friendly waves goodbye. If I had ever entertained the possibility that it was a "show for tourists," this evening dispels it. Once again, the boat carries Koreans along with a great number of tourists. It's a pleasant evening, more or less the same meal, the same entertainment program, but without the unique, electric dynamic of last time.

*

Pyongsong is located about thirty-five kilometers north of Pyongyang. The largest satellite city around the capital, it has a population of three hundred thousand. Pyongsong is known as the "Silicone Valley" of North Korea, and is home, inter alia, to the North Korean Center for Nuclear Research. In 1969, the decision was taken to establish the city around a train station. In 2012, the city was opened to tourists.

Our tour itinerary has not included a visit to Pyongsong in the past, but since we were supposed to sleep over here, a visit was included on the program. Although the sleepover at the hotel was canceled, we asked to go ahead with the visit. The road to Pyongsong passes through agricultural areas. Unlike the other main roads that we have traveled, the road here is narrower and winds its way through fields; there is more vehicular traffic, including bicycles, and also pedestrians. We enter the town and continue on the main road leading to the town square. The appearance of the entrance to Pyongsong makes it clear that this is quite unlike the other satellite towns we have seen so far –

Wonsan, Nampo, and Kaesong. Pyongsong is far nicer-looking, and in better condition. Not like Pyongyang, but even a Western tourist can feel at ease with the condition of the streets. The square is named after Kim Il-Sung, and boasts a giant statue of the Founding Father. I ask if we are required to bow to the Leader, and the local guide leaves it to our discretion. As usual, I follow my policy of cooperating with the rules of the game, and more than half of the group joins me.

Since I regard a trip to North Korea as a journey to an alternative reality, I try to merge into that reality as fully as possible. In other countries, we visit churches and remove our caps, respecting the local custom. Entering a mosque or a Buddhist temple, I remove my shoes. Those participants in the group who wish to get a feel for the local culture go along with this approach, and enter barefoot. I see no difference in principle between the bow in North Korea and the removal of my shoes, or the covering or uncovering of my head elsewhere. Aside from the matter of principle, when one shows respect towards the locals in North Korea, the bonus is that you gain their respect and appreciation, too. On all my tours – and this one especially – I discover the significance of this trust and confidence, built mostly on the genuine respect that I have for my North Korean hosts. After the bowing ceremony, we head for the Museum of the Revolution, adjacent to the square. It's an old-style museum: lots of pictures and certificates, and a few models of battlefields. The exhibition is a tribute to the personality, leadership, and vision of the freedom fighter, President Kim Il-Sung. The visit lasts about forty-five minutes – forty-five minutes of propaganda, all faultlessly recited by the local guide. As noted previously, the local guides at tourist sites in North Korea are completely unlike the guides attached to tourist groups in terms of the nature of their work and their understanding of Western mentality. Our tour guides are in constant, close contact with foreigners. They are chosen carefully for the job; they are all very smart, and each speaks a foreign language. Most of them have traveled outside of their country, and they have some idea of how life looks in the "other" world. In view of all this, it is not surprising that they have an easier time grasping what tourists want. The local guides, in contrast, live in a narrow world that is limited to the site to which each of them is assigned, and they simply rattle off their page of messages with little to no flexibility. The more visitors the site receives, the more flexible they become. When you go to a museum that attracts few tourists, this "robotic" sort of presentation is to be expected. It's best to simply regard it as an experience of the alternative reality of North Korea.

After a five-minute drive from the museum, we arrive at a school. A visit to a school is an itinerary item only in Third World countries. On a visit to a school in North Korea, it is manifestly clear that you are not visiting some random educational institution, but rather a school that has been set up for show. At the same time, even with the strict education towards discipline, it is difficult to suppress the innocence and outward show of emotions in children. Here, too, the further the school from the regular tourist trail, the less effect the preparation for the tourist visit has on them. With all of this in mind we are exceedingly happy to visit the school – and by the end we are even happier. Like the school I visited in Pyongyang, here too the investment in infrastructure is unimpressive. The minimalistic, functional building is nevertheless clean and adorned with decorations and artwork by the students. The children themselves, although clean, neatly combed, and in uniform, are still children: some try to attract our attention and that of the teacher; some cast their eyes shyly downward; some regard us with curiosity; some try to hide embarrassed smiles. After a few minutes of adjustment, their behavior becomes more relaxed and it becomes possible to communicate with them through exchanges of nods and smiles. We visit classrooms for music, painting, mathematics, and English. Afterwards, we are invited to the school hall, where we enjoy a performance of about half an hour including music, dancing, and singing. Although this is clearly a show for tourists, it is equally clear that such a performance cannot be created on the spot. The visit is enjoyable, unlike the propaganda show at the museum.

We all have lunch at the hotel where we were originally supposed to stay. I use the opportunity to have a look at the rooms. All in all, it's not terrible, but certainly not at the level of the hotel where we usually stay. After lunch, Miss Yong Mi informs me with a somber face, that we will have to leave the Koryo Hotel for the last two nights of the tour, and move to a different hotel in Pyongyang. When I ask why, and to which hotel, her response is to shrug her shoulders with a look that says, "I have no idea." I accept the verdict. After all, this is North Korea, celebrating its seventieth anniversary.

*

We are on our way back to Pyongyang, to see the circus. On each of our tours, we have requested an opportunity to see a show for a local audience – folklore, an opera, a musical – and our request has been granted. All the performances we have seen have been showpieces with a common theme of patriotism and glorification of the Leaders. Since the mass games are going on, there are no such shows available, and the only possibility of a local performance is the circus. I am somewhat skeptical for two reasons: firstly, it's clear to me that the top acrobats will not be part of the show, since they will be participating in the mass games. Secondly, it's hard to see how a circus in North Korea will be different from a circus anywhere else. What we're looking for is to see what is unique and special about this country. But since there aren't too many options, we go along with the idea.

*

During the journey back to the hotel, my wife, who always prefers to sit at the back of a bus, comes over to me with a worried
look and says, "Rachel (not her real name) has written a diary of
the trip. I think you need to see it." Rachel isn't young, and she's
the sort of interested tourist who listens to every word the guide
utters and notes every detail. I approach Rachel: "I understand
that you're writing a tour diary. Could I have a look and enjoy
it too?" Rachel proudly holds out a thick file, perfectly ordered,
detailing all our activities with pictures attached. I start reading,
with a smile expressing my appreciation of her impressive documentation. As I continue perusing it, I see pictures cut out of a
magazine that Rachel purchased at one of the souvenir shops.
My smile is slowly replaced by a frown of worry, and then more
urgent concern when I see pictures of the Leaders cut out to fit
into the available space on the page. The first request that the
North Koreans make of visitors is to respect their Leaders, and
this includes not photographing a picture or statue of the Leaders in such a way that any part of them is cut off; not to fold or
sit on pictures of the Leaders, not to throw their pictures into
the trash, and not to cut them out. Day after day, we remind our
tour participants of these rules, and at least once a day I remind
them, "Remember which country we're in."

"Is there a problem?" Rachel asks.

I don't answer her immediately, but ask her permission to
show the diary to our guide. "With pleasure," she answers. I
make my way to our head guide, Miss Yong Mi, hand her the diary, and tell her, "Rachel is keeping a diary of our trip. She's put
a lot of work into it, and she's proud of it. She asked that I show
it to you so you can review it and check that there's no problem
with her creation." Miss Yong takes the diary, and almost immediately her face grows long with worry. On page three, she

comes across a cut-out picture of the Chollima Monument. She lifts the edge of the picture, which has been stuck onto the page; on the other side is a picture of Chairman Kim Jong-Il. Now I am more than worried: not only is the picture of the Leader cut off, but his face is smeared with glue. Things are not looking good, but the fact (at least, as far as Miss Yong knows) that Rachel has presented the diary and asked for the guide's assessment and approval, offers some degree of reassurance. Miss Yong looks at me. Her face says it all, but she says, "I think we have a problem."

"I understand," I answer, "but you're aware that she's an elderly lady, who has prepared this diary in order to share her experiences in North Korea with her friends and relatives. More importantly, she acted innocently: she proudly asked that I show it to you."

Miss Yong listens with understanding and in agreement, and tells me that this will need to be dealt with. She calls the tourism company, and after a few minutes of conversation, she turns to me and asks that I find out from Rachel what she did with the remains of the cut-out pictures. Rachel tells me that she put them in the wastepaper basket in her room. Miss Yong makes another call, and then turns to us and says, "In order to bring this story to a conclusion, Rachel will need to meet with the company directors." I ask her to speak with Mr. Cha and to explain to him again that Rachel proudly asked to show the diary, etcetera. Mr. Cha answers and says that he understands, and believes that everything will be fine, but in order to conclude the incident there is a need for a meeting with her. "Since Rachel doesn't speak English," I tell him, "I will need to accompany her, and I have to be with the group, so could we perhaps do this after the circus?"

"It's best that we do it right away," he replies. At this point, Itai fortunately intervenes and offers his help as a translator. Mr. Cha agrees unhesitatingly, and so Itai and Rachel travel to the hotel. I continue with the rest of the group to the circus.

I sit with the group during the circus performance. Although I believe that if the problem is dealt with by Mr. Cha, all will be well and the saga will end with the meeting this evening, I am still tensely waiting to hear what is happening with Rachel and Itai.

*

After the circus, I meet up with Mr. Cha, Itai, and Rachel. Mr. Cha looks serious. I am sure that the incident with the diary has darkened his mood, but he brushes it off briefly and matter-of-factly, as something that happened and is now over. Then he repeats the "bad news": tomorrow, the entire Koryo Hotel where we are staying is being evacuated. Unlike the previous changes in plan, this time there's an explanation: the President of South Korea will be arriving on September 18th for a meeting with the Leader of North Korea. The preparatory teams from South Korea will be arriving earlier, and the hotel is being prepared for them. The story of Rachel and her diary pales into insignificance; the sort of "bad news" that we are accustomed to no longer concerns us, and – most interestingly of all – there is an explanation, and one that makes sense, for the change. My mood improves dramatically.

Rachel is all smiles, not at all agitated, but slightly upset with me since it is on my account that her diary has been confiscated. I dare say she simply didn't understand the significance of what she did, and its potential for problems. I had already imagined a scenario – not far-fetched by any means – in which at Pyongyang airport, during our departure, the officials decided to carry out an inspection like the one that is customary on the train when one leaves the country on land. I was covered with cold sweat, and my mind filled with ghastly images. Itai was smiling less than Rachel. In general, he is a very restrained and rational person, but I could see how nervous he had been. Putting on a calm face for the group, he allowed Rachel to take center stage; later he told me what had happened:

"We arrived at the hotel – Rachel, me, and the apprentice guide. Mr. Cha was waiting for us there, together with a woman. They looked through Rachel's diary and launched into a series of questions that were aimed to clarify beyond all doubt that she had acted in good faith. Mr. Cha posed the questions to me; I translated for Rachel, then translated her answer into English, which was then translated into Korean. The purpose of the question was to understand what had happened to the cut-out remains that weren't pasted into the diary. At some point, I was asked to read excerpts that Rachel had written, and to translate them into English. Fortunately, all the entries they chose at random were positive, or neutral and factual concerning the sights and experiences, so I had no problem providing a straight translation."

The diary was confiscated.

Rachel was asked to write a letter in which she explained that she had not intended to offend the Korean people.

The letter was written by Itai in English; Rachel copied it in her handwriting in English, and signed, and it was given to the Koreans.

The practical conclusions I draw from the bowing incident with Moshe, and – especially – from the episode of Rachel's diary, in addition to Mike's story (from my first tour), are simple:

Don't ever forget, even for a moment, the unique nature of the North Korean regime. Don't allow yourself to be lulled into the pleasant, comfortable routine that is created over the course of the tour. Remind the participants over and over again to respect the Koreans' requests, and to behave on their home turf in accordance with their rules. Their requests aren't unreasonable, and they can be followed without difficulty.

In the event of a problem, the simplest course of action is also the most effective: speak up immediately and honestly.

The Koreans have no desire to turn a deviation from their rules that was an honest mistake into a major incident. If they're intolerant, it's towards deliberately provocative behavior.

And – with all due modesty – it seems that my investment in building relationships with the Koreans, based on an understanding of their perception of reality, and on honesty and respect, paid dividends.

*

During dinner, with the episode of the diary behind us, I start to internalize the fact that this evening we have to leave the hotel. For the last two nights we have an "opportunity" to experience a different hotel – we don't know yet which. On our way from dinner back to the hotel, I update the group. They respond with cynical smiles, thinking to themselves, "Well, nothing's changed; we've been through this before." When we reach the hotel, the scene is reminiscent of a railway station: tourists are making their way out with their baggage; uniformed officials are walking about; citizens whose dress indicates that they hold senior positions are rushing about with worried expressions. After all, it's not every day that the President of South Korea arrives for talks with the Leader of North Korea, nor that delegations of senior personnel are on their way for work discussions. All of this is going to be happening in exactly one week's time. Indeed, we have arrived at an historical moment, and so we should take this inconvenience in our stride.

We give the group participants time to go up to their rooms so that they can pack and prepare for the move tomorrow. As is my custom, I stay behind to talk some more with the local guides. Itai is with me, and we have lots to talk about, considering all that has happened today. As we are sitting in the lobby, the in-defatigable Mr. Cha pops in and announces that there has been a change in the arrangements. He updates us: tonight our group will remain at the Koryo; only tomorrow night will we need to move to the other hotel. However, we will need to evacuate five of our rooms and move to different rooms. He gives me a list of the rooms that will be vacated, and the five new rooms. I imagine that they are carrying out a security check of the ho-tel, so they are emptying one floor or wing at a time. I look at the list of rooms that we need to clear, but it makes no sense. There is no common denominator. One of them is the room I am sharing with my wife; another is Itai's room. These and the other three rooms that must move are on the same floor, or in the same wing, as other rooms in which we are allowed to stay. I don't even try to understand the logic. I make an attempt to in-troduce some small adjustments in the list, so that women who are alone in their rooms are not alone on a floor, while neither Itai nor I have any problem occupying the group's only room on a floor. But Mr. Cha is short and decisive in his response: that's the list, and there's no possibility of any changes. Itai and I call the other three rooms in question and explain the situation. The relevant participants reconcile themselves to the instructions without too much complaining, and within an hour, the move is completed.

*

In the morning, with our baggage already packed up in our rooms, we are ready for our last day of touring. At breakfast, the dining room is less busy than on the preceding days; the occu-pancy is significantly lower; the hotel is indeed clearing all out the tourists. Our last morning here will be spent in Nampo; in the afternoon, we will complete our visits in Pyongyang; and before dinner, we will return to the hotel, curious to know which hotel we will be moving to. Dinner is scheduled to take place at the nearby grill restaurant which is within a short walking distance. Mr. Cha receives us as we arrive. He seems quite relaxed, in complete contrast to the tension that he has displayed over the past few days. After we exchange a few pleasantries, I ask him, "Well, which hotel will we be moving to?" fearing that his answer might be, "The hotel in Pyongsong" – meaning that we have a long night ahead after dinner, organizing ourselves with all our baggage in the bus and a fifty-minute drive. Mr. Cha smiles and answers, "Which hotel would you like?"

"The Koryo Hotel," I answer, knowing that this is impossible. Mr. Cha continues smiling and says, "Okay. You want it – you got it. We've made a special effort for you, and you're the only group that will stay at the hotel tonight." For a second I am skeptical, but immediately realize that it would make no sense in Korean culture to "play jokes" on tourists. I am happily surprised, and express my genuinely enthusiastic thanks and appreciation. We return to the final dinner at the grill restaurant. A dinner on a river boat, as enjoyable and successful as it may be, doesn't offer the proper conditions for the final dinner of a tour. Mr. Tang, Mr. Cha, the team of guides, the photographer, and the driver are all present. The waitresses sing and invite the participants to dance; the hall is small, and allows for conversation, speeches of thanks, and good wishes. All the participants understand that we have encountered North Korea in a most unique situation: the seventieth anniversary celebrations, combined with the atmosphere of the political spring that is taking place in the Korean peninsula. There are winds of change; time will tell whether this is indeed the beginning of a new era, or a balloon that pops when it floats too high. When we return to the Koryo Hotel, we find it almost emptied of all Western tourists. If we were not the only Western group left, we were certainly among the last.

*

It's our last morning in North Korea. My wife and I are, as usual, the first to enter the dining room for breakfast. Slowly the group assembles in the almost empty room. Mr. Cha was correct: we have indeed been shown special consideration; the other tourist groups all had to leave the hotel in anticipation of the arrival of the South Korean delegation.

On our way to the airport, we take our leave of the staff, as usual leaving a generous tip, even by Western standards. In my discussions with our office about the "unreasonable" level of the tip, I explain to them: it's a destination that I visit again and again, and it's not just any destination. We want the guides there to want to work with us and to cooperate with us – not only in terms of guiding the group, but in dealing with unanticipated situations and the sort of problems that only occur in North Korea. On this tour, more than on any other, I understood that the unexpected is what one has to be careful about. And it's best not to learn this in retrospect.

I am on edge. I remember all too well what happened to Otto Warmbier, at the airport, right before takeoff. Although the episodes of the bowing and the diary are behind us, I am still uneasy. My wife and I are the last to pass through border control and the last to board the flight. Of course, my attention is focused mainly on Rachel and Moshe. Only when everyone is on board and there is no longer reason to fear, do I finally allow myself to settle into calmness and the release of tension that comes after it's all over.

*

The general feeling among all the participants, including my wife, who for so long was so vehemently opposed to the idea of traveling to North Korea, is that the tour of North Korea has been a powerful and special experience. It has been thought-provoking and drives one to attempt to find answers to questions and issues which, in our comfortable routine, don't usually bother us.

The power of the North Korean experience lies in the encounter with the alternative reality in North Korea – the furthest place from Earth on the planet.

In the DMZ, a covenant of friendship between the North Korean army and Rimon Tarbutu, Israel. (On the right – Yaki, Co-owner of Rimon Tours; on the left – me)

CHAPTER 16

Thoughts in Conclusion, or:
Who Isn't "Disconnected from Reality?"

The seasons follow their fixed order. Winter makes way for spring, which heralds the coming of summer. The use of seasonal terms to describe political developments is convenient and picturesque, but doesn't necessarily match the reality; in this case it is misguiding. In January 1968, Communist Czechoslovakia saw its famous Prague Spring, which was brutally suppressed within a few days in August of that year. The "Summer" reached Czechoslovakia only in 1989, and with no connection to the "Spring" of 1968.

As described in the preceding two chapters, the events of 2018 created an optimistic atmosphere – a "Korean Spring." To date (2024), in the Korean instance, too, the spring of 2018 was not followed by a summer.

On February 27th, 2019, another meeting was held between the leaders of the US and North Korea in Hanoi, Vietnam (an ironic location, in view of the history of US relations with Vietnam). The meeting was shorter than expected, ending in less than a day, before the joint luncheon, with no agreement or statement of any kind.

This meeting ended the political "spring" in the Korean peninsula. What followed was not so much a summer as an autumn. The relations between North and South Korea remained slightly warmer than they had been in 2016-2017. The flames of the conflict seemed to have died down, and even intercontinental ballistic missile tests (carried out in March 2021 and April 2022) were given relatively less prominence in the Western media. News from North Korea made way for more "interesting" events.

The Korean conflict lost its centrality on the US foreign affairs agenda. Relationships with Iran, China and Russia, and the war in Ukraine, have certainly come to appear more problematic and urgent, and have accordingly been awarded priority over dealing with the Korean nuclear program.

North Korea may have benefitted slightly from the very existence of the summit meetings with the leaders of South Korea and the US. The calmer relations with South Korea are certainly convenient. But the return to routine in North Korea has been hard. The sanctions on the country are the most severe to have been applied to any country in modern history. With the outbreak of the COVID-19 pandemic, North Korea sealed off its borders, allowing no one to enter or leave, and its current isolation is certainly not helping the already problematic economic situation.

The Korean conflict isn't over. Its relegation to the inner pages of the news doesn't mean anything. Like a sore, simply covering it up may lead to a more severe eruption sometime in the future. The situation in the country, as per reports from time to time in the Western media, is worrying. History has shown that internal distress can be exploited by leaders to turn the public's attention to an external foe. And when that happens, there is always the danger of the situation igniting and spiraling out of control.

*

The division of Korea isn't fair; it isn't moral, and it doesn't make historical sense. Dividing the country of a homogeneous people that has consolidated itself over thousands of years in a well-defined territory, for no reason that makes sense internally, is an anomaly, and anomalies eventually resolve themselves.

Time will tell – will it happen? And if so – when, how, and at what price?

*

I am preoccupied with thoughts about North Korea. In my mind, I review those two-and-a-half years in which I visited the country eight times: two and a half years of change in North Korea, from the arrest and death of an American student, via the war of words that seemed to be leading inexorably to war, to the euphoria, the lowering of tensions, and the hope for change. Two and a half years of change from half-empty hotels to hotels full to capacity. Two and a half years of change from the frightening and anxiety-provoking unknown to a budding familiarity with people, leading to an understanding of their subjective mindset and logic – even if objectively they might be mistaken. Two and a half years in which I endeavor to identify navigational tools to help me find my way through the information, disinformation, and misinformation offered by the free Western media. Two and a half years of learning all over again that there are two (or more) sides to every coin. Eight visits over two and a half years, giving rise to a great deal of thought and insights, and the understanding that what seems self-evident isn't necessarily so obvious, and that there are some mysteries that may not be resolved.

I wonder, over and over again: what was it, in the encounter with North Korea, that grabbed me so powerfully?

I try to find an answer: perhaps it's that alternative reality, in which there are no banks, credit cards, internet, advertisements, or commercial billboards, but an abundance of notice boards and murals conveying patriotic messages; a reality in which a supermarket, pub, or gas station is a tourist attraction; a reality in which a country has a single international airport, and it shuts down after the single daily arrival; a reality in which a nation starts its day with a musical wake-up call; a nuclear power whose roads are empty and in disrepair; a reality in which there are a few lone highway restrooms, with no running water; breathtaking stage performances; tidy children who are taught "the right way to walk" in public spaces; a choice of four hairstyles for all citizens; grand monuments and public buildings that are brightly illuminated while the streets and homes around them are dim; and above all – a reality in which every citizen displays images of the Leaders on his lapel as part of a system of "religious" worship. Or is it perhaps the swift adaptation of visitors to this reality that amazes me more than anything else, whereby for a given time, phenomena that are strange and different become part of a logical routine?

Perhaps it's the insight as to the ease with which, in an isolated country under a totalitarian regime, one can engineer people's consciousness and manipulate their behavior?

Perhaps it's that the encounter with the North Korean reality shows that in the Western world, too, with its freedom and unlimited access to the media and to sources of information, we are constantly exposed to consciousness-engineering, with a stream of facts jumbled indiscriminately with opinions, theories, beliefs, myths, and fables?

My thoughts turn to *The Truman Show*, and the TV interview in which I was asked if I hadn't felt, like the hero of the movie, like someone walking around in the biggest show on earth, a show that was stage-crafted down to the last detail. Well, there's no question that a visit to North Korea includes many elements of a show for tourists. Still, there's no way of preventing exposure to the reality which the regime would prefer visitors not to see. The visitor has a sense of an engineered, closely controlled "alternative" reality that is different from the reality that we are familiar with. And this being the case, I go back to the interviewer's question and quote from the concluding scene of the film, where the producer addresses Truman, who wants to go out into the "real" world. He tells him,

"There's no more truth out there than there is in the world I created for you.

The same lies. The same deceit."

North Korea – state emblem

KOREA – HISTORY

Gojoseon Dynasty: 2100–100 B.C.E. ("Go" = "ancient")

The ancient Joseon dynasty was an Eastern kingdom of archers. The little that is known of its origins comes from earthen shards and Chinese manuscripts. Under the Gojoseon dynasty, the country's borders and independence had ups and downs as the Chinese emperors grew weaker or stronger. The dynasty came to an end in the year 109 B.C.E. with the Han conquest, under Wuju the Chinese.

The Three Kingdoms – Goguryeo, Silla, Baekje: 109 B.C.E.–688 C.E.

The Three Kingdoms arose after the fall of the Gojoseon dynasty, and for a period they existed in parallel. In fact, for a short time, there was a fourth kingdom that existed along with them.

For most of this period, the Goguryeo Kingdom was the strongest and most dominant among the three, which fought among themselves.

The Korean kingdoms shared similar background, language, and culture, and all operated on the basis of Buddhist and Confucian values.

During this period, there was an ongoing war against the Chinese Sui and Tang dynasties.

The Tang dynasty in China supported the Silla kingdom, which came to dominate the Korean kingdoms.

Silla dynasty: 668–935

The Silla kingdom was founded in the year 57 C.E., but only after the fall of the Goguryeo dynasty did it assume a central role in Korean history.

The Silla period is regarded as a lengthy period of quiet. It was during this time that "*idu*" developed: a system for writing the Korean language using Chinese characters ("*hanja*"). This was also the time of the development of the Seon Buddhist stream, better known by its Japanese name: Zen Buddhism. At the same time as the Silla Dynasty, there existed the Balhae kingdom, which was conquered by the Khitans.

Korea – "Middle Ages"

Koryo/Goryeo Dynasty: 918–1392

The fall of Balhae and the weakening of the Silla kingdom cleared the way for the appearance of the new Goryeo dynasty – the Koryo.

The Koryo dynasty ruled over almost the entire Korean peninsula, establishing a uniform system of laws and of imperial service and administration. It was during this period that Korea in fact coalesced into a single, unified political entity.

In terms of technological and cultural development, the Koreans take pride in two original contributions:

1. Celadon pottery with a bluish-greyish-jade green glaze.
2. In the 12th century, a technology developed in the Goryeo kingdom for movable metal type that anticipated the Western printing press.

The 11th and 12th centuries were dominated by wars against the Khitans, which weakened both kingdoms. The Mongol invasion of Korea during the 13th century turned Goryeo into a vassal state of the Yuan dynasty, although the Goryeo dynasty survived until 1392.

The Goryeo capital was the city of Kaesong, located in the territory of North Korea, but south of the 38th parallel (a fact of great patriotic symbolism for the North Koreans).

The Goryeo period is central to the Korean national narrative – especially in North Korea, but also in the South. The reunification plan proposed by President Kim Il-Sung proposed "Koryo" as the name for the merged states. Koryo is also the name of the national airline, as well as the national tourism company.

Joseon Dynasty: 1392–1895

In 1392, there was a coup d'etat led by General Yi Seong-gye, commander of the Korean army, with the support of the Chinese Ming Emperor, which put an end to the Goryeo dynasty. It was replaced by the last imperial dynasty to rule Korea: the Joseon.

The Joseon dynasty ruled under Chinese patronage for some five hundred years, making it the longest lasting Confucian dynasty. Upon its establishment, the capital was moved from Kaesong southward, to Hanseong (Seoul), where it remained.

In 1443, the Korean alphabet – Hangul – was introduced.

In 1592, and again in 1598, there were Japanese invasions, which were repelled with the help of China, but extensive damage had been caused, which weakened the kingdom. It became a vassal state of the Chinese Ming Empire.

In 1644, the kingdom remained a vassal state, this time in relation to the Manchurian Ching dynasty, which ruled China.

Between 1876 and 1895, Japan and China fought a war that ended with a Japanese victory. Korea became a vassal state of Japan.

In 1895, the Korean Empress was assassinated by the Japanese.

From 1895 until 1905, Russia and China fought over control of Korea, ending with a Japanese victory and the annexation of Korea.

Under Japanese Occupation (1905 – 1945)

Introduction: In 1868, a process known as the Meiji Restoration began in Japan, in which the emperor led Japan to become a military, political, and industrial power. As an island country with a large population and few natural resources, Japan sought to conquer eastern Asia, so as to gain control of strategic assets including agricultural land, as well as natural resources such as crude oil, rubber, and more. Korea, weakened and situated only a hundred and fifty kilometers away, was therefore an ideal bridgehead from which to pursue the conquest of eastern Asia. The campaign began at the end of the nineteenth century, and was completed during the Second World War.

Major milestones

1876 – The Treaty of Ganghwa is signed between the Japanese Empire and the Kingdom of Joseon. On paper, it is trade agreement that also grants the Japanese access to natural resources. In practice, it opens the door to significant Japanese influence in Korea.

April 1895 – Following China's defeat in the war against Japan, an agreement is signed guaranteeing Korea's independence from China, which is a step towards Japanese hegemony in the country. The same year, Empress Myeongsong, who had attempted to counter Japanese interference in Korea, is assassinated by Japanese agents.

1904 – Japan is victorious in war against Russia; Korea becomes a protectorate of Japan.

August 29, 1910 – An official agreement is reached between the Korean government and a representative of the Japanese Emperor annexing Korea to Japan. In Korea (South and North), this day is commemorated as the "Day of National Humiliation."

August 15, 1945 – Japan announces its unconditional surrender to the US. An agreement is signed on September 2nd, 1945. Korea is liberated, but in North Korea, there is no mention of Japan's unconditional surrender to the US and the Allied forces. Nor is there any mention of the atomic bombs on Hiroshima and Nagasaki. Here, the liberation of Korea comes about as the product of a heroic war of independence.

Overview of Japanese occupation of Korea

- Significant investment in infrastructure and development of roads, ports, mines, and industry.
- Heavy-handed suppression of opposition, massacre of demonstrators, and murder of farmers who refused to pay taxes.
- 1919 – Death (apparently by poisoning) of the last Korean Emperor. Declaration of Korean independence, followed by the Japanese response of a massacre of demonstrators (at least 7,000 in one specific incident). Establishment of a government-in-exile in China, which enjoyed widespread legitimacy among Koreans.
- Korean guerilla war, especially in Manchuria on the Korean border, China, and the USSR. Guerilla warfare with a Communist orientation.
- 1937 – Outbreak of the Sino-Japanese War, continuing in Asia into the Second World War:
- Increased oppression, with an attempt to eradicate any expression of Korean identity: prohibition on teaching the Korean language; prohibition on spoken or written Korean in the public sphere; prohibition on giving Korean names; Japanese Shinto the only permitted religion.
- Destruction and theft of artworks and artifacts from museums and burial sites. Items of value were transferred to Japan (after the war, the majority were returned to South

Korea, but many very valuable items were sold to museums and private collections, especially in the US).

- Forced laborers in Japan, Manchuria, and Korea (at least 700,000)
- Recruitment of over 100,000 Koreans for the Japanese army.
- Comfort Women – a euphemistic term for the despicable use of Korean girls and young women as sex slaves by Japanese soldiers. There are no exact data on the scope of this phenomenon, but estimates put the figure at 200,000 women. Japan later apologized to the Korean people and also paid reparations, but the episode keeps surfacing in Korea and continues to weigh heavily on the relations between Japan and Korea (both North and South).

Summary of the period of occupation and the war

- Over a million Koreans killed over forty years of Japanese occupation – approx. 5% of the population.
- Almost complete destruction of Korea's organizational and administrative infrastructure.
- Eradication of the country's administrative elite.
- Humiliation and acute damage to Korean national dignity.
- Division of Korea into two countries.

Liberation, Division, Independence (1945–1948)

- August 15th, 1945 – Korean liberation from Japanese occupation.

In North Korea, the liberation is presented as the result of a heroic war, led by the commander of the resistance – later to become President Kim Il-Sung.

Division of Korea

-   November 1943 – The Second World War is far from being over, but the Allied victories at Midway, Al-Alamein, Stalingrad, and Kursk, are indicating its direction. Two conferences take place in the midst of the war: the Cairo Conference, with the participation of the US, Britain, and China (Chiang Kai-shek), and later on the Tehran Conference, in which Stalin replaced the Chinese leader. Among the agreements reached was that Korea would be a free and independent state.
-   February 1945 – The Second World War is nearing its end. The Yalta Conference convenes and resolves, inter alia, that Korea would be temporarily placed under an international trusteeship, during which time it would be divided between the powers. As a gesture to Russia for joining the war in Asia, the USSR would enter northern China.
-   July 1945 – Two months after the Second World War ends in Europe, a conference is held in Potsdam, in the Soviet occupation zone, to plan the post-war agreements – including the proposed conditions for Japan's surrender. Despite the agreements, while the Second World War could be said to be over, what followed was not peace, but rather the Cold War.
-   August 8th, 1945 – Two days after the atom bomb is dropped on Hiroshima and a day before the bombing of Nagasaki, the USSR declares war on Japan, and its army begins moving swiftly southward (perhaps the first real act of the Cold War).
-   August 10th, 1945 – (The day after the bombing of Nagasaki) – The US, fearing that the USSR might seize control of Korea, suggests a partition of the country between the US and the USSR. Following some brief discussion, the two powers agree on the temporary division of Korea

into two areas of influence, on the two sides of the 38th parallel (the US insisted that Seoul, the capital, remain in the Western area of influence).

- August 15th, 1945 – Japan surrenders; Korea is liberated, and is divided along the 38th parallel.

From August 15th, 1945, until September 9th, 1948
South Korea

While the USSR arrives in North Korea well-prepared with Korean officers and guerilla fighters with a Communist orientation, and faces poverty-stricken masses who are enchanted by Communist ideology, the US finds itself completely unprepared for its role in taking charge over two thirds of the Korean population: It has no knowledge of either the language or the culture, and has to deal with the distinctly Communist-orientated government-in-exile that has now returned to the country. The US establishes a military administration under General John R. Hodge, completely ignoring the Korean government-in-exile and its legitimacy amongst the majority of Koreans.

An exiled Korean politician named Syngman Rhee (pronounced more like "Lee") had moved to the US in 1913. Despite his activities protesting the Japanese occupation in Korea, he was not a public figure and was virtually unknown. In September 1945, Rhee was flown to Tokyo on a military plane, despite the objections of the US Foreign Office. The next month he was flown to Korea on General McArthur's private plane, later to become the first President of the Republic of Korea.

- July 17th, 1948 – Promulgation of the First Constitution of the Republic of Korea.
- July 20th – Syngman Rhee is appointed President of the Republic, by 92% of the vote, in elections overseen by the South Korean army, with the support of the US forces.

Upon entering office, Rhee immediately introduced a hard-line, anti-Communist policy that squashed the opposition and set about eliminating the opposition – especially members of the Korean government-in-exile. The most widely publicized offense of his authoritarian regime was the massacre of around 14,000 demonstrators on Jeju Island, but there were many others. Dr. John Merrill, former chief of the Northeast Asia Division in the State Department's Bureau of Intelligence and Research, estimates the number of victims at about 100,000, while US historian of East Asia Bruce Cumings puts the figure at closer to 300,000.

- August 15th, 1948 – Declaration of the establishment of the Republic of Korea.

North Korea

- August 14th – The Red Army reaches the port city of Wonsan, by sea.
- August 24th – The Red Army reaches Pyongyang.
- "Popular Committees" appear in both parts of Korea. The USSR cooperates; the US ignores them.
- September 19th – Kim Il-Sung and other Korean officers of the Red Army reach Wonsan, and travel by train to Pyongyang.
- October 14th – Kim Il-Sung, presented as the commander of the guerilla forces and the liberating national hero, becomes the new leader of North Korea.

With the support of the USSR and the participation of the Popular Committees (reorganized on the basis of their support for him), he undertakes a long series of actions, including:

- Agrarian reform and nationalization of industry.
- A law granting full equality to women.
- Establishment of the Communist Party, integrating the Popular Committees.

- Establishment of the Korean People's Army, based on the guerilla forces. The USSR provides aid in the form of weapons and training.
- Extensive political purges.
  - 1946 – Legislation supported by the lower class (the great majority of the population) turning North Korea into a Communist country for all intents and purposes.
  - 1947 – Failure of encounters between the US and USSR concerning future reunification between the two parts of Korea.
  - July 1948 – Elections are held in South Korea.
  - August 1948 – One-party elections in North Korea, with the obvious result.
  - September 9th, 1948 (25 days after the declaration of the establishment of South Korea) – declaration of the establishment of the Democratic People's Republic of Korea (DPRK).

Two Koreas (heading for war)

As the Second World War ended, the Cold War was already well in progress. Divided Korea is one of the focuses of conflict, owing to its proximity to the USSR and to China. In China, a civil war is raging that will end with the establishment of the (Communist) People's Republic of China in October 1949.

- 1948 – Following the division of Korea, there are two separate declarations of two separate countries – South Korea and North Korea.
- June 1949 – Almost all US forces are withdrawn from South Korea, within the framework of President Truman's policy of budgetary restriction and commitment to Europe as the top-priority over Asia.
- January 1950 – US Secretary of State Dean Acheson, in a public address, defines the border dividing the Blocs

in Asia. The eastern border, according to his definition: Alaska, Japan, the Philippines, Taiwan. Accordingly, Korea is included in the Communist Bloc, along with China and the USSR. In view of this declaration, Kim Il-Sung hurries to Moscow to meet with Stalin, and requests approval to launch a military offensive to unite Korea under Communist rule. Stalin has his reservations, and does not approve the move.

- April 1950 – Kim Il-Sung again appeals to Stalin for his go-ahead to attack. Stalin, who had previously opposed the move for fear of complications, and had made it clear that the USSR would not intervene to help in that instance, now softens his stance and makes his approval conditional upon the agreement of the leader of China.

- May 1950 – Kim Il-Sung meets with Mao Zedong in Beijing. (It is worth remembering that it was only on October 1st, 1949, that China had declared its independence, following a cruel, bloody civil war that ended in December 1949). Mao was in favor of the invasion (apparently with the understanding that Stalin had already given his go-ahead): "The shell of war has already been loaded into the cannon's mouth!"

Korean War, June 25th, 1950, to July 27th, 1953

- June 25th, 1959 – In the early hours of the morning, North Korean soldiers start firing cannons; later, the army starts moving southward. The South Korean army falls apart and beats a hasty withdrawal. Three days later, on June 28th, Seoul, capital of South Korea, is captured. (According to the North Korean narrative, this was a counter-operation in response to an American attack – a somewhat

394

problematic narrative in view of the fact that the US had thinned its forces significantly.)

The UN Security Council met to discuss the North Korean aggression. The USSR and its allies boycotted the discussion. A resolution was passed to send a UN force to help South Korea. US forces comprised the vast majority of this force, along with smaller numbers from fourteen other countries, and symbolic forces from some others.

- The South Korean army, aided by the diminished US forces, is unable to halt the North Korean army. At the beginning of September 1950, other than an enclave around the port city of Busan in south-eastern Korea, almost the entire peninsula is under the North's control.
- September 15th, 1950 – A stunning amphibious landing is undertaken by the United Nations Command (mainly US soldiers), under the command of General Douglas MacArthur, at Inchon (west of Seoul). The North Korean army is trapped in the South. Seoul is liberated within two days. By the end of October, the South Korean forces have fought their way back to the 38th parallel.

The aim of returning to the division line had been attained, but under pressure from South Korean leader, Syngman Rhee, and dizzy with the ease with which the strategic reversal had been achieved, the forces of the South continued northward and eastward to the Chinese border.

- November 1950 – Most of the territory of Korea is under the control of the South Korean army, which now heads westward, to the Yalu River valley. MacArthur ignores China's warnings, and favors the idea of spreading a belt of radioactive waste along the Yalu River, and bombing Chinese industrial areas in Manchuria. The US announces that it will not invade China.

- November 26th, 1950 – China declines to place its faith in US promises, and its army launches a counterattack. The Chinese army numbers approx. half a million soldiers.
- January 1951 – The attack by the North is halted at Seoul. Again, a counterattack by the South is halted around the 38th parallel.
- April 1951 – US President Harry Truman dismisses General Douglas MacArthur.

January 1951 – July 1953

Two and a half years of fighting ensue, with the position on the ground remaining more or less a stalemate, while endless meetings and discussions are held.

During this period, there were a great many military casualties, and even more civilian victims. There was incessant bombing, especially in the North, which flattened cities, left millions homeless, and cost hundreds of thousands of civilian lives.

The main differences of opinion in the talks concern the freedom of choice for South Korean refugees and captives to be repatriated.

- January 1953 – US President-elect Dwight Eisenhower, true to his election promise, pushes for an agreement.
- July 27th, 1953 – A ceasefire agreement is signed, bringing the war to an end.

Korean War – Summary

- Civil war descends into an international conflict.
- This was the first active war of the Cold War period. The "domino effect" theory represented the West's "ideological" basis for fighting. The theory was later laid to rest in Vietnam, in 1975.
- For the first time, forces fought a war under the UN flag.

- This was the first war that included jet-powered dog-fights.
- Widespread war crimes on both sides of the conflict.
- Some two and a half million victims, of them a million and a half civilians (about a million of them North Koreans). Almost a million soldiers were killed: 600,000 Koreans, 400,000 Chinese, 50,000 UN soldiers, the majority of them Americans (based on Western sources; other sources offer different figures).
- The ceasefire has been maintained for 70 years (up until 2024) – the longest ceasefire in modern history.

Korea, alone of all the countries divided in the wake of the Second World War, remains divided. The ceasefire lines at the end of the war were very close to the original division.

- **The US, by refraining from using nuclear weapons, established a precedent: the atomic bombs used against Japan would remain a one-time event; the use of nuclear weapons is not legitimate.**

Summary of Korean history
from the (North) Korean perspective

Following a long and glorious history, during which we were conquered by various invaders when we were weak, in the 20th century our weakness brought about a series of catastrophes. We were conquered, trampled, humiliated, violated – and punished for it. We are the only country that was a victim of the Second World War, divided for no good reason. Owing to foreign interests, this division remains in force to this day.

We were drawn into another war of independence because of external forces that interfered in our homeland; a war in which more than two and a half million of our citizens died. Millions of

Koreans were exiled and abandoned the homeland, which was destroyed to its foundations in the war.

Korea is the only place where the conflict between the Blocs – the Cold War – was an active war.

The results of the events of the twentieth century include some three and a half million Korean casualties, representing about 15% of the country's population (!) – five times more than the proportionate number of casualties suffered by Japan, the aggressive conqueror.

The coarse intervention by the US, in bringing an American of Korean origin to the South and the elimination of the Korean government in exile, led to the creation of an artificial vassal state in the south of our country.

In their aggression, they even tried to seize control of the northern part of our homeland, and when we decided to take our fate in our hands, and to reunite, the US and its allies forcibly prevented this, using military force under the UN flag.

Only when we took our fate into our own hands, in a war of stunning heroism, led by our Leader, did we manage to defend half of the homeland and our dignity.

Korea is a single country. Its division is unnatural and unjust. We aspire to reunification, as difficult as it may be to achieve. Eventually it will be realized, in keeping with our Leader's vision: through peaceful means, and without foreign intervention.

ACKNOWLEDGEMENTS

Sincere thanks to...

Chaim Peres, CEO of Tarbutu, a member of the Rimon Tours group, who first thought of the idea of an Israeli group tour to North Korea.

Yaki Ben-Menahem, co-owner of Rimon Tours and my work partner who accompanied me on all my travels in North Korea.

My family and friends, who supported and encouraged me throughout my journey on this new and unfamiliar path.

And a special thank you to my beloved wife, Drora, without whose help and guidance this book would never have come to light.

And finally, to my friends and acquaintances in North Korea, who I long to meet again one day.

INDEX

A

Agricultural University 192, 194, 246, 284

Arch of Triumph 54, 100, 101, 143, 163, 164, 165, 203, 235, 274, 275, 300, 318, 344, 351

C

Children's Palace 222, 245, 248, 249, 253, 325

G

Grand People's Study House 93, 175, 177, 179, 202, 238, 343

I

International Friendship Exhibition 106, 220

J

Juche Tower 58, 61, 82, 87, 93, 100, 106, 179, 201, 202, 238, 343, 356, 360

K

Kim Il-Sung 34, 35, 53, 54, 55, 58, 59, 60, 67, 69, 70, 74, 76, 78, 80, 82, 83, 87, 93, 94, 95, 97, 98, 100, 106, 107, 112, 114, 116, 121, 133, 139, 150, 151, 153, 154, 156, 157, 162, 163, 164, 175, 176, 177, 179, 180, 183, 196, 203, 220, 221, 238, 262, 292, 294, 300, 301, 343, 353, 356, 357, 367, 386, 389, 392, 394, 401

Kim Il-Sung Square 55, 82, 83, 87, 93, 94, 150, 175, 179, 183, 238, 343, 353

Kim Jong-Il 27, 35, 58, 60, 69, 71, 76, 77, 78, 79, 81, 94, 106, 112, 116, 138, 139, 150, 151, 153, 154, 197, 220, 221, 240, 241, 255, 259, 262, 293, 324, 334, 357, 359, 371, 401

Kim Jong-Suk 60, 78, 139, 220, 221, 222

Kim Jong-Un 27, 35, 59, 61, 79, 94, 95, 105, 136, 139, 150, 151, 153, 154, 170, 180, 192, 196, 259, 260, 262, 268, 287, 288, 301, 315, 319, 332, 333, 334, 335, 361, 363, 401

Kumsusan 69, 71, 89, 106, 138, 169, 170, 171, 233, 266, 293, 294, 301, 354, 355, 356, 357, 358

M

Mangyongdae 72, 97, 180

Mansudae 54, 55, 58, 61, 89, 165, 203, 224, 225, 227, 236, 238, 239, 240, 256, 274, 294, 318, 323, 324, 343, 344, 351, 358, 401

Masikryong Ski Resort 85, 196

P

Pyongsong 248, 350, 352, 353, 355, 360, 366, 367, 376

R

Reunification Arch 188

Ryugyong Hotel 83, 94, 344

S

Sci-Tech Complex 181

Sinuiju 292, 305, 306, 309, 328, 344

Sonjuk Bridge 175

V

Victorious Fatherland Liberation War Museum 95, 206

W

Western Sea Barrier 134, 255, 256, 298, 340, 341

Workers Party Foundation Monument 323

People

Kim Il-Sung 34, 35, 53, 54, 55, 58, 59, 60, 67, 69, 70, 74, 76, 78, 80, 82, 83, 87, 93, 94, 95, 97, 98, 100, 106, 107, 112, 114, 116, 121, 133, 139, 150, 151, 153, 154, 156, 157, 162, 163, 164, 175, 176, 177, 179, 180, 183, 196, 203, 220, 221, 238, 262, 292, 294, 300, 301, 343, 353, 356, 357, 367, 386, 389, 392, 394, 401

Kim Jong-Il 27, 35, 58, 60, 69, 71, 76, 77, 78, 79, 81, 94, 106, 112, 116, 138, 139, 150, 151, 153, 154, 197, 220, 221, 240, 241, 255, 259, 262, 293, 324, 334, 357, 359, 371, 401

Kim Jong-Suk 60, 78, 139, 220, 221, 222

Kim Jong-Un 27, 35, 59, 61, 79, 94, 95, 105, 136, 139, 150, 151, 153, 154, 170, 180, 192, 196, 259, 260, 262, 268, 287, 288, 301, 315, 319, 332, 333, 334, 335, 361, 363, 401

Boxes

Instructions for Tourists in North Korea 31

Rules of Etiquette During a Tour to North Korea 32

Leaders of North Korea 35

History (20th century) 35

Mansudae – Monument and Myth 58

Juche 67

Great Leader Kim Il Sung 72

President Kim Il-Sung (according to Western sources) 74

Great Leader Kim Jong Il 76

Kim Jong-Il (according to Western sources) 78

Personality and leadership 79

Kimilsungia 80

Kimjongilia 81

The North Korean army 109

Songun 111

Kimchi 127

The Teachings of Confucius 130

Religions in Korea 131

Bombshell of a Tour 147

North Korea – Basic Facts for Tourists 153

Rules of Behavior for Visitors to North Korea 154

Arirang 198

Kim Jong Suk, 1917-1949 221

Kim Jong-Un (As per Western sources) 262

Leadership 263

Potemkin towns 310

Made in the USA
Monee, IL
16 April 2025